BRAIINS

BUILDING BITCOIN IN RUST

Lukas Hozda

BRAINS

Building bitcoin in Rust

Written by: Lukáš Hozda
Editor: Debbie Liebenberg
Technical reviewers: Daniela Brozzoni, Luukas Pörtfors, Pavel Šimerda
Cover design: Jiří Chlebus
Design consulting: Robert Blecha
Consultations: Jáchym Černý
Typesetting: Sabina Heyová
Marketing strategy: Kristian Csepcsar

Printed in the Czech Republic
978-80-909253-4-2

CONTENT

ACKNOWLEDGMENTS

"ACK! ACK! ACK!"
– Exclamation unique to pirate skeletons and the TCP protocol

Imagine this: At the end of the movie 'The Menu' (2022), Margot, a.k.a Erin, accuses chef Slowik of preparing food without love. He denies this but then agrees to make a delicious, greasy cheeseburger for the protagonist. It is a very different meal from the sterile intellectual exercises served earlier. Not as sophisticated or perfect, but far more human and welcoming.

Similar to that tasty cheeseburger, this book is made with lots of love and care, Eurobeat blasting on full volume, and numerous cans of Monster Ultra Zero™. It is intended to be genuine and authentic. Like almost every labor of love (and the Roman Empire[1]) it wasn't built in a day, and not by a single pair of hands either.

First and foremost, I would like to thank my grandma, Ing. Daniela Rambousková, for guiding me through my childhood and helping me become the person I am today.

I want to thank Braiins for giving me the opportunity and support to create this book. In particular, my gratitude goes to Sabina Heyová, Debbie Liebenberg, Milenko Rebić, Jáchym Černý, Jiří Chlebus, Martin Connor, and Kristian Csepcsar for not just expending tremendous effort in making this work of art a reality but also for putting up with my bullshit. Naturally, I must also thank our CEO, Eli Nagar, who approved the idea for this book in about two minutes over a random afternoon snack.

I am also very grateful to my other Braiins colleagues and former Rust-course students for providing valuable feedback on different parts of the book or helping me improve my teaching skills, especially my team members Mark Firman, Daniel Havlíček, and Vojtěch Mikulenka.

There is also a long list of friends who were not directly involved with the book's text but either inspired some part of the content or discussed something topical with me. To name a few: Connor Crawford, Vít Matějíček, Dawid Kubiś, Adam Sedláček, and Katka Zusková.

1 I think about Ancient Rome every day.

Gratitude also goes to Daniela Brozzoni, who spent a tremendous amount of time reading the book, providing precious feedback, and writing the foreword; Luukas "Luukasa" Pörtfors, who meticulously examined every page and provided both technical and grammatical suggestions; and Piia Huhta for creating her illustrated animal in the latter part of the book.

Finally, I would like to thank Pavel Šimerda for helping me get involved with the Czech Rust community around Charles University and reviewing this book.

Remember: Programming can be a fun and creative discipline. Experiment, build with purpose, learn with passion, and keep on keeping on, always. :)

Let's take a look at the book now.

Lukáš Hozda
Renaissance man 🦀

PRELUDE

Howdy, my name is Lukáš, and I am the author of this book. If all goes well, you hold a copy of our first published book in programming. It also happens to be my first book. Thank you for picking it up, and I wish you a pleasant journey if you continue reading it beyond this point.

Together, we will embark on a journey that should enhance your knowledge in two areas. In Rust, the programming language, and in bitcoin. To me, these are both exciting areas. I first learned about bitcoin in 2013 and started using Rust full-time in 2015. At the beginning of 2021, I joined Braiins, which let me work with Rust in a bitcoin-adjacent environment. Now, after almost a decade working with these, I want to share my passions with you.

Before we can do that, we need to answer the most significant question: Is this book for you?

WHO IS THIS BOOK FOR?

The primary target audience is people in the field of IT, both students and professionals. The optimal intersection is for those who like both bitcoin and programming. If you keep up with IT news, you have undoubtedly heard about Rust: the up-and-coming star programming language.[2] Bitcoin, conversely, remains the time-tested, golden standard of cryptocurrency.

You do not need to have an interest in both. This book may be the final bargaining chip to convince you that Rust is a great tool or that bitcoin does, in fact, represent sound money based on its technical merits alone.

If you are a Computer Science student looking to learn something new, welcome, you are in the right place. If you are a bitcoin enthusiast with some programming knowledge - perfect, you will have a great time. Programmers looking to learn Rust or to add another project to their portfolio? Come aboard!

WHO IS THIS BOOK NOT FOR?

No book is for everybody, and this one is no exception. In this text, we will practice learning through development. We will get our hands dirty and spend

2 Also the leading language in hot takes on Twitter and Reddit.

a considerable amount of time developing a project. Sometimes, you may get stuck thinking over an issue - Rust is a language with a steep learning curve and it pulls no punches.[3] Very often, you have to do things properly the first time and cannot take shortcuts.

I do my best to make things easier for you, but you need the time and the means to follow along in order to succeed. Keep in mind that programming languages are ultimately tools - and different tools perform differently for different tasks. Rust is a great programming language for systems programming, backend development, embedded systems, and networking. It is not the best tool for frontend developers (although it is improving rapidly in this domain!), for fast prototyping, for scientific programming, for mobile applications or for machine learning and data science. That being said, you can use almost any programming language for almost anything. There are people who have written toy operating systems in JavaScript.[4]

If you are a complete newbie to programming, this book may scare you with its seeming complexity. It is not *that* complex, but IT is a large field, and penetrating it requires much effort and learning. I like soft landings for my newcomer colleagues and soft launches for my students. If you fall into this category, start with something simpler.

Python is a great programming language as your first and has many great books and websites. There are also toy projects that are easier for beginners than a blockchain would be. Make a simple text game, an editor, a calculator, or a website to manage a database of recipes. In my case, the breakthrough projects were mods for Minecraft and Terraria. To misquote Shakespeare's *Merry Wives of Windsor*: "The world is your oyster."

So seize the day, one step at a time. You can return to this book later. I won't be mad, I promise.

ONLINE RESOURCES

We are all humans, and it is natural that it may be hard to keep track of all

3 Fighting the borrow-checker is an established phrase for Rust newbies.

4 The mere thought keeps me up at night. But people also made operating systems in Java, and made Linux run in JavaScript...

the code that we will be writing in this book. I have bundled up all the source code and some additional information into a repository here: https://github.com/braiins/build-bitcoin-in-rust

If you run into any issues, refer back into the repository. If you struggle with anything, don't be afraid to reach out to me on Twitter/X (**@LukasHozda**), or open an issue in the repository. :)

REQUIREMENTS

To make the most out of this book, you should meet a couple of requirements. This book is beginner-friendly, but it is only for some beginners. You need to know at least one other programming language. Statically-typed languages prepare you the best (Java, Kotlin, C#, C/C++...), but dynamically-typed are alright too (Python, JS...). Mastering a functional programming language (Haskell, OCaml, F#...) makes you a superstar, and learning Rust will be a breeze.

Furthermore, we will touch upon a few concepts from the realm of low(er)-level programming:

- Pointers
- Allocations
- Stack and the heap (in the context of memory management)
- Threads

While we will remind ourselves of technical terms when appropriate, you may have an easier time if you are already familiar.

Here is a brief description of all of these:

Pointers: Variables that store memory addresses of other data. They "point" to locations in memory, allowing direct access and manipulation of data at that address. Useful for dynamic memory management and efficient data structures. In Rust, you will mostly hear pointers being referred to as borrows, and apart from an address, they are also tagged with information about the lifetime of the data they are pointing to. Pointers (and borrows), can be read-only (also referred to as immutable, or shared, in Rust), or they can allow write access as well (making them mutable, or exclusive, in Rust).

Allocations: Process of reserving memory for program use. Can be static (resolved during compilation) or dynamic (at runtime). Dynamic allocation lets programs request memory as needed, but requires manual management to avoid leaks.[5] To put it slightly differently, memory is a managed resource. You have to ask the operating system to assign you memory you can use, and you have to return the memory once you no longer do. Forgetting to return the memory is a **memory leak**, while using memory that is not assigned to you is an **access violation** that may lead to a **segmentation fault**.

Stack: Fast, automatically managed memory for local variables. LIFO (Last--In-First-Out) structure, limited size (on your desktop, each program/thread has a default stack limit of units of megabytes). Your local variables live on the stack. Allocations on the stack are usually automatic, and so is their cleanup. However, you cannot resize allocations on the stack.

Heap: Larger, manually managed memory for dynamic allocation. Flexible but slower, requires explicit deallocation to prevent leaks. This is where vectors (dynamic lists), variable-sized strings, and bigger objects live.

Threads: Lightweight units of execution[6] within a process. Allow concurrent operations, sharing the same memory space. Useful for parallel processing and responsive applications, but require careful synchronization to avoid conflicts.

Back to the topic at hand.

Many online materials and videos on YouTube are available to explain each concept, so I have no doubt that you will be able to find ones that speak to you. Same goes for the Rust concepts - there are many ways to explain some of the most difficult concepts, and one explanation may suit you better than others. So do not consider this book in a vacuum, if you don't understand something on the first go, do not feel bad about it, try again, or try a different explanation, then come back to the text of the book.

Finally, you will also need a computer, an internet connection, and some peace and quiet. The final one is not a deal-breaker; we all know how hectic modern life can be.

---

5 Static allocation is the stack, and it is where local variables are usually located. Stack is small (single MBs), but very fast. Dynamic allocation is on the heap, which is slower, but much larger (essentially your entire RAM), and allows reallocation.

6 Such as sub-processes or tasks.

GOALS AND STRUCTURE

This book is not a complete overview of bitcoin nor a complete reference for Rust. Our journey aims to introduce new concepts one by one and immediately put them to good use.

We will begin by looking at the cornerstone of bitcoin - its whitepaper. The whitepaper is a remarkably short and well-written document, and we will read and examine it together.

As we do so, we will learn about bitcoin in theory. We can map out how to apply the theory based on our new knowledge.

We will do this by conceiving a plan and then executing it bit by bit, learning Rust along the way. Together, we will build the three necessary components of our toy bitcoin:

- the miner
- the CLI wallet
- the bitcoin node

When all the components are ready, we will deploy and kickstart our blockchain. You will then be able to enjoy the fruits of your labor, send fake sats to your friends, and include this project in your portfolio.

One thing to note is that we will neither be writing the perfect Rust, nor will we be making the perfect bitcoin. Compromises have to be made, otherwise this book would have been three times as long, and to be fair, maybe not as exciting.[7]

Sounds good? Let's get on with it. Have fun and enjoy the adventure.

NOTE: Having a place where to keep notes and things you want to go back to may be very valuable for you when tackling the contents of this book. I like pen and paper, but both it and digital forms are perfectly fine.

7 Read: our typesetting lady, who also happens to manage this project, would kill me.

FOREWORD

Bitcoin is the best form of money in the world, though I didn't understand that when I first started exploring it. What caught my attention was the incredibly complex engineering problem that bitcoin solves: achieving consensus on ownership of coins through a trustless, private, peer-to-peer network. This problem fascinated me, and I found myself going deeper and deeper down the rabbit hole. Over time, I discovered the many other aspects of bitcoin - how it can help us build a better world based on sound money, protect people's privacy and freedom, and allow self-sovereignty and security. Ultimately, it was my curiosity about the engineering that led me to become a bitcoin developer, but it's my love for the cause that still fuels me.

Similar to bitcoin, Rust also caught my attention by solving a challenging engineering problem: ensuring that dumb developers write safe and performant code. For me, learning Rust was a tough journey - as you'll soon notice, the compiler is pretty grumpy, and will complain relentlessly until you write code safe from issues like double-free memory bugs, dangling pointers and null references. Don't be intimidated, though: before switching to Rust, I was a Java developer with little experience using C/C++; yet, through a lot of trial and error, I learned the language and gained a deeper understanding of how computers work. Rust became more manageable with experience, though it never stopped being challenging - but ask yourself, as bitcoin developers, should we aim for easy code or for safe code?

Looking back, this book is exactly what I needed when I started. It provides a concise overview of bitcoin and Rust before diving straight into hands-on action. By the end, you won't be an expert in either, but you will have a practical understanding of both, along with your own pet project to improve and practice on.

You might think there are already many bitcoin developers, and it's true, but there's never enough. There is still much to improve, whether in privacy, UX, scalability, design, or many other areas. I don't know you, fellow reader, but I know you are different from all the other developers out there, and as such, you have something unique to contribute.

Let this book be the start of an amazing journey, and together, we can make bitcoin even better.

Daniela Brozzoni
Bitcoin developer

1 INTRODUCTION

Before me there were no created things,
Only eterne, and I eternal last.
All hope abandon, ye who enter in!"

– Dante Alighieri, Inferno, Canto III

Ha, I hope I didn't scare you with this quote. We are about to enter a new realm, but do not worry, ever since COBOL proved that programming languages should be designed by enthusiasts and academics (and not business committees) learning a new language is not abject misery, and, in fact, is not comparable to a descent into hell.

Rust, much like the vast and intricate circles of Dante's Inferno, is layered with concepts that are deep and sometimes seem daunting. Fortunately, and unlike the despairing souls in Dante's work, we as Rustaceans, are equipped with powerful resources, an enthusiastic and supportive community, and a language designed to empower us to write better programs (and indeed, many, myself included, have experienced that learning Rust made us write better programs in other languages). Our journey through Rust is one of enlightenment, where each concept we master and every line of code we write brings us closer to the divine comedy of creating software that is not only efficient and reliable but also a joy to craft.

Without further ado, let me be the Virgil to your Dante, and let me guide you safely through the world of Rust programming.[8]

WHY RUST AND BITCOIN ARE HANDSOME TOGETHER

If you know me, which is unlikely, you will see that I have certain "Finnic" relations. I am "in the know" with the finnic lifeforms, if you will. To put it bluntly, I am a Czech man uniquely surrounded by Finns. There are many of them; they are all stellar guys and gals, and one could say that I am one with' the sauna people. I have a good friend, a gentleman known as "Luukasa", which is a cleverly hidden compound word meaning "a pile of bones" (owing to his pre-army physique). He has this linguistic quirk where he calls technologies, programming languages, algorithms, or straight-up math concepts "handsome."

8 This line was revealed to me in a dream.

It is difficult to describe this handsomeness precisely, but I would tackle it this way. If something has quality, is somehow aesthetically pleasing, and makes sense, then it is handsome. Unfortunately, we cannot go further down into our analysis. If you want to know what quality is, you can read Pirsig's "Zen and the Art of Motorcycle Maintenance" and Kant for aesthetics. I am unaware of a book that would make sense out of making sense. Aristotle tried.

But I digress.

As it turns out, Rust is quite handsome. It underwent tremendous trial and error, research, experimentation, and discussion. It also maintains a level of cleanliness, clarity, and ergonomics. The language assumes a pragmatic philosophy - let's change what needs to change, let's keep what is tried and true. Like bitcoin, it was born from the creator growing tired of something. For Rust, it was a lack of robustness and rampart memory management errors. For bitcoin, it was the financial system, which, if you have ever had issues with your bank, makes it handsome too.

A principal motto for bitcoin is "Don't trust, verify". Rust, as a language, follows the same philosophy. By mandating safe and effective programming, it reduces the amount of trust you need to invest in other programmers. Using a 3rd party library in C requires a lot of trust; there may be dozens and dozens of instances of undefined behavior, memory leaks, and other errors. These are not possible in safe Rust.[9] If something is potentially unsafe, it is visible and limited to the smallest scope necessary, making it easy to audit these critical sections of code.

In other words, Rust offloads trust onto the compiler (and, more broadly, the language's design), while bitcoin offloads trust onto cryptography and its Proof-of-Work approach in general.

However, no security and cryptographical soundness is enough if a memory issue makes you print your deepest secrets. Such was the case with the famous **Heartbleed** security bug in the **OpenSSL** cryptography library, which allowed clients to ask for more data to be echoed back than they sent.

You could say:

---

9 Memory leaks are possible in safe Rust, although much harder to achieve. A memory leak is, however, not unsafe in and of itself. However, memory leaks may create unsafe conditions, so the safety of memory leaks is a topic for debate in some circles.

"Here is the string 'Hello, Braiins!' please send me back the first 512 bytes of this 15-byte string."

And OpenSSL would reply with "Hello, Braiins!" followed by whatever lies after it in the program's memory, which could be passwords, certificates, private keys, or whatever else your heart desires.

Thus, if we want bulletproof technologies, we are incentivized to use the most secure tools available. Rust is handsome. Bitcoin is handsome. Together, they make for the most "handsomest" combination.

I am far from the only one who has noticed that Rust works well with crypto. The Stratum V2 (a protocol miners use to talk to pools) has a reference Rust implementation. Almost everything Braiins makes is in Rust. SatoshiLabs is exploring Rust, too. Finally, a biblical flood of non-bitcoin crypto projects (mostly scams) use Rust. If you ever put Rust into your LinkedIn profile, these companies will spam you with job offers.

It is not only crypto, though. Rust, on its own, enjoys great popularity. Year after year, it wins StackOverflow's "most beloved language" category in its annual developer survey. It attracts attention from every type of programmer - hobbyists, students, professionals, and researchers. And I hope that it will entice you, too. But let's not get ahead of ourselves. We should start at the beginning. Let's take a look at the beginning of Rust and of bitcoin.

Here's Rust:

```
// main.rs
fn main() {
    println!("Hello, world!");
}
```

This code snippet is, as you know, the quintessential Hello World program, which is generally the first thing you learn in any language. When we are done analyzing the whitepaper, this is the first piece of code that we will run.

And here‘s bitcoin:

```
00000000 ................
00000010 ................
00000020 ....;£íýz{.²zÇ,>
00000030 gv.a.È.Ã^ŠQ2:Ÿ¸ª
00000040 K.^J)«_Iÿÿ...¬+|
00000050 ................
00000060 ................
00000070 ......ÿÿÿÿM.ÿÿ..
00000080 ..EThe Times 03/
00000090 Jan/2009 Chancel
000000A0 lor on brink of
000000B0 second bailout f
000000C0 or banksÿÿÿÿ..ò.
000000D0 *....CA.gŠý°þUH'
000000E0 .gñ¦q0·.\Ö¨(à9.¦
000000F0 ybàê.aÞ¶IÖ¼?LÏ8Ä
00000100 óU.å.Á.Þ\8M÷°..W
00000110 ŠLp+kñ._¬....
```

Here, you see the genesis block of bitcoin: the very first one mined and therefore the beginning of the blockchain (commonly also referred to as timechain by BTC developers). Notice how the creator of bitcoin, Satoshi Nakamoto, was lovingly tongue-in-cheek with his inclusion of that day‘s newspaper headline about bank bailouts. Subtlety is a most gentle art.

Let’s read the whitepaper together now.

2

ANALYZING THE WHITEPAPER

BRIEF HISTORY AND OVERVIEW OF BITCOIN

Bitcoin started in 2009, created by someone using the name Satoshi Nakamoto.[10] It is a digital currency, different from traditional money because there‘s no authority. Instead, bitcoin runs on a computer network that tracks all transactions on a public ledger (the blockchain).

To ensure every transaction is secure, bitcoin uses a process called mining. Miners run a math algorithm (SHA-256, to be exact) to confirm transactions. A successful verification rewards the miner with bitcoin. This process also creates new coins, mimicking how we mine gold from the earth, but digitally. Over time, bitcoin grew from a novelty to a significant player in the financial world. Now, it challenges how we think about money.

These two paragraphs should give you the briefest introduction to what bitcoin is (if Rust brought you to this book and not bitcoin). Unfortunately, discussing bitcoin‘s history and economics is beyond the scope of this book. If this is something that interests you, check out our other books:

- *Bitcoin: Separation of Money and State* (by Josef Tětek)
- *Bitcoin Mining Economics* (by Daniel Frumkin)
- *Bitcoin Mining Handbook* (by Daniel Frumkin)

All of the aforementioned books are freely available on the Braiins website.

THE WHITEPAPER PULLED APART

What follows is the text of Satoshi‘s whitepaper. I have taken some slight liberties with it by omitting the abstract and the sources. Since the whitepaper is a public document, you can find these without issue.

Before we start, there are a couple terms you may be unfamiliar with:

- ***Hash** - A number produced by a hashing function. A hashing function takes input data of any length, and produces one number[11]. Ideally, the smallest change in the input should generate a completely different hash, and it should be impossible to calculate the original data from the hash. Some examples of*

10 Speculation about who Nakamoto is is one of the only sources of bitcoin controversy. Personally, I hope it was either aliens or a disgruntled blue-collar worker.

11 In more general terms, a hash function produces data of fixed length.

hashing functions are the SHA family, MD5 or Adler32.

- ***Node*** *- A node is a member of a network. In the context of bitcoin, a node is a program (we can call the computer running the program a node also), which stores either a complete or a partial copy of the timechain, and takes care of validation, propagation, and formerly, in some cases, mining.*
- ***Private and public keys*** *- Cryptography can be either symmetric (there is only one key that does both decryption and encryption), or asymmetric (there is a private key with more capabilities than the public key). In the context of encryption, the public key can only encrypt data, but not decrypt. In the context of digital signatures, the public key can only verify signatures, but cannot sign. The private key can do both and the public key is typically calculated from it. Asymmetric cryptography is typically slower than symmetric, and so it is commonly used to securely exchange a symmetric key when you want to establish encrypted communication with another party.*

Introduction

Commerce on the Internet has come to rely almost exclusively on financial institutions serving as trusted third parties to process electronic payments. While the system works well enough for most transactions, it still suffers from the inherent weaknesses of the trust-based model. Completely non-reversible transactions are not really possible, since financial institutions cannot avoid mediating disputes. The cost of mediation increases transaction costs, limiting the minimum practical transaction size and cutting off the possibility for small casual transactions, and there is a broader cost in the loss of ability to make non-reversible payments for non-reversible services. With the possibility of reversal, the need for trust spreads. Merchants must be wary of their customers, hassling them for more information than they would otherwise need. A certain percentage of fraud is accepted as unavoidable. These costs and payment uncertainties can be avoided in person by using physical currency, but no mechanism exists to make payments over a communications channel without a trusted party.

This paragraph focuses on the commercial need for bitcoin, but we can start considering the technical needs first. For starters, transactions must be irreversible, so our implementation should not allow cancellation. The user should have no power over the transaction after creating and sending it to the network. It may, however, time out.

What is needed is an electronic payment system based on cryptographic proof instead of trust, allowing any two willing parties to transact directly with each other without the need for a trusted third party. Transactions that are computationally impractical to reverse would protect sellers from fraud, and routine escrow mechanisms could easily be implemented to protect buyers. In this paper, we propose a solution to the double-spending problem using a peer-to-peer distributed timestamp server to generate computational proof of the chronological order of transactions. The system is secure as long as honest nodes collectively control more CPU power than any cooperating group of attacker nodes.

Transactions

We[12] define an electronic coin as a chain of digital signatures. Each owner transfers the coin to the next by digitally signing a hash of the previous transaction and the public key of the next owner and adding these to the end of the coin. A payee can verify the signatures to verify the chain of ownership.

As mentioned above, a hashing function takes any data, and by calculating the hash again, we can verify the integrity of data (if the data is unchanged, it will generate the same hash). Private and public keys can be used as a secure proof of ownership of your coins. Some hashing functions are very secure, others less. We need to use ones that are secure enough.

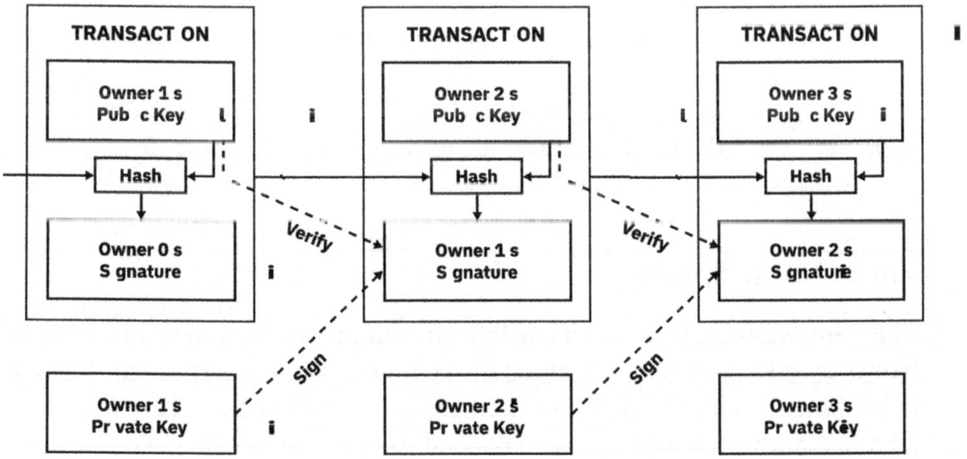

12 Who's the "we" in Satoshi's paper? Is it CIA? I am hoping for the Spanish Inquistion.

The problem of course is the payee can't verify that one of the owners did not double-spend the coin. A common solution is to introduce a trusted central authority, or mint, that checks every transaction for double-spending. After each transaction, the coin must be returned to the mint to issue a new coin, and only coins issued directly from the mint are trusted not to be double--spent. The problem with this solution is that the fate of the entire money system depends on the company running the mint, with every transaction having to go through them, just like a bank.

We need a way for the payee to know that the previous owners did not sign any earlier transactions. For our purposes, the earliest transaction is the one that counts, so we don't care about later attempts to double-spend. The only way to confirm the absence of a transaction is to be aware of all transactions. In the mint-based model, the mint was aware of all transactions and decided which arrived first. To accomplish this without a trusted party, transactions must be publicly announced, and we need a system for participants to agree on a single history of the order in which they were received. The payee needs proof that at the time of each transaction, the majority of nodes agreed it was the first received.

> *Transactions, blocks and block headers are the main data structures that we will need to model in our application. We can take some inspiration from real bitcoin, but we will simplify our implementation a bit.*
>
> *Furthermore, we will be able to be flexible with the underlying byte format, as we do not need to match the format used by the bitcoin network (naturally, it is possible to do that, but it would complicate our implementation with little educational benefit).*
>
> *This will simplify things greatly, as we will be able to use an established binary format, and automatically convert to and from it with the* `serde` *library.*

Timestamp Server

The solution we propose begins with a timestamp server. A timestamp server works by taking a hash of a block of items to be time stamped and widely publishing the hash, such as in a newspaper or Usenet post[13]. The timestamp proves that the data must have existed at the time, obviously, in order to get

13 A distributed discussion system predating the World Wide Web, ask your IT grandpa :-)

into the hash. Each timestamp includes the previous timestamp in its hash, forming a chain, with each additional timestamp reinforcing the ones before it.

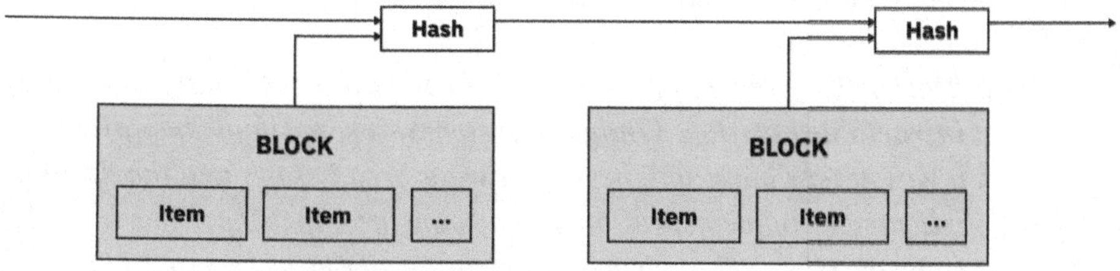

The timestamp server is the node of our network. It is a network application which maintains our timechain and talks to other nodes in the network. We will create our own simple fake bitcoin node, and later teach it to talk to other nodes.

Nodes that talk to each other have to be able to reach a consensus. We will simplify things here a little bit.

Proof-of-Work

To implement a distributed timestamp server on a peer-to-peer basis, we will need to use a proof-of-work system similar to Adam Back's Hashcash [6], rather than newspaper or Usenet posts. The proof-of-work involves scanning for a value that when hashed, such as with SHA-256, the hash begins with a number of zero bits. The average work required is exponential in the number of zero bits required and can be verified by executing a single hash.

Adam Back's Hashcash is a proof-of-work system for combating spam from 1997. Many moons ago, spam email seemed like a real problem. It still is, but the sheer power of our internet infrastructure can handle it pretty well. Spam traffic does not critically maim contemporary mailing services. We implemented spam filters capable of stopping (or at least moving out of sight) the majority of it.[14]

Back in the day, the situation was different. Malicious actors could spam relatively freely, and DoS attacks were a real threat. Measures to prevent users from sending emails quickly, as spammers do, were considered. One straightforward and more insidious way of combating this was introducing fees per email sent.

14 These spam filters are fairly centralized, though, and it is a question if that is a good thing.

This proposal was not popular with many people, and one of those people was Adam Back. He suggested an alternative, where the payment for an email would not be money but the computational performance of the sender by hashing. This "hashing fee" is why Back called his idea Hashcash.

The Hashcash PoW system requires the user to compute a moderately challenging but not intractable function. While this system saw some implementations for emails, it was never ubiquitous, never saw widespread usage, and the situation was complicated by implementations often being incompatible with each other. For example, the Microsoft implementation, naturally, lacked compatibility with anything else.

For our timestamp network, we implement the proof-of-work by incrementing a nonce in the block until a value is found that gives the block's hash the required zero bits. Once the CPU effort has been expended to make it satisfy the proof-of-work, the block cannot be changed without redoing the work. As later blocks are chained after it, the work to change the block would include redoing all the blocks after it.

A nonce (apart from its British meaning where it, I believe, describes the average politician) stands for "number only used once". Essentially, we add a counter to our block header, and keep incrementing it. In real bitcoin, the difficulty is high enough that we need an additional source of randomness - an extra nonce. This nonce is embedded in the coinbase transaction.

You will see that throughout this text, Satoshi Nakamoto mentions the word CPU. This is because in the early days, bitcoin would be mined on the CPU. A few years into bitcoin's history, we figured out we can calculate SHA-256 on our graphics cards, and GPU mining became a thing. Later on, we started making ASIC machines (Application Specific Integrated Circuit), which used chips that could only compute SHA-256, but nothing else, however, very effectively.

We are still using ASICs today.

The proof-of-work also solves the problem of determining representation in majority decision-making. If the majority were based on one-IP-address-one--vote, it could be subverted by anyone able to allocate many IPs. Proof-of-work is essentially one-CPU-one-vote. The majority decision is represented by the longest chain, which has the greatest proof-of-work effort invested in it. If a majority of CPU power is controlled by honest nodes, the honest chain will grow the fastest and outpace any competing chains. To modify a past block, an attacker would have to redo the proof-of-work of the block and all blocks after it and then catch up with and surpass the work of the honest nodes. We will show later that the probability of a slower attacker catching up diminishes exponentially as subsequent blocks are added.

To compensate for increasing hardware speed and varying interest in running nodes over time, the proof-of-work difficulty is determined by a moving average targeting an average number of blocks per hour. If they're generated too fast, the difficulty increases.

> *In real bitcoin, the block time should average out to one block every ten minutes. Of course, we are working with statistics and random chance, and sometimes there is only a couple seconds between blocks. Sometimes, there have been hours between blocks.*
>
> *Difficulty is adjusted every 2016 blocks, which corresponds to exactly two weeks if every block takes 10 minutes on average. If it takes less, difficulty is increased, if it takes more than that, difficulty is decreased.*
>
> *We will write our blockchain in such a way that we can configure both the block time and the adjustment period, so that development is faster. It would be a real slog, if we had to wait two weeks to see if our code works, haha!*

Network

The steps to run the network are as follows:

1. New transactions are broadcast to all nodes.

   Transactions will be created by our wallets, which connect to one or more nodes. The nodes will then broadcast the transactions to other nodes they know. Naturally, we will need a mechanism to verify that we do not have the same transaction multiple times. Luckily, we can simply hash them.

   New transactions are stored in something called the "mempool". We can consider this to be a list of unprocessed transactions. Whether it is actually a list is an implementation detail. There are other data structures that can make it easier for us to detect duplicate transactions.

3

SETTING UP

Before we get into programming, we should have a proper Rust setup that we can work with. In the case of Rust, it is easy to get started. Before installation, you will need the following:

- A laptop, computer, or a Samsung Smart Fridge[21]
    - Rust can compile and run on pretty much any laptop, including toasters. Still, its compilation is a performance-demanding process, so if you are less patient, consider choosing a device with a good CPU and a reasonable amount of RAM.
    - I am an impatient creature and so I develop remotely on a powerful server, but in a pinch, my 8-year-old Lenovo Thinkpad still manages to keep up and compile Rust just fine.

- A recent operating system
    - Windows, MacOS, and Linux are all fine (OpenBSD/FreeBSD enjoyers are also welcome)
    - I mainly develop software on Linux, and solutions for our use cases on MacOS and Linux should be identical.
    - There might be slight differences on Windows - I will try to accommodate them as much as possible.

- At least 10GB of free space
    - We must fit a Rust toolchain, an editor, and some build artifacts, which can get large in the debug profile.

These are all the hard requirements for installing Rust. For some parts of this book, you will need to have an active internet connection. Rust deliberately has a small standard library, following the maxim of "the standard library is where code goes to die"[22] In fact, neither random number generation nor datetime manipulation is included in the standard library, and so we will need to rely on the ecosystem a lot.

This may re-open old wounds in those traumatized by NPM dependency hell (boy, I love it when my "hello world" project has 900 dependencies and 30k files in node_modules/!), but the situation with Rust is nowhere near as

21 Seriously, if you manage to get the Rust compiler running on a fridge, you are probably too smart for this book.

22 The exact origin of this quote is a bit hard to pin down, but in 2019 this quote, uttered by Amber Brown at the Python Language Summit, made Guido van Rossum (the language's creator) storm out of the room in anger - Python notoriously took a "kitchen-sink" approach to the standard library.

bad. The biggest projects I have ever worked on only reached low hundreds of dependencies, I suspect ours will have just dozens at most.

INSTALLING RUST

When I want to do small experiments I often play around with the **Rust Playground** (found at https://play.rust-lang.org/) or **Godbolt** (https://rust.godbolt.org/) if I need to see the generated instructions. For example, consider the following short example (it does not matter that the syntax is still very new or unknown to you at this point, we will explain everything later - the comments, starting with // tell you what you need to know):

```
/// factorial implemented with an iterator
fn factorial_iter(num: usize) -> usize {
  (1..num)
      .fold(1, |acc, x| acc * x)
}
/// factorial implemented with a loop and a mutable variable
fn factorial_loop(num: usize) -> usize {
  let mut sum = 1;
  for x in 2..num {
      sum *= x;
  }
  sum
}
/// fibbonaci implementation with a loop
fn fibbonaci(n: usize) -> usize {
  let mut a = 1;
  let mut b = 1;
  for _ in 1..n {
      let old_a = a;
      a = b;
      b += old_a;
  }
  b
}
fn main() {
  let x = factorial_iter(12);
```

```
    let y = factorial_loop(20);
    let fib = fibbonaci(35);
    println!("factorial 1: {}, factorial 2: {}, fibbonaci: {}",
  x, y, fib);
}
```

I use this snippet of code to demonstrate Rust's strong static analysis and aggressive optimization practices. If you build this small program in release mode, and run it, it will print the following:

```
factorial 1: 39916800, factorial 2: 121645100408832000, fibbo-
naci: 1493035
```

These are the correct values, but things get more interesting if we look in Godbolt at the assembly. We will see this:

```
...
mov qword ptr [rsp], 39916800
movabs rax, 121645100408832000
mov qword ptr [rsp + 8], rax
mov qword ptr [rsp + 16], 14930352
...
```

These numbers look awfully familiar, don't they? That's right, in this case, Rust is able to evaluate the algorithms at compile time and embed the results directly into the binary. It's the same as if we would have written the following pseudo code:

```
function main():
    print("factorial 1: 39916800")
    print("factorial 2: 121645100408832000")
    print("fibbonaci: 14930352")
    print("\n")
```

These tools are nice and very useful for demonstrations such as this one, but if we are to develop a serious project, we need to grow beyond these online tools. So it is time to install Rust.

Rustup vs native packages

On all mainstream desktop operating systems besides Windows, you are presented with a choice: Install Rust via a package manager (e.g. **apt** or **homebrew**), or via **rustup**?

Many Linux users prefer to install software via a package manager, as it generally makes for a less messy system. In the case of Rust, however, this is not the ideal solution. In Rust, it is common to switch versions of the compiler, add and remove components of the toolchain, and enable new targets for cross-compilation.

If you install a **rust** package from your distribution's repository, you are robbing yourself of this functionality, which may complicate things for you.

The main reason for Rust being tracked in package repositories is that other packages are written in Rust, and for a particular version of an operating system, you want to be consistent and have a Rust version available in your package ecosystem to build the other packages with.

Therefore, if you can, install Rust via **rustup** by running the following command on your Linux or Mac machine (or BSD, if you are so inclined[23]):

```
curl --proto '=https' --tlsv1.2 -sSf https://sh.rustup.rs | sh
```

On Windows, you will need to download an installer from the following link:

```
https://rustup.rs/
```

23 Rust supports FreeBSD, OpenBSD, NetBSD, and to a lesser degree (barely functional), DragonflyBSD, my favorite:(

Please, refer to the website above if the Linux/Mac/BSD command did not work. While the installation process has been the same since about 2016, it may change. The rustup installation will show you the following text, assuming all went correctly:

```
info: downloading installer
Welcome to Rust!
This will download and install the official compiler for the
Rust
programming language, and its package manager, Cargo.
Rustup metadata and toolchains will be installed into the Rus-
tup
home directory, located at:
  /root/.rustup
This can be modified with the RUSTUP_HOME environment variab-
le.
The Cargo home directory is located at:
  /root/.cargo
This can be modified with the CARGO_HOME environment variable.
The cargo, rustc, rustup and other commands will be added to
Cargo's bin directory, located at:
  /root/.cargo/bin
This path will then be added to your PATH environment variable
by
modifying the profile files located at:
  /root/.profile
  /root/.config/fish/conf.d/rustup.fish
You can uninstall at any time with rustup self uninstall and
these changes will be reverted.
Current installation options:
   default host triple: x86_64-unknown-linux-gnu
     default toolchain: stable (default)
                   profile: default
  modify PATH variable: yes
1) Proceed with standard installation (default - just press
enter)
2) Customize installation
3) Cancel installation
>
```

Note that the host triple and which profile files will be modified will change depending on your OS and what shells you have installed. For Windows users, I believe this will be just PowerShell.

You can press Enter here - no need to customize anything. For me, the installation looked like this:

```
info: profile set to 'default'
info: default host triple is x86_64-unknown-linux-gnu
info: syncing channel updates for 'stable-x86_64-unknown-linu-
x-gnu'
info: latest update on 2024-03-28, rust version 1.77.1
(7cf61ebde 2024-03-27)
info: downloading component 'cargo'
info: downloading component 'clippy'
info: downloading component 'rust-docs'
 14.9 MiB /  14.9 MiB (100 %)   9.7 MiB/s in  1s ETA:  0s
info: downloading component 'rust-std'
 26.6 MiB /  26.6 MiB (100 %)  10.3 MiB/s in  2s ETA:  0s
info: downloading component 'rustc'
 60.5 MiB /  60.5 MiB (100 %)  10.1 MiB/s in  6s ETA:  0s
info: downloading component 'rustfmt'
info: installing component 'cargo'
info: installing component 'clippy'
info: installing component 'rust-docs'
 14.9 MiB /  14.9 MiB (100 %)   9.3 MiB/s in  1s ETA:  0s
info: installing component 'rust-std'
 26.6 MiB /  26.6 MiB (100 %)  13.3 MiB/s in  2s ETA:  0s
info: installing component 'rustc'
 60.5 MiB /  60.5 MiB (100 %)  13.2 MiB/s in  4s ETA:  0s
info: installing component 'rustfmt'
info: default toolchain set to 'stable-x86_64-unknown-linux-g-
nu'
  stable-x86_64-unknown-linux-gnu installed - rustc 1.77.1
(7cf61ebde 2024-03-27)
Rust is installed now. Great!
To get started you may need to restart your current shell.
This would reload your PATH environment variable to include
Cargo's bin directory ($HOME/.cargo/bin).
```

```
To configure your current shell, you need to source
the corresponding env file under $HOME/.cargo.
This is usually done by running one of the following (note the
leading DOT):
. "$HOME/.cargo/env"  # For sh/bash/zsh/ash/dash/pdksh
source "$HOME/.cargo/env.fish"  # For fish
```

If yours is anything like this, you are done. You can now verify that Rust is installed correctly by running the following two commands (If the text above suggests a different highlighted command to this one, use that one instead):

```
$ source $HOME/.cargo/env
$ cargo --version
```

The second command should print the following (Rust version will likely be different - a new version releases every 6 weeks):

```
cargo 1.77.1 (e52e36006 2024-03-26)
```

If that's it, hooray! You have Rust installed!

INSTALLING VS CODE AND/OR RUST ANALYZER

Now that we have installed Rust, we need to set up a development environment. Unfortunately, Rust is not a language that is easy to just eyeball without any guide, so a good editor with a language server is a great help.

If you already have an editor that you prefer and are familiar with, you can visit the following website to see how well it is supported and what steps you need to take to have proper Rust integration installed:
https://areweideyet.com/

Note that by virtue of the Rust community being very passionate about the craft, many editors are supported, including ones that are not listed at **Are We IDE Yet?** I use the **kakoune** editor, which is not on this list, and it works perfectly fine.

For this book though, it is best to follow the conventions and use mainstream tools, since they have the best support, and you can always find someone who will help you troubleshoot. In the case of Rust, the mainstream editor is **Visual Studio Code** with the **rust-analyzer** extension.

Installing Rust Analyzer

Rust Analyzer is the main LSP implementation for Rust. **LSP** stands for **Language Server Protocol** - a protocol to provide hints, diagnostics and other nice tools and pieces of information to editors, letting you transform editors into bona fide IDEs just by setting up the extension that provides LSP support.

The **rust-analyzer** extension in VS Code is able to install Rust Analyzer by itself, but especially if you are using a different editor, it is useful to know how to do it by hand.

It is very simple, just run this command:

```
rustup component add rust-analyzer
```

This is the output if the command succeeds:

```
info: downloading component 'rust-analyzer'
info: installing component 'rust-analyzer'
```

And we can verify that it works:

```
$ rust-analyzer --version
rust-analyzer 1.77.1 (7cf61eb 2024-03-27)
```

If you try running **rust-analyzer** by hand, it will not show you any output. The LSP server is meant to be started by editors and does not provide human-readable output by default.

Note that if you see this:

```
error: Unknown binary 'rust-analyzer' in official toolchain
'stable-x86_64-unknown-linux-gnu'.
```

Then the installation was not successful. Most likely, the **rustup component add** command failed. Try running it again, it should not harm anything.

There are a number of toolchain components that you can install via **rustup**. You can see the complete list by running:

```
$ rustup component list
```

You will see tons of standard library distributions for different architectures. Rust supports cross-compilation quite well, in part thanks to its implementation with the LLVM project as its compiler backend. However, there is a different mechanism for adding targets for cross-compilation.

There is one more component you may want to consider installing now:

```
$ rustup component add rust-src
```

Several tools in the Rust ecosystem provide better diagnostics if they have the source code of the standard library available, and this is the command that makes that happen.

Installing and setting up VS Code

To install Visual Studio Code, first head to its official website and select the download option that matches your operating system: Windows, macOS, or Linux. Visit the following link:
https://code.visualstudio.com/

And follow the instructions.

For Windows users, the process involves downloading an `.exè file and running it. During installation, it's recommended to choose the option to "Add to PATH," which simplifies launching the editor from the command line.

Mac users will download a `.zip̀ file, then need to extract it and move the Visual Studio Code application to the Applications folder. macOS users might also find Visual Studio Code available through Homebrew, a package manager that can install the software more seamlessly.

Linux users have a variety of installation methods available, depending on their distribution. Many Linux distributions offer Visual Studio Code directly in their repositories, allowing installation via the distribution's package manager with a simple command. For distributions that don't include it, or for users preferring a manual installation, downloading a `.tar.gz̀ file from the Visual Studio Code website and extracting it to run the `codè binary is the alternative method.

Here is how to install VS Code on some mainstream Linux distributions:

1. Ubuntu/Debian and derivatives (Mint, Linux MX, Deepin, Pop_OS, Elementary OS) using apt:

- Command: **`sudo apt update && sudo apt install code`**
- Note: You may need to add the Microsoft repository first (only do this if the above commands do not work - note that these are three commands, each a single line - it might not be clear from the way the lines are broken):

```
wget -qO- https://packages.microsoft.com/keys/microsoft.asc |
gpg --dearmor > packages.microsoft.gpg
sudo install -o root -g root -m 644 packages.microsoft.gpg /
usr/share/keyrings/
sudo sh -c 'echo "deb [arch=amd64 signed-by=/usr/share/key-
rings/packages.microsoft.gpg] https://packages.microsoft.com/
repos/vscode stable main" > /etc/apt/sources.list.d/vscode.
list'
```

2. Fedora/Red Hat and derivatives (using dnf)

- Command: `sudo dnf check-update && sudo dnf install code`
- Note: Visual Studio Code may be available in the repositories directly or through third-party repositories like RPM Fusion.

3. Arch Linux (using pacman)

- Command: `sudo pacman -S code`
- Note: Visual Studio Code can be installed from the Arch User Repository (AUR) as `code` for the official version or `visual-studio-code-bin` for the binary distribution.

4. openSUSE (using zypper)

- Command: `sudo zypper refresh && sudo zypper install code`
- Note: You might need to add the Visual Studio Code repository first depending on your setup.

5. CentOS (using yum)

- Command: `sudo yum check-update && sudo yum install code`
- Note: As CentOS is closely related to Fedora/Red Hat, the process may require enabling EPEL or other third-party repositories first.

6. Gentoo (using emerge)

- Command: `sudo emerge --update --newuse code`
- Note: Visual Studio Code may need to be unmasked by adding it to /

`etc/portage/package.accept_keywords` depending on your stability requirements and Gentoo's categorization of the package.

7. Snap Package (Universal for Linux distributions)

- Command: `sudo snap install code --classic`
- Note: Snap packages are distribution-agnostic and require snapd to be installed. This method works across many different Linux distributions.

8. Flatpak (Universal for Linux distributions)

- Command: `flatpak install flathub com.visualstudio.code`
- Note: Similar to snap, Flatpak is a universal package system that works across various Linux distributions. You'll need to have Flatpak installed and the Flathub repository added.

On MacOS, if you have **homebrew** installed, you can also install VS Code like this:

```
brew install --cask visual-studio-code
```

This is the preferred method for MacOS systems that have **brew** available.

Once installed, Visual Studio Code can be launched from your applications or start menu, ready for use. If you want to run VS Code from the command line, you can:

```
$ code
```

This will run VS Code and fork into the background, meaning you can close the terminal window.

Next, install the rust-analyzer extension. First, click on the extension icon:

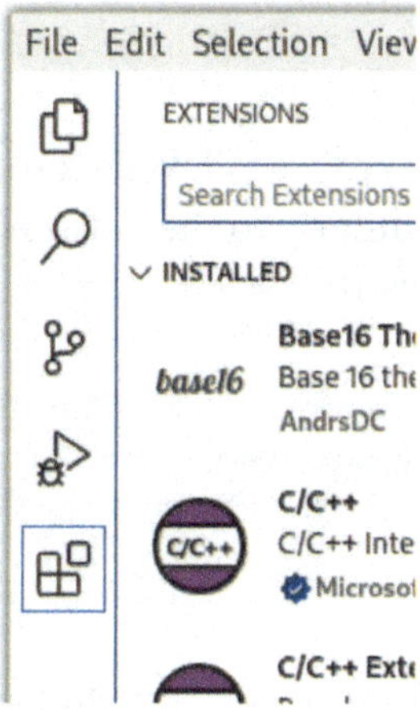

Then search for **rust-analyzer:**

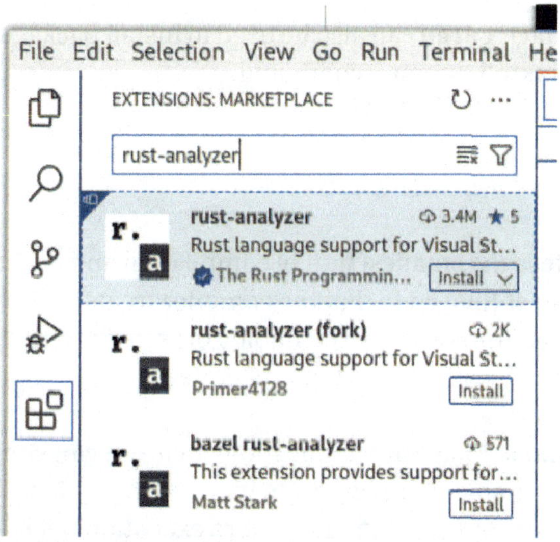

Install the highlighted extension and that should be it. The extension may then ask you for some initial setup configuration - you can leave all options to be the default, no additional changes should be necessary.

CREATING A WORKSPACE AND STARTING WITH RUST

At last, we have everything we need to start developing Rust but before we begin, there are some quirks about Rust development we need to get out of the way first.

First and foremost, it is very rare to invoke the compiler directly. The compiler, called **rustc**, behaves similarly to the various **C/C++** compilers, and we can invoke it directly, if we want:

```
rustc main.rs -o my_program
```

However, this would make working with dependencies difficult (actually, just as difficult as it is in C/C++). The toolchain comes bundled with the **Cargo** tool. **Cargo** is a package manager as well as a build system. It is responsible for both fetching and configuring your dependencies, and for building your project.

As a matter of fact, **Cargo** can also be used to install packages to your system via the **cargo install <name>** command.

Crates

In Rust, **a crate** is the smallest unit of compilation and packaging. It‘s essentially a package of Rust code that the compiler treats as a single unit. Crates can be compiled into binary executables or into libraries that other crates can link against. There are two types of crates:

1. **Binary Crates**: These are applications that you can compile into a standalone executable. A binary crate has a `main.rs` file as its entry point, containing the `main()` function where execution begins.

2. **Library Crates**: These are collections of code intended to be used as dependencies by other crates. A library crate doesn‘t have a `main()` function and instead provides functions, types, and constants that can be used by other crates. The entry point for a library crate is typically `lib.rs`.

A crate can have both a binary and library part. As we will see later, there can be multiple executable binaries produced by a crate, but only one library.

Crates can be published on crates.io, which is Rust's official package registry, allowing developers to share their code with the community. We will take a closer look at crates.io when we start adding dependencies to our project. When you create a project using cargo, Rust's package manager and build system, automatically manages your project as a crate. This includes compiling your project, downloading and compiling dependencies, and more.

A key feature of crates is their support for modularity and reusability. By organizing code into crates, developers can easily share and reuse code across projects. Crates also allow for versioning and dependency management, making it simpler to manage complex projects with many dependencies.

Dependency management

In Rust, dependency management is fairly streamlined and efficient, thanks to Cargo, Rust's build tool and package manager. Dependencies for a Rust project are declared in a file named `Cargo.toml`. This file contains all the necessary information about a project, including which external crates the project depends on. Here's how dependencies might look in a `Cargo.toml` file:

```
[package]
name = "my_project"
version = "0.1.0"
edition = "2021"
[dependencies]
serde = "1.0" # a library for de/serialization
log = "0.4" # a logging facade, in binary crates, you need to
add an implementation crate, too
```

In this example, the project depends on two crates: `serde` and `log`, with specified versions. This explicitness in declaring dependencies makes it clear what the project needs to build and run, avoiding ambiguity and ensuring consistency.

NOTE: serde is a library for serialization and deserialization into a variety of commonly used formats (such as JSON, YAML, TOML and binary formats like CBOR). The serde library itself contains no formats, it is purely generic over them, you usually also need to include a backend with one, such as serde_json. The log library is a facade for a variety of logging backends.

When it comes to managing these dependencies, Cargo commands play a crucial role. Here are a few key commands:

Adding a New Dependency: Instead of manually editing the `Cargo.toml` file, you can add a new dependency with Cargo by running:

```
cargo add serde_json
```

This command automatically finds the latest version of `serde_json` and adds it to your `Cargo.toml`.

Updating Dependencies: To update your project's dependencies to their latest permissible versions according to the specifications in `Cargo.toml`, use:

```
cargo update
```

This will update the `Cargo.lock` file, which tracks the exact versions of each dependency being used. If you come from the Javascript world, you will be familiar with similar lockfiles (package.lock, yarn.lock).

Building a Project: To compile your project along with its dependencies, run:

```
cargo build
```

This command compiles the project, downloading and compiling the dependencies if they're not already compiled.

Running a Project: To run your project directly, use:

```
cargo run
```

This compiles the project and its dependencies (if necessary) and then runs the resulting executable.

Cargo's design around the `Cargo.toml` and `Cargo.lock` files ensures that all team members working on a project use the same versions of dependencies, leading to consistent builds and reducing "it works on my machine" problems, which are always fun to debug. This straightforward approach to dependency management keeps Rust projects organized and their builds reproducible. Furthermore, Rust has a mechanism for "deleting without deleting". Crates can be **yanked**, which will prevent new projects from depending on them (or on particular versions of a crate), without breaking software that already depends on it. Keep in mind that crates.io does **not** support deletion, so do not publish things you do not want to publish.

A tiny Cargo command reference

This table includes some of the most commonly used Cargo commands that you might find helpful for your Rust projects.

Command	Description
cargo new <project_name>	Creates a new Rust project in a new directory.
cargo init	Initializes a new Rust project in the current directory.

`cargo build`	Compiles the current project and all of its dependencies.
`cargo run`	Compiles and runs the current project.
`cargo test`	Runs the tests for the current project.
`cargo check`	Quickly checks your code to ensure it compiles but does not produce an executable.
`cargo clean`	Removes the target directory with the compiled artifacts.
`cargo update`	Updates dependencies as recorded in the local lock file.
`cargo doc`	Generates documentation for the current project's dependencies.
`cargo publish`	Packages and uploads the current project to crates.io.
`cargo bench`	Runs the benchmarks of the current project. (Note: Requires a nightly

You can see the help information for all of the commands by either writing **cargo <command> --help** (short reference) **cargo help <command>** (opens manual page). However, there is a number of flags that are supported across multiple commands and are commonly used:

Flag	Applicable Commands	Description
`-v, --verbose`	Most commands	Increases the verbosity of the command output. Can be used multiple times for increased effect.
`-q, --quiet`	Most commands	Reduces the amount of output from Cargo, opposite of `--verbose`.
`--release`	`build, run, test, etc.`	Compiles the project in release mode, with optimizations.
`--debug`	(Custom builds)	Compiles the project in debug mode, without optimizations. This is the default for some commands.
`-p <package>, --package <package>`	`build, run, test, check, etc.`	Specifies a specific package to operate on in a workspace.
`--all`	(Deprecated in favor of `--workspace`)	Operates on all packages in the workspace. Deprecated in favor of `--workspace`.
`--workspace`	`build, run, test, check, etc.`	Operates on all packages in the workspace.
`--bin <name>`	`build, run, test, etc.`	Compiles or runs the specified binary.
`--example <name>`	`build, run, test, etc.`	Compiles or runs the specified example.

--lib	build, run, test, etc.	Compiles or tests the library target.
--tests	test, build, etc.	Compiles or runs the test targets.
--all-targets	build, check, test, etc.	Builds all targets (lib, bins, examples, tests, and benches).
--features <features>	build, run, test, etc.	Enables specified space-separated list of features.
--no-default-features	build, run, test, etc.	Disables the default features.
--target <TARGET>	build, run, test, etc.	Compiles for the specified target triple.
--jobs <N>, -j <N>	build, run, test, etc.	Limits the number of parallel jobs, equivalent to Makefile's -j.

You can find more detailed documentation for Cargo online:
https://doc.rust-lang.org/cargo/index.html

Workspace setup

A Cargo workspace is a feature for managing multiple related crates in a single overarching environment. Its primary merit lies in its ability to compile multiple crates together, optimizing compile time and sharing dependencies across them. This is especially useful in large projects with several crates that may depend on each other, as it allows for a unified handling of all dependencies from a single location. Workspaces ensure that all member crates use the same version of each dependency, preventing conflicts and ensuring consistent behavior across the entire project.

Workspaces also simplify project management by having a shared `Cargo.lock` file for binary crates, ensuring that all crates within the workspace are built with the same set of dependencies. This uniformity is crucial for the coherence of the project, ensuring that changes in one part of the workspace do not inadvertently break another. Moreover, workspaces allow for shared output directories, making it easier to run and test the binaries and libraries in the development process.

Let's set up a Cargo workspace, which we will name "rsbtc" with the specified crates. First, create a folder called rsbtc:

1. **Create a Workspace Configuration File**: Start by creating a new file named `Cargo.toml` in the root of the **"rsbtc/"** folder. This file will declare the workspace configuration and its members.

2. **Specify Workspace Members**: In the `Cargo.toml` file, define the workspace and its member crates like so:

```
[workspace]
resolver = "2"
members = [
    "lib",
    "miner",
    "node",
    "wallet",
]
```

3. **Initialize Each Crate**: For each of the specified folders (lib, miner, node, wallet), navigate into the folder and initialize a new crate. For the library crate (`btclib`[24]), use the `--lib` flag; for binary crates, the default `--bin` flag applies. Here are the commands for each:

24 After you create the "lib", open its Cargo.toml and rename it to "btclib" for clarity.

```
cd rsbtc
cargo new --lib lib
cargo new --bin miner
cargo new --bin node
cargo new --bin wallet
```

Note: --bin is the default and this decision is in no way permanent. You can have both, this just makes Cargo generate either a **lib.rs** or a **main.rs** file to start with.

Cargo will complain along the way, but after all of the crates are created, running **cargo check**, should work just fine:

```
    Locking 4 packages to latest compatible versions
    Checking miner v0.1.0 (/root/rsbtc/miner)
    Checking node v0.1.0 (/root/rsbtc/node)
    Checking lib v0.1.0 (/root/rsbtc/lib)
    Checking wallet v0.1.0 (/root/rsbtc/wallet)
    Finished `dev` profile [unoptimized + debuginfo] target(s) in
0.17s
```

After running these commands, each folder will contain its own `Cargo.toml` file and a source directory (`src`) with a default source file (`lib.rs` for the library crate and `main.rs` for binary crates). You can then edit each crate's `Cargo.toml` to set the correct package name to match the crate names provided (`btc_lib, miner, node, wallet`).

4. **Building and Running the Workspace**: With the workspace configured, you can build all crates in the workspace by running `cargo build` from the root "rsbtc" folder. To run a specific crate, navigate to the crate's directory and use `cargo run`.

Now is the time to write some Rust.

RUST: THE FIRST CONTACT

Before we start designing the shared library, we will experiment with the language a bit to get the hang of it.

First, create a new binary crate called **hello_world**, either inside of the **rsbtc/** folder as a member of the workspace, or outside of it as a freestanding crate. You can simply run:

```
cargo new --bin hello_world
```

Then, open the **hello_world** folder in either VS Code, or your editor of choice.

Hello world

If you navigate to the src/main.rs file, you will see the following:

```
fn main() {
  println!("Hello, world!");
}
```

This is the quintessential hello world program we all know and love. You can run the programming by running either of the following two commands:

- cargo run
- cargo build; target/debug/hello_world

Rust builds output final binaries and intermediate artifacts in the **target/** folder by default. In this folder, there are subfolders for each build profile. Most of the time, we are only interacting with two build profiles, the default **debug** profile (which produces unoptimized binaries with debugging information embedded in them), and the **release** profile, which produces optimized binaries.

Let's look at the source code bit by bit:

- The **fn** keyword declares a function
- The function is named **main**, and takes no arguments, hence the empty parentheses "**()**"
- Function argument lists are followed by code block, delimited by **{ }**, that serves as the body of the function

Inside the function, we have a single statement, **println!("Hello, world!").** This statement is used for printing to the standard output and is not a function call, but rather a macro.

In Rust, we encounter macros quite often. The reason why **println!** and similar macros are macros and not functions is twofold - Rust has no variadic functions, and using a macro lets us do useful checks at compile time. If you've never heard of the term **variadic function**, it is a function that can take any number of parameters, and process them one by one. This is needed if you want to print multiple values ergonomically.

We can take a look at the useful checks provided by the **println!** Macro.

Let's adjust our code to the following (feel free to substitute with your own name):

```
fn main() {
    let my_name = "Lukáš";
    println!("Hello, {}!");
}
```

Now try running it.

You should get the following error:

```
error: 1 positional argument in format string, but no argu-
ments were given
 --> hello_world/src/main.rs:4:22
  |
4 | println!("Hello, {}!");
```

```
  |                         ^^
error: could not compile `hello_world` (bin "hello_world") due
to 1 previous error
```

Here, the compiler tells you that it expected something to be substituted inside the format string, but nothing was provided.

If you forget to provide an argument to the similar **printf()** function from the C standard library, your program may still compile and you may only discover the error at runtime. It is much safer if your program just plainly does not compile at all until issues like these are fixed.

Note that macro will detect the inverse error as well:

```
fn main() {
    let my_name = "Lukáš";
    println!("Hello, world!", my_name);
}
```

Gets you:

```
error: argument never used
 --> hello_world/src/main.rs:4:31
  |
4 | println!("Hello, world!", my_name);
  |          ---------------  ^^^^^^^ argument never used
  |          |
  |          formatting specifier missing
error: could not compile `hello_world` (bin "hello_world") due
to 1 previous error
```

The correct version is:

```
fn main() {
    let my_name = "Lukáš";
    println!("Hello, {}!", my_name);
}
```

And running should display something like:

```
Hello, Lukáš!
```

This demonstrates another nice feature of Rust - UTF-8 strings by default. It does not matter where you are from, if the font in your command line window can handle the characters in your name, it will print correctly. This is not a given in other languages, and you may need to reach for special, separate functions for UTF-8 strings.

In recent Rust, you can also write the previous example as:

```
fn main() {
    let my_name = "Lukáš";
    println!("Hello, {my_name}!");
}
```

Which may be more readable to some. It still provides the same checks and protection. Let's take a look at the first statement in this updated version:

```
    let my_name = "Lukáš";
```

This is how you declare variables (mostly referred to as bindings in Rust). You start with the **let** keyword, followed by a **pattern** (more on that later), which can be a plain identifier, an **equals** sign, and the value you want to store in the variable followed by a semicolon.

After the pattern, you can optionally specify the type of the variable. In the previous case, it would be:

```
    let my_name: &str = "Lukáš";
```

The **&str** type is pronounced as **string slice**, and we will discuss it more in detail later. One of the more difficult things about Rust for newcomers is that it has many string types.

Here are a couple more examples:

```
    let age: i32 = 30; // i32 is a 32-bit signed integer
    let temperature: f64 = 20.5; // f64 is a 64-bit floating
point
    let is_active: bool = true; // Boolean type
    let initial: char = 'A'; // char represents a Unicode sca-
lar value
    let count: u32 = 100; // u32 is a 32-bit unsigned integer
    let distance = 15.0; // Rust automatically infers distance
to be f64
```

You can see two things in this snippet:

- Names of primitive types are written in all lowercase letters and tend to be very short (e.g. **u32** stands for **unsigned 32-bit integer**)
- Single-line comment start with // characters, similar to how it is done in JavaScript, C/C++, C# or Java

In Rust, there are three more comment types, making it four in total:

```
// this is a single-line comment
/*
   This is a multi-line comment
   Multiline comments can be nested /*
       /*
           /*
               Doktor, turn off my nesting inhibitors!
            */
        */
    */
   */
*/
/// This is a documentation comment that supports full mar-
kdown
/// It documents the following item (function, struct, module,
etc.)
//! This is a documentation comment, similar to previous one,
but
//! documents the items that contains it (typically used with
modules and crates)
```

We will discuss doc-comments more in-depth later. Let's now intentionally run into a hurdle, by trying to re-assign the name variable to name of Rust's mascot, the lovely crab named **Ferris**:

```
fn main() {
   let my_name: &str = "Lukáš";
   // As all know, carcinization is the final stage of evolu-
tion,
   // and I am already growing pincers B)
   my_name = "Ferris";
   println!("Hello, {my_name}!");
}
```

This will, once again, not compile, with the following complaints:

```
warning: value assigned to `my_name` is never read
 --> hello_world/src/main.rs:2:9
  |
2 | let my_name: &str = "Lukáš";
  |         ^^^^^^^
  |
  = help: maybe it is overwritten before being read?
  = note: `#[warn(unused_assignments)]` on by default
error[E0384]: cannot assign twice to immutable variable `my_
name`
 --> hello_world/src/main.rs:5:5
  |
2 | let my_name: &str = "Lukáš";
  |         -------
  |         |
  |         first assignment to `my_name`
  |         help: consider making this binding mutable: `mut
my_name`
...
5 | my_name = "Ferris";
  | ^^^^^^^^^^^^^^^^^^ cannot assign twice to immutable varia-
ble
For more information about this error, try `rustc --explain
E0384`.
warning: `hello_world` (bin "hello_world") generated 1 warning
error: could not compile `hello_world` (bin "hello_world") due
to 1 previous error; 1 warning emitted
```

First, we get a warning that the original value of the variable is never read. This is not an error in and of itself, but it is a waste, and it is nice that the compiler warns us about this behavior, since it can indicate that either we are doing something wasteful, or we forgot to use the original value even though we intended to use it.

Then we get an error saying we **cannot assign twice to an immutable vari-**

able. This is because in Rust, **variables and arguments are immutable by default**. This is very useful for optimization reasons, more on that later. It also helps to prevent some mistakes on the programmer's part.

There are two ways to fix this. First, we want to keep **my_name** immutable, we can do:

```
fn main() {
    let my_name;
    // As all know, carcinization is the final stage of evolu-
tion,
    // and I am already growing pincers
    my_name = "Ferris";
    println!("Hello, {my_name}!");
}
```

This is the same as the very first example with this variable, but we have delayed the value assignment by a couple of lines. Note that you cannot use the **my_name** variable until it has been assigned, which prevents a plethora of possible errors caused by the usage of uninitialized variables.

Something similar will not compile:

```
fn main() {
    let my_name;
    println!("My name is now {my_name}");
    my_name = "Ferris";
    println!("Hello, {my_name}!");
}
```

Producing the following error:

```
error[E0381]: used binding `my_name` is possibly-uninitialized
```

```
 --> hello_world/src/main.rs:3:30
  |
2 | let my_name;
  |       ------- binding declared here but left uninitiali-
zed
3 | println!("My name is now {my_name}");
  |                          ^^^^^^^^^ `my_name` used here
but it is possibly-uninitialized
  |
  = note: this error originates in the macro `$crate::format_
args_nl` which comes from the expansion of the macro `println`
(in Nightly builds, run with -Z macro-backtrace for more info)
For more information about this error, try `rustc --explain
E0381`.
error: could not compile `hello_world` (bin "hello_world") due
to 1 previous error
```

The second way that we can approach this problem is by declaring **my_name** as mutable:

```rust
fn main() {
    let mut my_name = "Walter Hartwell White";
    println!("My name is {my_name}. I live at \
        308 Negra Arroyo Lane, \
        Albuquerque, \
        New Mexico, \
        87104."
    );
    my_name = "Ferris";
    println!("Hello, {my_name}!");
}
```

The **mut** keyword is universally used to make things mutable. It is involved in every single language feature governing mutability (with the possible exception of interior mutability, which is a bit special, and will be discussed later).

Note that there are two ways to break multi-line strings in Rust. The previously shown way with the backslash character "\" skips new line characters and all leading whitespace on the next line. You can also omit the backslash, which will preserve all whitespace.

With backslashes, the output is:

```
My name is Walter Hartwell White. I live at 308 Negra Arroyo
Lane, Albuquerque, New Mexico, 87104
Hello, Ferris!
```

Without:

```
My name is Walter Hartwell White. I live at
    308 Negra Arroyo Lane,
    Albuquerque,
    New Mexico,
    87104.
Hello, Ferris!
```

Sometimes, one is more useful than the other. Let's now spice up our program by making the **universal text transmogrifier™.**

Extended example

The **universal text transmogrifier** is just a wacky name for a simple command line program which takes two parameters - the name of the operation and input text, then applies the operation to the text and prints it out.

Let's specify a couple of operations:

- **Reverse** - reverses a text
- **Invert** - makes lowercase letters uppercase and vice versa

- **Uppercase** - makes all letters uppercase
- **No-spaces** - removes all spaces from the text
- **Leet** - leetifies text
- **Acronym** - creates an acronym

Our program will be invoked in the following way:

```
$ hello_world op text
```

Or, via Cargo, this would be:

```
$ cargo run -- op text
```

First, we need a way to read command-line arguments. In many languages you may be familiar with, command-line arguments are passed as arguments to the **main()** function of the program.

In Rust, arguments are available via the **std::env::args()** function, which is globally available. This is quite practical, since any part of the program, and even any library you import, can access the arguments without you having to do anything special to make that happen.

Let's start with this:

```
use std::env;
fn main() {
    let args = env::args();
    for a in args {
        println!("{a}");
    }
}
```

In Rust, we import items from the standard library (and any other library, and other parts of our program) with the **use** keyword. This example imports the **std::env** module a whole. The **use** keyword is quite flexible to help you organize your imports in a way that is clear to you and most ergonomic to a particular use case:

```
// Basic import
use library::utils::print_greeting;
// Importing a struct (type) and a function
use library::geometry::{Rectangle, area};
// Import variants of an enum (more on enums later)
```

```
use library::TrafficLight::{Green, Red};
// Nested wildcard import
use library::geometry::*;
// Import both the geometry module as a whole and the Point
type in it specifically
use library::geometry::{self, Point};
```

The **env** module contains items related to the environment in which the program is running. That constitutes arguments, environment variables, the location of the executable and the current directory, among other things. You can look at the full documentation here:
https://doc.rust-lang.org/std/env/index.html

We use the **args()** function from the env module to get access to the arguments, and store them in a variable:

```
let args = env::args();
```

Then, we can iterate through them with a for loop:

```
    for a in args {
        println!("{a}");
    }
```

The **for loop** in Rust is a bit smarter than the one in C. It can iterate through anything that is an iterator (anything that can be iterated through). That is a bit of a convoluted definition, but we will discuss iterators in detail later.

Finally, we are printing each argument.

If we invoke the program with the following command:

```
cargo run -- one two three four
```

This will be the output:

```
/some/path/hello_world/target/debug/hello_world
one
two
three
four
```

The first argument is in many languages the name the program was invoked with. Some programs change their behavior if you invoke them with different names, for example **busybox** is an implementation of many common Unix commands in a single binary, and distributions using **busybox** make many links to the same binary with the name for each command contained in it.

Now, we must do something about our **args**. We know the following:

- There should be precisely three arguments in total
- We want to skip the first argument

- The second argument is the name of the operation
- The third argument is the data to do the operation on

First, we have to collect the arguments into a list, so that we can take a look at how many there are (which is not possible with iterators by default without also consuming the iterator). Change your source code to this:

```
use std::env;
fn main() {
    let args: Vec<String> = env::args().collect();
    for a in args {
        println!("{a}");
    }
}
```

Now we have collected the arguments into a vector of strings[25]. If you have never encountered the term before, a vector is a dynamically-sized list that you can add to and remove elements from.

We need to specify the type of the **args** variable here because there are many choices for what you can collect an iterator into and are valid for the surrounding statements, so the compiler does not know what to choose and we need to provide a hint.

You will notice that running the program at this stage made no changes to how it works yet.

Let's adjust the program to verify the correct argument count:

```
use std::env;
use std::process::exit;
fn main() {

   let args: Vec<String> = env::args().collect();
```

25 Vec<T>, where T is any type you want, is the type of vector in Rust.

```
    if args.len() != 3 {
        eprintln!("Usage: {} <op> <text>", args[0]);
        exit(1);
    }
    for a in args {
        println!("{a}");
    }
}
```

In Rust, if-statements do not have mandatory parentheses around the condition, but they have mandatory **brackets around the body of the if-statement.** Therefore, in general, if-statements look like this:

```
if condition {
    // code
} else if another_condition {
    // other code, else-if blocks can be repeated
} else {
    // code if nothing else matches
}
```

The if statement in our program will be triggered if the length of the **args** vector is not exactly **3**. If it isn't, the following statements will execute:

```
        eprintln!("Usage: {} <op> <text>", args[0]);
        exit(1);
```

The **eprintln!()** macro works the exact same way as the **println!()** macro, except it prints to the **standard error output**. Then, we use the **exit(1)** statement to exit the program with exit code set to 1, which is universally recognized as "something went wrong".

You can try running the program now.

Now that we have established that we have the correct number of parameters, we can store the text and the operation into separate variables.

```
use std::env;
use std::process::exit;
fn main() {
    let args: Vec<String> = env::args().collect();
    if args.len() != 3 {
        eprintln!("Usage: {} <op> <text>", args[0]);
        exit(1);
    }
    let op = &args[1];
    let text = &args[2];
    println!("op: {op} text: {text}");
}
```

If you have a rust-analyzer with inlay-hints set up, you will see the type of the **op** and **text** variables is **&String**. String is a string type that manages its own memory allocation. It is the most versatile type for strings if you want to store them somewhere. The ampersand character (&) denotes a borrow, meaning a reference to a value. Here, we are not pulling the values out of the vector, merely referring to them.

For now, it is enough if you remember that borrows may not live longer than the values they are borrowing, this is one of the main safety guarantees Rust provides. Similar to bindings, they come in two flavors, **immutable (created with the & operator)**, also called **shared borrows**, and **mutable (created with the &mut operator)**, also called **exclusive borrows**.

You can create a mutable borrow like this:

```
    let mut val = String::new();
    let ref_mut = &mut val;
```

Notice that the reference does not need to be mutable so long as you do not intend to re-assign it. Sometimes, you may also want to lose the mutability of variables. You can do this via **shadowing:**

```
let mut val = String::new();
let val = val;
```

The second, immutable **val**, shadows over the first one. Shadowing is a fairly commonly used technique in Rust, so don't be afraid to do it if you need to.

If you run the program above, it will print the following:

```
$ cargo run -- one two
op: one text: two
```

Now, let's check that we have the correct operations:

```
let res = match op.as_str() {
    "reverse" => ...,
    "invert" => ...,
    "uppercase" => ...,
    "no-spaces" => ...,
    "leet" => ...,
    "acronym" => ...,
    _ => {
        eprintln!("Invalid operation: {}", op);
        exit(1);
    }
};
```

The **match** statement is the counterpart to the **switch statement** found in many languages. In Rust, it also happens to be an expression (just like the if-else statement is, if it has an else block), and we can assign it to a variable directly.

A quirk of the **match** statement is that it always has to be exhaustive, meaning all possible values for the expression we are matching on have to be covered by one arm in the statement. In our case, the last arm **_ = > { .. }** is a catch-all that shutdowns the program if we encounter an unknown operation.

Also note that we are not matching on **op** directly, but we call **op.as_str()**. This is because we need to convert the **String** into an **&str,** which is the type of the string literals in Rust.

So far, this will not compile, we need to fill out all of the branches of the match statement.

The simplest operation is **uppercase,** since we have a handy function ready:

```
        "uppercase" => text.to_uppercase(),
```

Reversing the string is fairly straightforward also:

```
        "reverse" => text.chars().rev().collect::<String>(),
```

Here, we are taking an iterator over the characters of the string, reversing it and collecting it into another string (remember how we mentioned that there are many things we can .collect() into)

Inverting is a bit longer to write, but still simple:

```
        "invert" => text
            .chars()
```

```
        .map(|c| {
            if c.is_uppercase() {
                c.to_lowercase().to_string()
            } else {
                c.to_uppercase().to_string()
            }
        })
        .collect::<String>(),
```

Once again, we are taking an iterator over every character of the string, and then inverting it in via an if statement. Note that the **.to_lowercase()** and **.to_uppercase()** methods return new characters. The **.map()** method takes a so-called closure (an anonymous function), taking a single character as input parameter, denoted in **|c|**, and returns the result of whatever expression follows it.

Similar to **C/C++/C#/JS** and many other languages, Rust has a **return** keyword. However, it is only used when you need an early return:

```
/// returns doubled 32-bit integer
/// -> denotes the return type of a function
fn double(x: i32) -> i32 {
    x * 2
}
```

Is the same as:

```
fn double(x: i32) -> i32 {
    return x * 2;
}
```

The closure above could be written also as:

```
fn invert(c: char) -> String {
    if c.is_uppercase() {
        c.to_lowercase().to_string()
    } else {
        c.to_uppercase().to_string()
    }
}
```

And using **.map(invert)** in the match arm above. To be honest, closures can do a bit more than functions because they "close over their environment", but let's leave that for later.

Now that we know the magic of the **.map()** and the **match** statement, we can implement **leet**:

```
        "leet" => text
            .chars()
            .map(|c| match c {
                'a' | 'A' => '4',
                'e' | 'E' => '3',
                'i' | 'I' => '1',
                'o' | 'O' => '0',
                's' | 'S' => '5',
                't' | 'T' => '7',
                _ => c,
            })
            .collect::<String>(),
```

Just a simple **match** for substitutions. The **no-spaces** operation is similarly simple:

```
        "no-spaces" => text
            .chars()
            .filter(|c| !c.is_whitespace())
            .collect::<String>(),
```

The **.filter()** also takes a closure, but this closure has to return a boolean value specifically (either **true** or **false)**. We can use the **.is_whitespace()** method on **char** to check if we should filter out the given character. The **!** operator negates a boolean value, meaning the closure will return true if the character is not whitespace. Finally, we have the **acronym**:

```
        "acronym" => text
            .split_whitespace()
            .map(|word| word.chars().next().unwrap())
            .collect::<String>()
            .to_uppercase(),
```

Here, the **.split_whitespace()** separates the text into words by splitting on whitespace, then we can try to get the first character of every word. The **.unwrap()** method is needed here because the **.next()** method returns **Option<char>**. Option is a type that indicates a value may not be present, since an iterator might be empty. We need to acknowledge this possibility explicitly, and **.unwrap()** is a simple way to do that by conceding and telling Rust to safely shutdown our program if that happens.

We can finish our program by printing the **res** variable at the end of our main function:

```
use std::env;
use std::process::exit;
fn main() {
    let args: Vec<String> = env::args().collect();
    if args.len() != 3 {
        eprintln!("Usage: {} <op> <text>", args[0]);
```

```
        exit(1);
    }
    let op = &args[1];
    let text = &args[2];
    let res = match …;
    println!("{}", res);
}
```

The program should work now as expected:

```
$ cargo run -- invert ahoj
AHOJ
$ cargo run -- reverse ahoj
joha
$ cargo run -- leet leet
1337
$ cargo run -- acronym "Big F. Gun - 9 0 0 0"
BFG-9000
```

Congratulations, you have made your first program that interacts with the world! Before we get into the nitty gritty of Rust, it may be helpful to learn how to navigate the Rust documentation.

Referring to Rust documentation

Rust comes bundled with many nice resources for orienting yourself in the language, compilation errors and the standard library.

First, let's tackle the compilation errors. Let's remind ourselves of an error we encountered in the first half of this chapter:

```
error[E0381]: used binding `my_name` is possibly-uninitialized
 --> hello_world/src/main.rs:3:30
  |
```

```
2 | let my_name;
  |     ------- binding declared here but left uninitiali-
zed
3 | println!("My name is now {my_name}");
  |                          ^^^^^^^^^ `my_name` used here but
it is possibly-uninitialized
  |
  = note: this error originates in the macro `$crate::format_
args_nl` which comes from the expansion of the macro `println`
(in Nightly builds, run with -Z macro-backtrace for more info)
For more information about this error, try `rustc --explain
E0381`.
error: could not compile `hello_world` (bin "hello_world") due
to 1 previous error
```

Errors in Rust have a code, and we can ask the compiler to explain the error to use. We can run the suggested command:

```
$ rustc --explain E0381
```

That will show you this:

```
It is not allowed to use or capture an uninitialized variable.
Erroneous code example:
fn main() {
    let x: i32;
    let y = x; // error, use of possibly-uninitialized variable
}
To fix this, ensure that any declared variables are initiali-
zed before being used. Example:
fn main() {
    let x: i32 = 0;
    let y = x; // ok!
}
```

Short and sweet, and gets straight to the point. If you do not understand why you are getting a particular error, try looking at the error codes. If you prefer to view the errors in your browser, you can go to the following website: https://doc.rust-lang.org/error_codes/error-index.html

And find the error in the list.

It is also quite handy to have the standard library reference open. It is available either online, found at:
https://doc.rust-lang.org/std/

Or you view the very same document locally by running:

```
$ rustup doc
```

And navigating to the **Rust API reference**. Alternatively, you can run **rustup doc --std** directly.

Finally, it can be also helpful to have the language reference at hand:
https://doc.rust-lang.org/stable/reference/

Alternatively opened locally by running **rustup doc --reference.** Note that the reference may be a little difficult to digest at first.

But things which are difficult to digest is the topic of the next chapter, so we will be able to get you up to speed in no time.

4
TAMING RUST'S LEARNING CURVE

Rust is a bit deceptive to newcomer programmers because it looks very similar in many ways to languages they already know, but then they run into a wall when they encounter new concepts that are entirely foreign to them. In this chapter, we will take a look at the concepts that newbie programmers struggle with the most.

MEMORY MODEL

You might have already heard that Rust does not have a garbage collector, and manages its memory manually, but you might be surprised to learn that its model is a different one to the one used in C.

NOTE: If you do not know what a garbage collector is, it is a mechanism for reclaiming memory from values that are no longer used. There are many ways of implementing garbage collection in programming languages, but in general, we can think of a garbage collector as an entity, which periodically probes for unused values that have gone out of scope and frees (returns to the system) their memory. If you have played Minecraft in the early 2010s like I did, you may be familiar with the **Lag Spike of Death,** where the game would run great for a bit, then sharply lag, then run well for a bit, and so on. The reason was that you had too little available RAM memory and Java's garbage collector would freeze the process. This is because Java is an enterprise language ("enterprise" I believe to be ancient Greek for terrible design decisions ;-)).

Rust's memory management is lexical (with an increasing amount of exceptions for the sake of ergonomics), which means that memory is allocated when a variable (or just a value) is created, and freed when it goes out of scope in terms of the syntax (the closing brace of the block it is created in) unless it is moved. When something is determined to be out of scope by the Rust compiler, the compiler also ensures that there are no dangling pointers left. The part of the compiler responsible for this is called the borrow checker.

You will hear many newbie Rust developers talking about "fighting the borrow checker", or "arguing with the borrow checker". Usually, the crux of the issue is that the developer does not realize their code is in one way or another incorrect; however, there is a small category of correct programs rejected by the borrow checker.

Rust enforces **RAII (Resource Acquisition Is Initialization)**, so to put it simply, initializing a variable gives you memory or other resources (such as opening a file), and when an object goes out of scope, its destructor is called and its resources are returned to the system (sockets and files are closed, memory is freed).

In order to implement this effectively, Rust introduces a couple of new concepts. Here is a short list with some succinct definitions from **Pascal Hertleif** (in quotes):[26]

(I strongly suggest you **run the examples in Rust Playground**, Rust's compiler errors are usually very descriptive and can help provide you insight into what is going on)

> ***Ownership**: You own a resource, and when you are done with it, that resource is no longer in scope and gets deallocated.*

In Rust, to denote that you own something, you simply use its type plainly without any fluff around it:

```
fn main() {
    // I own this string in this function, by creating this
variable,
    // I have allocated memory
    let the_11th_commandment = String::from("Braiins OS
rocks!");

    // the memory used by the string will be freed here, since
    // we have not passed its ownership elsewhere and main()
ends here
}
```

> ***References** to a resource depend on the **lifetime** of that resource (i.e., they are only valid until the resource is deallocated).*

26 https://deterministic.space/rust-ownership-and-borrowing-in-150-words.html

Often, you only want to give a reference to something. This is the Rust equivalent of a `const <type>*` pointer. It only allows read access. You can create as many of these as you want:

```
// in serious Rust, you'd use &str for flexibility,
// as &String can convert to it automatically
fn print_my_string(string: &String) {
    // compare to `const char * const string`,
    // which would be the C equivalent
    println!("{}", string);
    // the reference to string is destroyed here
}
// the print_my_string() function does not take the ownership
// of the string, so you can pass it multiple times; for refe-
rences
// rust creates copies if necessary
fn main() {
    let the_11th_commandment =
        String::from("Opps want an initiative - blow up their
entire quadrant!");
    print_my_string(&the_11th_commandment);
    print_my_string(&the_11th_commandment);
    // you can also create a reference and store it in a vari-
able
    let string_ref = &the_11th_commandment;
    print_my_string(string_ref);
    // <- string_ref is destroyed here
    // <- the_11th_commandment is destroyed here
}
```

However, as stated in the excerpt from Pascal, references are only valid for as long as the resource exists. This is a common pitfall for new Rust programmers:

```
// this function won't compile
//
// we have to specify a lifetime explicitly here through the
'name syntax
```

```
// in the < > brackets,
// otherwise Rust assumes you maybe want to return
// constants, which have a 'static lifetime, and
// as such live forever
fn give_me_a_ref<'a>() -> &'a String {
    let temp  =
        String::from("Opps want an initiative - blow up their
entire quadrant!");
    &temp // same as return &temp;
      // <- temp would be freed here,
    //    the returned reference cannot outlive it
}
```

Move semantics means: Giving an owned resource to a function means giving it away. You can no longer access it.

This is a major difference to languages with C-like semantics, which use copy semantics by default, i.e. to give a parameter to a function means to create a copy which is then available in the said function.

In Rust, however, you take the value you have and give it to a function, and then you can no longer access it:

```
fn completely_safe_storage(value: String) {
    // <- value is immediately freed
}
fn main() {
    let x = String::from("1337 US Dollars");
    completely_safe_storage(x);
    // ↑ ownership of x was moved to completely_safe_storage()
    println!("{}", x);
    // ↑ this does not compile, as we no longer have the owner-
ship of x
}
```

We then say that `main()` owns `x` until `completely_safe_storage()` is called, at which point ownership is handed to it (= `x` is *moved* into the function), and `completely_safe_storage()` owns `x` until it is dropped.

> ***To not move a resource****, you instead use borrowing: You create a reference to it and move that. When you create a reference, you own that reference. Then you move it (and ownership of it) to the function you call. (Nothing new, just both concepts at the same time.)*

We have already kinda demonstrated this two examples ago, but we can make a more annotated example:

```
fn takes_reference(my_ref: &String) {
    // <- reference is moved into this function
    println!("{}", my_ref);
    // ↑ this macro actually takes all arguments by reference
    // so a &&String is created here, which is moved into the
    // internals of the macro


    // <- my_ref is destroyed here
}

fn main() {
    let x = String::from("Hello, world!");
    // ↑ allocate and initialize new string x to
    // "Hello, world!"
    // main() now owns x

    let reference = &x;
    // ↑ create a reference to x
    // main() owns this reference
    // we call this "borrowing x (immutably)"

    takes_reference(reference);
    // ↑ reference is moved into takes_reference();
    // x is freed here
}
```

To manipulate a resource without giving up ownership, you can create ***one mutable reference****. During the* ***lifetime*** *of this reference, no other references to the same resource can exist.*

To prevent issues with pointer aliasing and `memmove()`'d [27] resources, and a whole plethora of possibilities for memory corruption, Rust prevents you from having more than one reference to a resource, if said reference is mutable. For example, you can't do this:

```
fn main() {
    let mut bitcoin = String::from("bitcoin");

    // Rust is actually pretty smart,
    // so if it sees you are not using mut_ref
    // after you have created ro_ref, it will
    // destroy it early, this is a relatively
    // recent change for ergonomics in Rust
    // called Non-Lexical Lifetimes
    let mut_ref = &mut bitcoin;
    // ↑ borrow bitcoin mutably
    // mut_ref is of type `&mut String`,
    // given that the variable itself is immutable,
    // this corresponds to `char* const ptr` in C
    let ro_ref = &bitcoin;
    // ↑ borrow bitcoin immutably
    // this is what makes this example not compile
    // as bitcoin is already borrowed mutably
     println!("{}", ro_ref);
    // ↑ use the immutable borrow
     mut_ref.push_str(", the cryptocurrency");
    // ↑ use the mutable borrow
}
```

We briefly also touched on the concept of **a lifetime**. A lifetime denotes how long a resource exists or is accessible from start to finish. Mostly, we speak about these in terms of references.

27 Memmove() is a C function for "Moving" - actually copying - memory to a different destination.

Rust uses the **'ident** syntax to denote lifetimes, as we have seen in the invalid reference-returning example before. Just like in the previous parameter, they usually appear as generic parameters. What you call them is up to you, although usually, single letters starting with **'a** are used. The only thing you can do with these explicit lifetimes is verify if they are equal, or rather, if one satisfies the other (e.g. lifetime **'a** lives as long or longer than **'b**)

The exception is the **'static** lifetime, which denotes references that are valid for the entirety of the program's run from anywhere, You mainly get these via constants and statics.

```
static NUMBER_REF: &'static i32 = &42;
```

To fully illustrate the concept of lifetimes, we can annotate the previous example with appropriate lifetime scopes for values. This is more of a pseudo-code, so this example is kind of for looking only:

```
fn main() {
    'bitcoin_lifetime: {
        let mut bitcoin = String::from("bitcoin");
        'mut_ref_lifetime: {
            let mut_ref = &mut bitcoin;
            // ↑ borrow bitcoin mutably
             'ro_ref_lifetime: {
                let ro_ref = &bitcoin;
                // ↑ borrow bitcoin immutably
               println!("{}", ro_ref); // <- use the immutable
borrow
                mut_ref.push_str(", the cryptocurrency");
                // ↑ use the mutable borrow
            } // <- ro_ref goes out of scope here ┐
             //                                  ├ these refs
can't coexist,
        }     // <- mut_ref goes out of scope here ┘ hence the
issue
    } // <- bitcoin goes out of scope here
}
```

To illustrate how you can ensure two references live for the same **duration:**

```
// This denotes:
// for two references left and right, which live the same,
// return a reference that lives as long as these two
//
//
// It is important to keep in mind, that Rust can accept
// parameters of varying lifetimes by shortening one of them
// in the perspective of the function
fn max_ref<'a>(left: &'a i32, right: &'a i32) -> &'a i32 {
    if *left < *right {
        right
    } else {
        left
    }
}
```

You can also specify other types of requirements:

```
// for two lifetimes 'a and 'b, such that 'a lives
// as long as 'b or longer
fn foobar<'a, 'b>(_x: &'a i32, _y: &'b i32)
where
    'a: 'b
{
    // code...
}
```

That's it. And it's all checked at compile-time.

This is only a very brief introduction, for a more complete overview, please check out the following links:

- https://doc.rust-lang.org/book/ch04-01-what-is-ownership.html
- https://depth-first.com/articles/2020/01/27/rust-ownership-by-example/
- https://blog.logrocket.com/understanding-ownership-in-rust/

Note: *Formally, the model used in Rust is called "stacked borrows". You can read more about it in Ralf Jung's et al. paper "Stacked Borrows: An Aliasing Model for Rust*[28]

Strings in Rust

A peculiarity of Rust is that it does not have a single string type in the standard library, but rather seven (there may be more when you read this text):

- &**`str`** / &mut **`str`** - primitive string slice type behind a standard reference
- Cow<str> - Clone-on-Write wrapped string slice, works for both owned and borrowed values, not seen very often (which is unfortunate, since they can be really handy!)
- String - owned string
- OsStr - borrowed platform-native string, corresponds to `str`
- OsString - owned platform-native string, corresponds to `String`
- CStr - borrowed C string, corresponds to `str`
- CString - owned C string, corresponds to `String`

From these, you are most likely to encounter `str` and `String`, and `str` is the primitive type that is always available regardless of if you have `std` and `core` lib present.[29] Strings are very important in any programming language, and they are a great tool to illustrate the nuances of Rust's memory model, so we will introduce them here.

`str` is a slice type, which comes with some features:

- slices are views into collections regardless of where they are present, string slices can exist on the stack, heap, or compiled into the binary

28 Ralf Jung, Hoang-Hai Dang, Jeehoon Kang, and Derek Dreyer. 2020. Stacked Borrows: An Aliasing Model for Rust. Proc. ACM Program. Lang. 4, POPL, Article 41 (January 2020), 32 pages. https://doi.org/10.1145/3371109

29 The core library is the platform-independent, bare-metal-available part of the standard library.

(whereas Strings are on the heap)

- slices' size is not static or always known at compile-time, so just like trait objects, they can only exist behind a reference, so you'll generally encounter string slices as `&str` or `&mut str`

In Rust, string literals are string slices too:

```
fn my_ref() -> &'static str {
    "Hello world!"
}
```

In the previous example, I have annotated the lifetime of the reference we got. Since string literals are compiled into the library, they are by default valid for the entire run of the program.

Normal conditions for working with references and ownership still apply. You can't return a string slice of a string you've created in the function you are returning it from:

```
fn my_ref() -> &str {
    let my_string = String::new();
    &my_string
    // ↑ doesn't compile, return value references temporary
value
}
 fn my_ref2(input: &String) -> &str {
    &input
    // ↑ compiles, since input is known to live longer than the
span
    // of this function
}
```

The error here says "missing lifetime specifier" because it correctly deduces that there is nowhere outside (meaning parameters) to deduce the lifetime and borrow the value, so it assumes you must want to return a reference to either a static or a string slice literal (which also has a static lifetime, given it is compiled into the binary).

An important feature is that you can create string slices from other string slices without copying data by re-borrowing:

```
fn main() {
    let my_str = "Hello, world!";
    let hell = &my_str[..4];
    println!("{} {}!", my_str, hell);
}
```

We can do this, since we are working with immutable references, and the mutable reference cannot exist so long as immutable ones exist.

```
fn main() {
    let my_str: &mut str = "Hello, world!";
}
```

This does not compile because string literals are always immutable (see that the error says "types differ in mutability"). And no, you cannot circumvent this by doing &mut *"Hello, world" ;-) that would be very unsafe.

> ***TIP:*** *By the "types differ in mutability" error, you might deduce that a borrow and its mutability make for separate types, that is* `T is not the same type as &T is not the &mut T`*. Keep that in mind when you have to enter a generic parameter somewhere or create a trait implementation.*

Let's also look into owned **Strings**, as they are extremely common. Owned strings do not have a lifetime because they manage their own heap allocation.

```rust
fn my_string() -> String {
    String::from("Hello, world");
    // or "Hello, world".to_string()
}
```

You usually use **owned** strings wherever &str is impractical or you need mutability. `&String` coerces into `&str`, so it is always the proper choice when needing read-only string function parameters:

```rust
// don't
fn my_fun1(_input: &String) {}
// do
fn my_fun2(_input: &str) {}
fn main() {
  let my_string = String::new();
  my_fun1(&my_string); // both work
  my_fun2(&my_string);
  // however, this wouldn't work:
  //
  // my_fun1("Hello!")   <- type mismatch, expected &String,
got &str
}
```

As you can see, using **`&str`** provides greater flexibility.

Lifetimes of owned vs unowned values

Sometimes when looking into Rust, you might hear that owned values have static lifetimes. The static lifetime here means that the value is not a borrow of anything else, and so no other value imposes a lifetime on it. This makes owned values type-check where `'static` is required.

```
fn main() {
    let owned_string = String::from("I'm not static, but I'm
owned");
    print_static(owned_string);
}
// This function expects an instance of any type with a 'sta-
tic lifetime.
// We can pass in string despite it not having any lifetime
expli
```

```
citly
// attacked to it
fn print_static<T: 'static>(value: T) {
    println!("Value: {:?}", value);
}
```

If a type is holding a borrow to something, then it needs to have the lifetime of the contained reference(s) as a generic parameter, and its lifetime will be bound by the shortest-lived contained reference (this is to, once again, prevent memory unsafety). Another way to put it is that the type holding the borrows needs to be valid, and it can only be valid for as long as all of the borrows are valid. Therefore, its lifetime is that of its shortest living field.

```
// In more technical terms, lifetimes are generic parameters,
// and Holder needs to be generic over the lifetime of the
// reference.
struct Holder<'a> {
    reference: &'a str,
}
fn main() {
    let text = String::from("Hello");
    let holder = Holder { reference: &text };
    println!("{}", holder.reference);
}
```

The lifetime of an owned value is bound by the scope of the function (or rather *code block*) it was declared in, provided it isn't moved. Without creating a reference, owned values can only be moved and possibly copied if it is allowed for said type.

```
fn main() {
    let x = String::from("hello");
    {
        let y = x; // x is moved to y
        println!("{}", y);
    } // y goes out of scope here, meaning it is dropped, and
deallocated
    // println!("{}", x); // Error: x was moved
    let a = 5; // i32 implements Copy, and so it can be copied
    {
        let b = a; // a is copied to b
        println!("{}", b);
    }
    println!("{}", a); // still valid
}
```

Types in Rust fall into two categories - types with copy semantics and types with move semantics. In the previous example, i32 is a copy type - it is copied whenever it is passed somewhere else, and the old copy is still valid. However, String has move semantics, if we pass it somewhere else, it is moved, rather than copied, and the previous variable that stored the String is no longer valid. In C and other languages that do pass-by-value as opposed to passing around references implicitly, copy semantics are used by default. In Rust, move semantics are the default, and copy semantics are opt-in via the Copy trait.

Finally, the lifetime of a reference is bound by both the scope of the function it was declared in, and by the lifetime of the owned value it is borrowing. References themselves are values and types also (remember from a couple of lines above: Rust considers `&T` to be a distinct type and you can implement traits on it), so rules of ownership apply to them as well.

```
fn main() {
    let outer;
    {
        let owned = String::from("hello");
        let reference = &owned;
        outer = reference; // Error: `owned` does not live long
enough
        println!("{}", reference);
    } // `owned` is dropped here
    // println!("{}", outer); // Would not compile
    let mut ref1 = &5;
    {
        let x = 10;
        ref1 = &x; // ref1 now points to x
        println!("{}", ref1);
    } // x is dropped, ref1 now dangling
    // println!("{}", ref1); // Would not compile
}
fn print_ref<T: std::fmt::Display>(r: &T) {
    println!("Reference value: {}", r);
}
```

In this example we can see that we cannot use references to leak owned values to the outside. We cannot create dangling references to values that would be dropped sooner than the reference is last used. Let's also quickly illustrate that references are their own distinct types:

```
trait SayHi {
    fn say_hi(self);
}
impl SayHi for Hello {
    fn say_hi(self) {
        println!("This hi! will cost me my life - I am owned
value");
    }
}
```

```rust
impl SayHi for &Hello {
    fn say_hi(self) {
        println!("Hi, I am a reference to Hello!");
    }
}
impl SayHi for &&Hello {
    fn say_hi(self) {
        println!("Hi, I am a double reference to Hello!");
    }
}
fn main() {
    let hello = Hello;
    (&hello).say_hi();
    (&&hello).say_hi();
    hello.say_hi();
}
```

As you can see, we have three distinct implementations of the same trait - one on **Hello**, another on the reference **&Hello**, and finally one on **&&Hello**. You wouldn't be doing these multiple implementations in regular Rust without a good reason, but here they serve to let us know that references are distinct types. If you run this program, you get the following output:

```
Hi, I am a reference to Hello!
Hi, I am a double reference to Hello!
This hi! will cost me my life - I am owned value
```

There is a bit of trivia to be known about the properties of references:

- `&T` is `Copy`, meaning the compiler will create and pass around copies as applicable
- `&mut T` is not `Copy`, meaning it follows move semantics and when used as a parameter, it gets *moved* rather than *copied*

This comes from the definition of borrowing rules written above, and may lead to unexpected surprises when you don't pay attention to it.

Here's an example:

```
// in the business, we call this foreshadowing ;-)
struct MyStruct<'a> {
    remainder: Option<&'a str>,
}
// ↑ here, we have created a struct which holds
//   a reference to an Option of a string slice.
//
//  string slices without the 'static lifetime are views
//  into strings, and cannot outlive them, hence the
//  lifetime parameter
// impl blocks are used to create methods for types,
// we need to respect the generic lifetime parameter
impl<'a> MyStruct<'a> {
    // this will keep returning the first character
    fn pop_first_char_as_string(&mut self) -> Option<&str> {
        // surprise! remainder here gets copied,
        // so we are not modifying which pointer is
        // stored in self, but only a copy on the stack
        let remainder = &mut self.remainder?;
        let c = &remainder[0..1];
        if remainder.len() != 1 {
            *remainder = &remainder[1..];
            Some(c)
        } else {
            self.remainder.take()
        }
    }
}

fn main() {
    let mut broken = MyStruct {
        remainder: Some("Hello"),
    };

    for _ in 0..5 {
        println!("{:?}", broken.pop_first_char_as_string());
    }
}
```

If we run this, we will get the following output:

```
Some("H")
Some("H")
Some("H")
Some("H")
Some("H")
```

The reason why this code does not work as you might expect is that the underlying immutable reference got copied and *then* we took an immutable reference to said reference.
We still need a `&mut &'a str` to properly solve this, however, we need to prevent the copy. The solution is to borrow mutably while still inside the option either through pattern matching or by using a handy dandy `.as_mut()` method on Option, the result of which is another option containing a mutable reference to the contents of the original Option, if it was **Some**.

> *Note that the above example is still not ideal - it will panic if an* **Option::Some("")**, *that is, Some with an empty string slice, is passed. In a more serious setting, we would be performing checks to prevent this panic, or using methods which cannot panic.*[30]

Here is how to pattern-match borrow:

```
if let Some(ref mut contents) = Some("Hey") {
    // ...
}
```

The if-let will bind the value to the right of the equation sign to the pattern on the left side, if the pattern matches the value.

`ref` and `ref mut` are special pattern modifiers that borrow whatever matches

30 Typically, the standard library and 3rd party crates document if something can panic and when - check the documentation if you are unsure about something.

them. Sometimes, new developers confuse it with (or question why it isn't) `Some(&mut contents) = Some("Hey")`.

The latter is a valid syntax also, but it does the opposite, it pattern matches mutable references and binds the data it points to to contents, which is what we don't want in this case.

If you want to know more about slices and string slices, please check out the following links:

- https://doc.rust-lang.org/book/ch04-03-slices.html
- https://doc.rust-lang.org/std/primitive.str.html

Pattern matching

Pattern matching has been briefly mentioned in the paragraph above. You have likely already encountered it and will encounter it many more times doing common tasks in Rust.

If you want to learn more about pattern-matching, check out the section on the sidebar.

In general, there is two types of patterns, constant patterns and bindings.

Constant patterns limit which values are acceptable by set pattern, for example, in the following pattern:

```
if let Some(val) = some_option {}
```

The Some(...) part is constant -> nothing other than an Option::Some will match this, whereas val is binding, it will bind whatever is in that spot in said value to the name val, which is then available in this if.

Some patterns are also invariant (also called irrefutable), whereas others are not (called refutable):

```rust
let (first, second) = a_tuple_of_two;
```

Here, this pattern is always true (so it is invariant, irrefutable), we know if we get a tuple, we can always destructure it into its constituent elements. The fact that it is a tuple of two here is the constant factor, ie. (.., ..).

Patterns can be nested as much as you want or need:

```rust
if let (Some(4), Err(MyErrorEnum::Other(err))) = a_pair {

}
```

Here, this pattern will only match on a pair of Option and Result, if the Option is of the variant Some and Result of the variant Err. Furthermore, the Option must contain the integer **4**, and the Err must contain a `MyErrorEnum::Other` variant of the supplied error type. We then bind the inner error in this type into the name `err`, which then becomes available inside the if-let.

Global "variables" in Rust

While you are unlikely to run into these soon, this seems to be the correct place to mention a major difference in approach between Rust and other mainstream programming languages.

To put it bluntly, Rust *really, really, doesn't like global variables*. This is with regards to two of its stated goals, name explicitness and safety.

Global variables are generally pretty bad when it comes to safety especially across threads, and using them properly requires synchronization mechanisms. Adding these implicitly is beyond the "explicitness" goal of Rust, so the Rust way of doing things is to restrict them severely.

In Rust, global variables are called *statics*, which speaks to their nature as often being static and requiring static initialization only.

Statics are declared with the `static` keyword, have to have their type typed out (no, or very little, type inference):

```
static N: i32 = 5;
static mut M: i32 = 15;
```

Mutable statics are quite problematic, and they can only be used in unsafe code, since you are prone to running into issues with multithreaded code, data races, race conditions etc.
If you need mutable shared states, you have to use one of the types with interior mutability, such as a `Mutex`. (More on that later)

However, only literals and constant function calls are allowed in static context (and all references to types have to have the static lifetime), so you need to use a crate that provides lazy static functionality.

OBJECT-ORIENTED PROGRAMMING IN RUST

OOP in Rust is one of the biggest culture shocks newcomers experience:

- Rust does not have classes
- Rust does not have type inheritance

Visibility and privacy

Just like you might be used to from your other languages, Rust has methods and visibility modifiers to facilitate encapsulation and information hiding.

For instance:

```
#![allow(unused_code)]
pub fn public_function() {
  println!("Available from everywhere");
}
```

```rust
fn private_function() {
  println!("Only accessible by this module and its descen-
dants");
}
pub(crate) my_public_in_crate_function() {
   println!("Accessible from the same crate");
}

/// This is roughly equivalent to the following file structure
///
/// my_module.rs
/// my_module/
///      - child_module.rs
///     - child_module/
///         - grand_child_module.rs
///     - other_child.rs
mod my_module {
  pub mod child_module {
      pub mod grand_child_module {
          pub(super) fn public_in_grand_child() {
              println!("only accessible from this module \
                       (and its descendants) and its parent
 (super)");
          }
          pub(self) fn public_in_self() {
              println!("Only accessible by this module and its
 descendants, \
                       effectively same as private");
          }
          pub(in crate::my_module) fn public_in_my_module() {
              println!("Public from my_module onwards");
          }
      }
  }
  pub mod other_child {
      pub(super) fn public_in_my_module() {
          println!("Accessible from my_module onwards");
      }
  }
}
```

As you can see, Rust allows a fair amount of control over visibility and privacy. You can read up on it more here:
https://doc.rust-lang.org/reference/visibility-and-privacy.html

Methods

Methods are split from data via an implementation block:

```
pub struct AveragedCollection {
    list: Vec<i32>,
    average: f64,
}
impl AveragedCollection {
    pub fn add(&mut self, value: i32) {
        self.list.push(value);
        self.update_average();
    }

    pub fn remove(&mut self) -> Option<i32> {
        let result = self.list.pop();
        match result {
            Some(value) => {
                self.update_average();
                Some(value)
            }
            None => None,
        }
    }
    pub fn average(&self) -> f64 {
        self.average
    }

    fn update_average(&mut self) {
        let total: i32 = self.list.iter().sum();
        self.average = total as f64 / self.list.len() as f64;
    }
}
(taken from rust book [17.2])
```

User-defined types (structs and enums)

In place of classes, Rust's user-defined types fall into these two categories:

- **structures** - can be C-like structs or tuples. Rust also allows empty, zero--sized structs (also called ***unit structs***) as a useful abstraction for working with traits
- **enums** - essentially algebraic data types you might be used to from Haskell / ML / OCaml / Scala and so on. In Rust, they are implemented as tagged unions[31]

> ***BTW:*** *Rust also supports plain C-like* **unions**, *however, these are very rarely used, and their handling requires unsafe code, since the compiler can't always guarantee you select the correct union member. (Compare with enums where the valid union member is stored in the tag, so it is always known to the compiler)*

There are certain conventions observed when working with structs and enums, which you can read about here:

- https://doc.rust-lang.org/book/ch05-01-defining-structs.html

Traits

The heavy lifters of Rust's OOP story are not structs or enums, but rather *traits*. A trait describes common behavior, in less abstract terms, it is essentially a set of methods

a type is expected to provide, if it implements (satisfies) the trait. There is no such thing as **duck typing** in Rust, so you have to *pledge allegiance* to a trait manually:

```
trait Quack {
    fn quack(&self);
}
struct Duck;
// Duck implements Quack
// it has the trait method quack()
impl Quack for Duck {
    fn quack(&self) {
```

31 https://en.wikipedia.org/wiki/Tagged_union

```
        println!("quack");
    }
}
struct Human;
// Human does not implement Quack
// it has a **type** method quack()
// but that is no substitute for the real
// art
impl Human {
    fn quack(&self) {
        println!("I quack, therefore I am");
    }
}
```

> ***TIP:*** *A trait may also have zero methods. We refer to these as* ***marker traits****. Several of these are found in the compiler and they are usually ascribed special meaning, for example, the std::marker::Copy trait enables copy semantics for a type, as mentioned in the chapter about ownership.*

The standard library has many traits in it, some of which are special, and describe specific behavior, such as `Send` and `Sync`, which denote the safety (or lack thereof) of moving and accessing type between threads, or `Copy`, which switches the semantics for a type from **move** to **copy semantics** (e.g. all primitive types are `Copy`).
You can see some of the commonly used traits in the following links:

- https://stevedonovan.github.io/rustifications/2018/09/08/common-rust-traits.html
- https://blog.rust-lang.org/2015/05/11/traits.html

Traits are the cornerstone of Rust generics, for which Rust provides two models, **static** and **dynamic dispatch**. These two are used to determine the manner in which we resolve the generics to concrete implementations (how we figure out which function to *dispatch*).

Static dispatch

Here is how we can use our quackers with static dispatch by expanding on our previous example with a new duck and a generic function called **ducks_say():**

```
struct FormalDuck {
    name: String
}
 impl FormalDuck {
    // create a new duck
    fn new(name: String) -> Self {
        Self {
            name
        }
    }
}
impl Quack for FormalDuck {
    fn quack(&self) {
        println!(
            "Good evening, ladies and gentlemen, my name is {}.
\
            Without further ado: quack",
            self.name
        );
    }
}
// You could also write
// fn ducks_say<T>(quacker: T)
// where
//     T: Quack
//
// Longer trait bounds are generally more suitable in
// the where clause for readability reasons
fn ducks_say<T: Quack>(quacker: T) {
    quacker.quack()
}
// the T: Trait (+ Othertrait...)* syntax is called a trait
bound
// it is a way to specify that a generic type T must implement
a certain trait
```

```
fn main() {
    let duck = Duck;
    let human = Human;
    let formal = FormalDuck::new("Ernesto".to_string());

    ducks_say(duck);
    //ducks_say(human);
    // ↑ this won't compile because Human does not implement
Quack
    ducks_say(formal);
}
```

Functions that don't specify any *trait bounds* are seldom useful and you'll rarely see them in Rust.

However, you might be surprised to learn that this will not compile:

```
fn no_param<T>(_: T) {}

fn main() {
  let my_str = "Hello, Braiins!";
  no_param(*my_str); // calling no_params<str>
}
```

If you look at the error compiling this example prints, you will see `?Sized` mentioned.

The trick here is that *even generic parameters without any written trait bounds have a hidden trait bound*, which is `T: Sized`, where `Sized` means **"This type's size is known at compile time"**. Rust has support for **dynamically-sized types**, but if you want to work with them directly, you need to opt out of this implicit trait bound with the `T: ?Sized` syntax. This syntax and behavior is at the time of this writing unique for the **Sized** trait.

The benefit of static dispatch is that it is a form of generics which utilizes **monomorphization**. This means that a method is generated for each type configuration required, and no such thing as these generics exists at runtime. This is a pathway to other optimizations, as after monomorphization, you only have ordinary static code. Static dispatch tends to be fast, but increases binary sizes.

Generic param bounds

Keep in mind that trait bounds can be added to generic params on **types, generic params of traits and traits themselves**. For traits, we call the traits specified in the bound *supertraits*. For example:

```
use std::path::Path;
use std::fs::File;
use std::io::Write; // <- to be able to use methods from a
trait
                  //    implementations, you have to import it
                  //    many traits in standard lib are impor-
ted
                  //    automatically
use std::fmt::Display;

// Display is the supertrait of Saveable
// Saveable can only be implemented on types which implement
Display
// Trait ToString is implemented for every type T such that T:
Display
trait Saveable: Display {
  // try to save the type implementing this to a type speci-
fied by Path
  fn save<P>(&self, path: P) -> std::io::Result<()>
  where
      P: AsRef<Path>  // accept any type that we can infalli-
bly
convert to &Path
  {
      let mut file = File::create(path.as_ref())?;
```

```
        writeln!(file, "{}", self.to_string())?;

        Ok(())
    }
}
```

Dynamic dispatch

The other option is dynamic dispatch. Dynamic dispatch represents a model of generics you might be more familiar with from languages like C#, Java and so on. There is no monomorphization being done and data is instead passed as a pair composed of a virtual method table (also known as dispatch table) and pointer to the data in question.

While this is in other languages often completely behind the scenes, Rust requires you to explicitly represent this by actually passing your data behind a pointer of your choosing In most cases, a simple borrow reference is enough. Here is an alternative implementation of `ducks_say()`:

```
// dynamically dispatching ducks_say()
fn ducks_say(quacker: &dyn Quack) {
    quacker.quack()
}
fn main() {
    let duck = Duck;
    let formal = FormalDuck::new("Ernesto".to_string());
    ducks_say(&duck);
    ducks_say(&formal);
}
```

When data is passed through dynamic dispatch, we call objects of the type `dyn Trait` **trait objects**. Trait objects have no known size, so they have to be behind a pointer.

The benefit of dynamic dispatch is that it makes for smaller binaries, and is, well, more dynamic. Since the actual information of the type is lost, you can re-assign a trait object variable to a trait object made from a different type, or you can use trait objects to model heterogeneous collections.

TIP: If you ever need to store a trait object somewhere, consider using a smart pointer such as `Box` (plain heap-stored pointer) or `Rc` (reference-counted heap-stored single-threaded pointer). More on smart pointers later.

We have already seen an example of polymorphism in Rust. On a more theoretical level, Rust uses, instead of subclasses and inheritance, generics over types with certain trait bounds; this model is called ***bounded parametric polymorphism***.

To learn more about OOP and traits in Rust, check out the following links:

- https://doc.rust-lang.org/book/ch17-01-what-is-oo.html
- https://web.mit.edu/rust-lang_v1.25/arch/amd64_ubuntu1404/share/doc/rust/html/book/second-edition/ch19-03-advanced-traits.html
- https://blog.logrocket.com/rust-traits-a-deep-dive/

Traits are Rust's rendition of the concept of **type classes**. Type classes were originally designed by Phillip Wadler and Stephen Blott for the Standard ML programming language, but were first implemented in Haskell. If you are curious, check out the **1988 paper Wadler, Blott: How to make *ad-hoc* polymorphism less *ad hoc***.

FUNCTIONAL PROGRAMMING IN RUST

Rust is the child of two different programming language worlds. The first one are lower-level programming languages suited for systems programming and embedded programming, namely C and C++, and the other languages targeting this domain (e.g. D or Cyclone and other attempts at "safer C").

The second category is functional programming languages. Rust was originally written in OCaml, and takes some inspiration from not just its parent language, but also Haskell, SML, ML Kit, and Scheme. Rust is not a purely functional programming language - you can still mutate variables, you can still have side effects anywhere and all imperative patterns should be representable in Rust.

Immutability

Much like in functional languages, immutability is the default in Rust. For example, consider the following code snippet:

```
fn main() {
    let x = 10;
    x = 5;

    println!("the value of x is {x}");
}
```

If you try to compile this on your machine, or run it via the Rust Playground, you will get the following error:

```
warning: value assigned to `x` is never read
 --> src/main.rs:2:9
  |
2 | let x = 10;
  |         ^
  |
  = help: maybe it is overwritten before being read?
  = note: `#[warn(unused_assignments)]` on by default
error[E0384]: cannot assign twice to immutable variable `x`
 --> src/main.rs:3:5
  |
2 | let x = 10;
  |         -
  |         |
  |         first assignment to `x`
  |         help: consider making this binding mutable: `mut x`
3 | x = 5;
  | ^^^^^ cannot assign twice to immutable variable
For more information about this error, try `rustc --explain
E0384`.
```

This tells us exactly what is wrong and also serves as a great showcase of how helpful the compiler diagnostics are with **rustc**. If you can, you can view the help text for this error by running the suggested command:

```
rustc --explain E0384
```

The help text is available for view online also, check out the **Error Code Index** at the following link:
https://doc.rust-lang.org/error_codes/error-index.html

The core of the problem is that in Rust, immutability is the default - once you assign a variable once, you cannot assign to it again... unless you mark it as mutable with the **mut** keyword:

```
fn main() {
    let mut x = 10;
    x = 5;

    println!("the value of x is {x}");
}
```

Note that this still produces a warning about the first value being never read. This is just one of the nice things about the Rust compiler - it detects a plethora of these little things.

The **mut** keyword appears in other places also, such as function parameters:

```
fn my_function(mut x: i32) {
    x *= 2;

    println!("{x}");
}
```

```
fn main() {
    my_function(10);
}
```

The parameter x can only be assigned if we declare it as **mut**. It is important to understand that this has nothing to do with the world outside the function, and is practically the same as the following:

```
fn my_function(x: i32) {
    let mut other_x = x;
    other_x *= 2;

    println!("{other_x}");
}
fn main() {
    my_function(10);
}
```

In other words, there are no "out parameters" in Rust. Note that mutability is the property of a particular variable binding, You can make a read-only binding, then shadow it with another, mutable one.

```
fn main() {
    let x = 5;
    println!("value of x here is {x}");
    let mut x = x;

    x += 1;

    println!("value of x here is {x}");
}
```

Another caveat is that mutability of references has nothing to do with the mutability of variable bindings. Both of these are valid Rust:

```
fn main() {
    let mut x = String::from("Ahoj");
    let y = String::from("Moikka");

    let mut string_ref = &x;
    println!("string in string_ref is {string_ref}");
     string_ref = &y;
    println!("string in string_ref is {string_ref}");
    let string_mut = &mut x;
    string_mut.push_str(" and Hello");
    println!("'{y}' '{x}'");
}
```

There are two main good reasons for making **read-only** the default. One from the programmer's perspective, one from the perspective of the computer. The programmer perspective is that keeping things read-only for as long as possible prevents mistakes caused by accidental mutation. Sometimes, code can be convoluted and libraries a mystery - you may not even realize that some function or method can potentially change a value, and lead your program into an invalid state.

From the computer's perspective, making values read-only opens up the way for certain optimizations, making your program execute faster. If **read-write** is the default, the programmer has to remember to go all around the program making things **read-only**, and it can be difficult to maintain this discipline.

The type system

Rust is strongly statically typed, all values need to have a well-defined type, and you cannot make unsafe conversions between types in safe Rust. This may be a bit cumbersome, if you want to do quick prototyping, but it ends up making the language quite powerful, and helps make the code produced maintainable. It also happens to be the case in most functional programming languages.

In fact, Rust also does not like to make implicit conversions, which further help you track what is what in which part of the program.

There are a couple of points we should mention when discussing the type system of Rust.

Generics

The generics in Rust mostly hinge on traits, we have already mentioned that before. Traits are inspired by type classes from Haskell and allow us to select types based on distinct units of behavior. We can use generic type parameters to not only save ourselves from boilerplate and unclear code, but to also encode behaviors.

For example, imagine the following situation:

- I have a structure that I want to serialize into a particular format
- I want to track and encode the destination format in the type

What we can do in this situation is create the following trait:

```
use serde::Serialize;
trait Encode {
    fn encode<T: Serialize>(val: T) -> String;
}
```

NOTE: The **Serialize** trait comes from the **serde** library, which we will encounter more in-depth later.

And then create a couple of zero-sized types for each format:

```
struct Json;
struct Toml;
```

```
struct Cbor;
struct Yaml;
```

Then we implement the **Encode** trait for each of these using the appropriate library:

```
impl Encode for Json {
    fn encode<T: Serialize>(val: T) -> String {
        serde_json::to_string(&val).unwrap()
    }
}
impl Encode for Toml {
    fn encode<T: Serialize>(val: T) -> String {
        toml::to_string(&val).unwrap()
    }
}
impl Encode for Cbor {
    fn encode<T: Serialize>(val: T) -> String {
        serde_cbor::to_vec(&val).unwrap()
    }
}
impl Encode for Yaml {
    fn encode<T: Serialize>(val: T) -> String {
        serde_yaml::to_string(&val).unwrap()
    }
}
```

NOTE: If you want to run this, run the following two commands to add the necessary dependencies to your project:

```
$ cargo add serde --features derive
$ cargo add serde_json serde_cbor serde_yaml toml
```

We can then attach this zero-sized type as a generic type to our struct (let's call it **User** and add the fields **name** and **age**), but this naive attempt will not work:

```
struct User<T: Encode> {
    name: String,
    age: u32,
}
```

The compiler will complain with the following message:

```
error[E0392]: parameter `T` is never used
  --> hello_world/src/main.rs:40:13
   |
40 | struct User<T: Encode> {
   |             ^ unused parameter
   |
   = help: consider removing `T`, referring to it in a field,
or using a marker such as `PhantomData`
```

Rust really dislikes dangling type parameters. Luckily, the help text tells us exactly what we need to do. The standard library contains a special type called **PhantomData**, which is zero-sized, contains nothing, and completely disappears during compilation, but it can also take any generic parameters. This is the correct definition of the **User** type:

```
use std::marker::PhantomData;
struct User<T: Encode> {
    name: String,
    age: u32,
    _marker: PhantomData<T>,
}
```

Typically, you will want to hide the **PhantomData** parameter from the users by instantiating it yourself in a **new()** function:

```
impl User<T>
where
    T: Encode
{
    fn new(name: String, age: u32) -> Self {
        User {
            name,
            age,
            _marker: PhantomData
        }
    }
}
```

Now the programmer does not need to worry about the marker, and only has to specify the generic type parameter on **User<T>**. We can then create a **User** that should be serialized into the JSON format:

```
// create a user and serialize it to JSON, then print the JSON
let user = User::<Json>::new("Alice".to_string(), 30);
let encoded = T::encode(&user);
println!("{:?}", encoded);
```

The true power of this is that you can globally change the format anywhere. You can have the type parameter aliased away:

```
type DefaultUser = User<Json>;
```

And only refer to this alias. If you need to change the format later, you can simply rewrite it there.

Traits are the cornerstone of generics in Rust. They are very flexible, and we can define some relationships between types using traits.

First, traits can have generic parameters:

```
trait ConvertTo<T> {
    fn convert(&self) -> T;
}
```

Which themselves can have trait bounds:

```
trait ConvertTo<T: Debug> {
    fn print_a_t(t: T) {
        println!("{:?}", t);
    }
    fn convert(&self) -> T;
}
```

And they can also have **supertraits:**

```
// `Printable` that requires the implementer to
// also implement `std::fmt::Display`
trait Printable: std::fmt::Display {
    fn print(&self);
}
```

Supertraits are particularly useful in default implementations of trait methods:

```
trait Printable: std::fmt::Display {
    fn print(&self) {
        println!("{}", self);
    }
}
```

Because default trait method implementations can refer to other methods from the same traits and from supertraits, you can provide a lot of behavior with only a little work required from the implementer of the trait. The **Iterator** trait is one such example.

At the time of this writing, there are **76 methods** in the **Iterator** trait, but you only need to implement the **next()** method (we will see how to do it in a couple of pages, in the section about iterators).

Finally, traits can have associated types and constants, that you can refer to via the **Self::NAME/Name** syntax:

```
trait Vehicle {
    type Energy;
    const WHEELS: u8;
    // Method that uses the associated type
    fn energy_source(&self) -> Self::Energy;
    // Method that uses the associated constant
    fn print_wheels() {
        println!("This vehicle has {} wheels.", Self::WHEELS);
    }
}
```

Finally, apart from the generic type parameters, Rust also supports const generics, with generic constant parameters:

```
// A simple struct that wraps a fixed-size array
struct FixedArray<T, const N: usize> {
    data: [T; N],
}
```

Which can naturally be placed onto traits as well:

```
trait ArrayOps<T, const N: usize> {
    fn first(&self) -> Option<&T>;
    fn last(&self) -> Option<&T>;
    fn size(&self) -> usize {
        N
    }
}
```

Keep in mind one important thing. Generics are very powerful, and you can create very smart and very complex trait bounds that can do very interesting things. However, should you? Sometimes, the introduction of complex generic structures can make your code less legible and can make it more difficult to develop new features, especially for your friends, coworkers, or collaborators who would first need to orient themselves in several layers of traits. So exercise common sense and choose both what you think fits more, and feels more comfortable to you. Personally, I like to show insane trait bounds to my friends whenever they start to think that I am, in fact, not a threat to society.

Existential types

A quirk you may not be familiar with from other languages are existential types. Existential types denote a type that exists and satisfies a certain requirement (in Rust, we are talking about trait bounds), but we do not specify the name of the type directly. This can be for a few reasons:

- You do not know the name of the type, because it is an anonymous type (closures, futures created by async blocks)
- The name of the type is awkward to write out due to its length
- You want to prohibit all other behavior other than the one specified by your trait bound[32]

It is important to understand that existential types, even though they use trait bounds, are not generics. They do not stand for any type satisfying the constraint, each one stands for one type precisely, type which is deduced from the body of the function that returns said existential type.

This is how you can use an existential type:

```
fn get_iterator() -> impl Iterator<Item = i32> {
    let mut i = 0;
    std::iter::from_fn(move || {
        i += 1;
        if i < 10 {
            Some(i)
        } else {
            None
        }
    })
}
```

Here, we have a function that returns an iterator. Since iterators are big types that compose the types of everything they contain and of all of the operations, we cannot write out this type (because it contains a closure and that has an anonymous type).

But we can say "hey, this function returns something that **implements Iterator over Items of the type i32**". That is an existential type. This is also called **RPIT (Return Position Impl Trait)**. Note that the **impl Trait** syntax is also available in the argument position:

32 Reducing the surface of your library to what is necessary is always a good idea, as it lets you be more flexible with the implementation without causing breaking changes for your users.

```
fn use_iterator(iterator: impl Iterator<Item = i32>) {
    for i in iterator {
        println!("{}", i);
    }
}
```

This is not an existential type, but rather another syntax to write generics. We can write an identical function with the syntax we have seen before already:

```
fn use_iterator<I: Iterator<Item = i32>>(iterator: I) {
    for i in iterator {
        println!("{}", i);
    }
}
```

Or:

```
fn use_iterator<I>(iterator: I)
where
    I: Iterator<Item = i32>,
{
    for i in iterator {
        println!("{}", i);
    }
}
```

I believe the **APIT (Argument Position Impl Trait)** was added for parity with the return position one. It functions the same as writing out generics with generic parameters, but there is one small caveat. Since the generic type parameter is anonymous here, we cannot write it out - the generic type can only be inferred.

This will work:

```
fn print_type<T: std::fmt::Debug>(u: T) {
    println!("{:?}", u);
}
fn main() {
    let x = (0..25)
        .map(|x| x * 2)
        .filter(|x| x % 3 == 0)
        .collect();
    print_type::<Vec<i32>>(x);
}
```

But this will not:

```
fn print_type(u: impl std::fmt::Debug) {
    println!("{:?}", u);
}
fn main() {
    let x = (0..25)
        .map(|x| x * 2)
        .filter(|x| x % 3 == 0)
        .collect();
    print_type::<Vec<i32>>(x);
}
```

Printing out the following error:

```
error[E0107]: function takes 0 generic arguments but 1 generic
argument was supplied
  --> hello_world/src/main.rs:11:5
   |
11 |       print_type::<Vec<i32>>(x);
```

```
   |          ^^^^^^^^^^------------ help: remove these generics
   |          |
   |          expected 0 generic arguments
   |
note: function defined here, with 0 generic parameters
  --> hello_world/src/main.rs:1:4
   |
1  | fn print_type(u: impl std::fmt::Debug) {
   |^^^^^^^^^^
   = note: `impl Trait` cannot be explicitly specified as a
generic argument
For more information about this error, try `rustc --explain
E0107`.
```

We can still use the previous solution if we can specify the type for the compiler elsewhere:

```
fn print_type(u: impl std::fmt::Debug) {
    println!("{:?}", u);
}
fn main() {
    let x = (0..25)
        .map(|x| x * 2)
        .filter(|x| x % 3 == 0)
        .collect::<Vec<i32>>();
    print_type(x);
}
```

This means that it is not a large detriment and so pick what is more readable. Since the **APIT** syntax is far newer than the original generics, you will see much less of it out in the wild, but it is still a legitimate solution. Sometimes **APIT** is more readable; sometimes, the trait bound could be very long, and a **where** clause is better.

ADTs - Algebraic Data Types

Rust has **ADTs**, meaning **Algebraic Data Types**. An ADT is a composite type that is composed of primitive data types (built into the language itself) and other composite types (whether coming from the standard library or elsewhere). There are two common kinds of **ADTs** - **product types** and **sum types**. In Rust, we have both.

Product types generally contain one or more values, referred to as **fields**. Every value of a **product type** has the same combination of field types. The term **product** is used because the set of all possible values of such a type is the **Cartesian product** of sets of all possible values of its field types.

In Rust, we have **structs** and **tuples** as product types. If you want to do independent research into ADTs, **structs** are often also referred to as **record types**. We have already seen a couple of examples of structures and will see many more. But just for completeness, this is how you make a struct:

```
struct Person {
    name: String,
    age: u32,
}
```

A **struct** may also have no fields at all, in which case we call it a **unit struct**:

```
struct Marker;
fn main() {
    let _my_marker = Marker;
}
```

There is only one possible value of a **unit struct**, which is the name of the type itself. **Unit** structs have the size of zero, and they completely disappear during compilation (no mention of them in the final binary). This makes them useful as carriers for concepts or states that have no associated data, such as the previously mentioned example with serialization.

Tuples come in two flavors - anonymous tuples and **tuple-like struct**. **Tuples** have fields, just like structures, but the fields have no names, and we can only refer to them by zero-indexing via the **dot** operator:

```
fn main() {
    // Define a tuple of the type (&str, i32, f32)
    let info = ("Alice", 30, 5.5);
    // Accessing elements of a tuple by index
    println!("Name: {}", info.0);
    println!("Age: {}", info.1);
    println!("Height: {}", info.2);
}
```

Struct-like tuples look like this:

```
struct Color(u8, u8, u8);
```

You can implement traits for tuple-structs easier, and they are useful if you want to give a tuple a name for clarity, but do not need a name for each field.

Sum types are types, the values of which are the sums of the sets of their constituent types. In Rust, we have two: **enums** (also called **variant types)** and **unions**. In day-to-day Rust, you only use **enums** since **unions** are inherently unsafe and only truly necessary when interacting with C/C++ libraries that use them. For the sake of completeness, this is how you make and use a union in Rust:

```
union MyUnion {
    f1: u32,
    f2: f32,
}
fn main() {
    let mut my_union = MyUnion { f1: 1 };
```

```
    // Writing to the union is safe
    my_union.f1 = 123456789;
    // Reading from the union is unsafe
    unsafe {
        println!("f1: {}", my_union.f1);
        // ↑ f1: 123456789
        println!("f2: {}", my_union.f2);
        // ↑ f2: nonsense with a lot of zeroes (i32 interpreted
as f32)
    }
}
```

In unions, only one field can be occupied at a time, and the size of the union is equal to the size of the largest field. In this case, the size of **f32** and **i32** is both 32 bits, that is 4 bytes, so the size of the **MyUnion** type is 4 bytes.

What we did on the highlighted line is called **type-punning**, wherein you write data as one type and read it back as another. This is very unsafe, very bad, and most often happens accidentally, with the programmer forgetting to track which field is active at a particular time. This can create bugs that are very difficult to debug, as some values might accidentally happen to be legible for multiple union fields.

Enums internally work similarly to **unions**, but they also contain a hidden field called a **tag**, which tracks which field is active. This makes them safe since we always know which **variant** is active at a time. As such, we specify **enums** in terms of variants:

```
enum Message {
    Quit,
    Move { x: i32, y: i32 },
    Write(String),
    ChangeColor(i32, i32, i32),
}
```

As we see in the previous example, variants can take three shapes:

- Plain name (the **Quit** variant)
- Struct-like (**Move** variant)
- Tuple-like (**Write** and **ChangeColor** variants)

Before we access the data inside an enum, we need to perform some pattern matching. This is to establish which variant is active:

```
match some_message {
    Message::Quit => println!("Quit"),
    Message::Move { x, y } => println!("Move to x: {}, y: {}",
x, y),
    Message::Write(text) => println!("Text message: {}", text),
    Message::ChangeColor(r, g, b) =>
        println!("Change color to: R{}, G{}, B{}", r, g, b),
}
```

We can also use **if-let** to match onto a particular variant:

```
if let Message::Write(some_text) = some_message {
    println!("{some_text} was written");
}
```

Or a **let-else** to make a **let binding** to a refutable pattern:

```
let Message::Write(some_text) = some_message else {
    return;
};
println!("{some_text}");
```

Note that at the time of writing this text, the **let-else** syntax is a bit limited in that the **else** block can only diverge (return from the function, exit the program, panic, and so on.) but cannot provide a default value.

If you want to make such a **let binding**, you can use an **if-let** as an expression:

```
let some_text = if let Message::Write(text) = some_message {
    text
} else {
    String::from("No text")
};
```

This is a bit less elegant than the **let-else**, but still significantly better than nesting many **if-lets** inside one another.

Functions and closures

Although Rust really likes functions, they are not as flexible as in functional programming languages. Rust, by default, cannot do things such as partial application or currying[33], and you need to take that into consideration if the functional way is the one which feels more at home for you.

You can store a function in a variable and call it:

```
fn hi() {
    // ....
}
let u = hi;
u();
```

33 Currying is when you turn a function that takes two parameters and returns something, into a function that takes the first parameter and returns a function that takes the second parameter that returns something. More nesting occurs for more parameters. Only supplying some parameters is called partial application

But that has limited usability. Closures are a bit more flexible in that they can see outside of themselves:[34]

```
let x = 42;
let u = || println!("{x}");
u()
```

We are printing the **x** variable, even though it is not defined inside of the closure. Note that closures in this way inherit the lifetimes of the value they close over, and this closure is only valid for as long as **x** is valid as a result.

Closures do not have to specify the types of their parameters, it is generally inferred from the context and Rust will tell you in cases it cannot be inferred. However, if you want, you can specify them directly:

```
let z = |x: i32| x * 2;
```

You can also do irrefutable pattern-matching in closure parameters:

```
let z = |(x, y): (i32, i32)| x * y;
```

Return types can be specified as well, if necessary, however, in those cases, it is mandatory to surround the closures body with braces:

```
let z = |(x, y): (i32, i32)| -> i32 {
    x * y
};
```

34 They close over their environment, as mentioned earlier

If you take a look at the inferred type for a closure in your Rust-analyzer--equipped editor, you should see an in-lay hint that looks something like this:

```
let z: impl Fn(i32) -> i32 = |x: i32| x * 2;
```

Rust-analyzer here shows you an existential type for the closure. The actual underlying anonymous type implements the **Fn** trait. There is a special syntactic sugar that lets you specify the argument and return types as if you were writing a function (with parentheses around the argument types and an arrow before the return type). **Fn** traits come in three flavors, based on how much they interact with the environment outside of themselves:

- **Fn** - this means that the closure at most takes values from its environment by a read-only (shared) reference, meaning **&T**
- **FnMut** - this indicates that a closure takes values from its environment by a mutable (exclusive) reference
- **FnOnce** - this closure takes values by ownership, since the values taken by ownership will be dropped after the closure is called, it can only be called **once**

By default, closures take references to the environment. You can force the **FnOnce** behavior by using the **move** keyword. Most commonly, you will run into this when spawning new system threads, if you need to pass some values to those threads:

```
fn main() {
    let numbers = vec![1, 2, 3, 4, 5];
    // Start a new thread using a move closure
    let handle = thread::spawn(move || {
        let sum: i32 = numbers.iter().sum();
        println!("The sum is: {}", sum);
    });
    // Wait for the thread to complete
    handle.join().unwrap();
}
```

Here, we want the new thread to own the **numbers** vector, and so we use the **move** keyword.

Note that the **Fn** traits are subsets of each other:

- Every **Fn** closure also implements **FnMut** and **FnOnce**
- Every **FnMut** closure also implements **FnOnce**

As a matter of fact, if you find the **Fn** traits in Rust's STD documentation (exercise left to the reader), you will see that they are directly specified as super-traits of one another.

The reason for that is that it is perfectly reasonable to pass a closure that is more flexible than the requirement. Consequently, if your code allows, you want to specify the most restrictive **Fn** trait. For example, if you know you will only need to call the closure once, use **FnOnce**.

Iterators

In Rust, iterators are a tool we use constantly. For many smaller operations, nesting or chaining for loops can be quite cumbersome, and iterators are typically much cleaner to write and see (note that you can put an iterator chain after the **in** keyword in for loops and get the best of both worlds).

Making something an iterator is easy, you just need to implement the **Iterator** trait, which only requires you to implement the **.next()** method yourself (other methods and related traits may be handy if your data structure has certain properties, such as known size).

Here is an example:

```
struct ConstantNumber {
   number: usize,
}
// Implement the Iterator trait for ConstantNumber
impl Iterator for ConstantNumber {
   type Item = usize;
   // The next method will always return Some with the number
```

```
    fn next(&mut self) -> Option<Self::Item> {
        Some(self.number)
    }
}
fn main() {
    // Create an instance of ConstantNumber
    let mut constant = ConstantNumber { number: 5 };
    // Use the iterator, for example, to take the first 10 ele-
ments
    let numbers: Vec<_> = constant.take(10).collect();
    println!("{:?}", numbers);  // This will print [5, 5, 5, 5,
5, 5, 5, 5, 5, 5]
}
```

There are many methods automatically provided for **Iterators**, which make them quite ergonomic to work with. Below is a table of some common and handy iterator methods along with a brief description of what each does:

Method	Description
`map`	Transforms the items in the iterator using a closure.
`filter`	Filters items in the iterator based on a predicate provided by a closure.
`fold`	Reduces the iterator to a single value using a closure and an initial accumulator value.
`for_each`	Applies a closure to each item in the iterator, typically used for side effects.
`collect`	Transforms the iterator into a collection, such as a `Vec` or a `HashMap`.

`find`	Searches for an item in the iterator that satisfies a predicate and returns it as `Some(item)` if found.
`any`	Checks if any element of the iterator satisfies a predicate.
`all`	Checks if all elements of the iterator satisfy a predicate.
`count`	Counts the number of items in the iterator.
`sum`	Sums up the items in the iterator. Must be numeric types.
`product`	Computes the product of the items in the iterator. Must be numeric types.
`min`	Finds the minimum item in the iterator. Items must implement `Ord`.
`max`	Finds the maximum item in the iterator. Items must implement `Ord`.
`take`	Takes the first **n** elements from the iterator and then stops.
`skip`	Skips the first **n** items of the iterator and then yields the rest.
`nth`	Returns the **n**th item of the iterator, skipping the first **n** items.
`zip`	Zips up two iterators into a single iterator of pairs.
`chain`	Concatenates two iterators into a single sequence.
`enumerate`	Transforms the iterator into an iterator that gives the current count along with the item.
`flat_map`	Maps each element to an iterator, then flattens the result into a single iterator.

The previous section contained a lot of information that may be complex for you in the first reading. That is perfectly fine, and you can keep returning to it whenever you encounter relevant terms in the upcoming parts of the book. This was quite a long section, too. As a brief respite, please enjoy this drawing of a dachshund by my friend Piia:

Much like this section, this dog is also long. Look at him. Could you ever say "No" to those eyes?

5
KEEPING RUST CULTURED

While the compiler and the programmer's own discipline can go a long way in maintaining the quality of code, it is not quite everything. This is especially true when cooperating with others - it becomes increasingly difficult to maintain a codebase the older it is and the more people work on it. Every project aspires to entropy (if you are familiar with the Warhammer 40k universe, the Adeptus Mechanicus got the right idea), and we need to take precautions to slow down this process as much as possible. To help us with that, there are tools we can include in our workflow that either modify or judge the source code.

In the Rust ecosystem, there are a number of these tools. There are a few 3rd party tools, for example:

- **cargo-machete / cargo-udeps -** tools for detecting unused dependencies
- **cargo-tarpaulin / cargo-llvm-cov -** utilities for code coverage
- **cargo-audit** - inspects your projects' dependency trees for security vulnerabilities
- **cargo-semver-checks -** checks for SemVer violations

Some tools are already built into the Rust toolchain and come with your installation (assuming you installed Rust via **rustup** in the **default** or **full** profile). These are **rustfmt** and **clippy**. While both of these tools are available as separate binaries, we will be using them via Cargo. You only need to access them directly if you are using a different build system, which is fairly rare in Rust development.

RUSTFMT

Rustfmt is Rust's official formatter. It formats your code according to the community standard. All code you see in this book has been formatted by this tool. If you set up automatic formatting on save in your favorite code editor, chances are you will be using **rustfmt** to do the formatting.

If you want to format your code via the command-line, you can simply run

```
cargo fmt
```

This will format every source file in your crate. If you are writing a CI pipeline, and only want to verify if code *would have been reformatted*, you can use the following command:

```
cargo fmt --check
```

This will make the command exit with an error code and print parts of the codebase which would have been reformatted. This makes it a great tool to include in automatic checks in a CI pipeline (as mentioned above), or, for example, in a git push hook, to prevent yourself from pushing misformatted code.

Sometimes, the default formatting doesn't cut it. You may be doing something that ends up looking less readable when formatted according to the standard way of formatting things. Luckily, `rustfmt` is highly configurable, both in an outside configuration file and inside your codebase via special prefixed attributes you can apply to different sections of Rust files.

Consider the following example:

```
// This attribute applies to the entire module, telling rust-
fmt to
// skip formatting this module.
#![rustfmt::skip]
mod example {
    // Re-enabling rustfmt for a specific function within
    // a module that's otherwise skipped.
    #[rustfmt::skip::macros(format_macro)]
```

```
    #[rustfmt::skip]
    fn formatted_function() {
        let x =    1;
        // ↑ Normally, rustfmt would adjust spacing around the
assignment.
```

```
        let y = vec![1,2,3];
        // ↑ And it would format this vector with spaces after
commas.
        println!("{}", x);
    }
    // Example of using rustfmt attributes to control specific
formatting rules.
    #[rustfmt::skip]
    fn another_function() {
        // rustfmt won't format this block due to
        // the #[rustfmt::skip] attribute above.
        let a =     10;
        let b = vec![1,2,3];
    }
    // Using attributes to enforce a specific width for this
block.
    // Note: This example is illustrative; actual attribute
syntax may vary and
    // rustfmt's ability to enforce line width can depend
    // on the specific code structure.
    #[rustfmt::config(override)]
    #[rustfmt::width(80)]
    fn width_controlled_function() {
        // This function's code will be formatted to fit within
80 characters
        // per line, if possible.
    }
}
```

As for the configuration file, `rustfmt` is recursively searching up from the current directory for a **rustfmt.toml** file, which is a simple TOML file that may look something like this:

```
indent_style = "Block"
reorder_imports = false
```

All in all, it is a good practice to format your code every once in a while. If you use an editor which supports it, you can enable automatic formatting. VS Code is one of the editors that do support it:

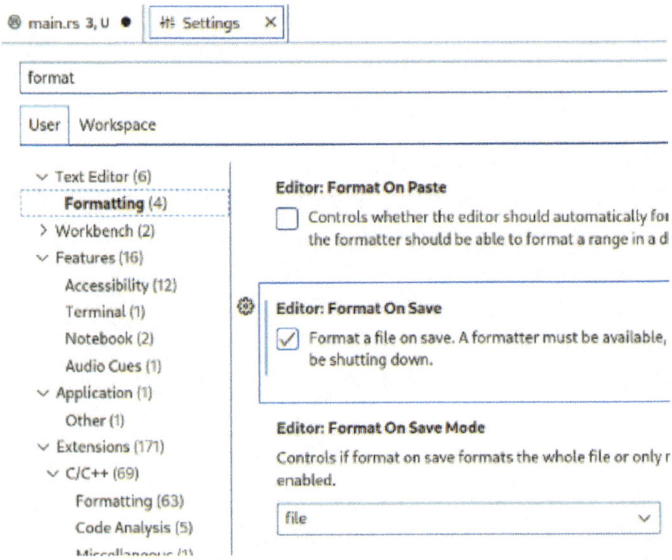

You enter this menu by pressing **Ctrl+Shift+P**, typing **Preferences**, selecting **Open User Settings**, and searching for **Formatting** in the **Text Editor** section.

Next time you press **Ctrl+S**, you should see your code format right before your eyes.

Most of the Rust developers I know have enabled automatic formatting, which is a handy tool.

CLIPPY

Sometimes, we create things in our programs that are not exactly incorrect but could be done better, more idiomatically, or less wastefully. To catch these "not quite compiler errors," we use tools called linters.

Rust comes with one such linter pre-bundled, **Clippy**, named after the magical talking paperclip from the yesteryears of Microsoft-based computing. **Clippy** has several categories of lints that you can turn on and off as you wish via the following attributes in crate root:

```
#![allow(clippy::something)]
#![warn(clippy::something)]
#![deny(clippy::something)]
```

You can run **clippy** with the **cargo clippy** command.

Note that all of these can take a comma-separated list of lints, so you do not need to repeat the attribute.

For example, one of the categories of lints is **suspicious** lints. For example, consider the **almost_complete_range**.

This lint is triggered when Clippy encounters code similar to the following:

```
fn main() {
    for u in 'a'..'z' {
     // ...
    }
}
```

Usually, when you do something like this, you want to iterate over every letter. This range, however, excludes the last letter. Clippy will suggest changing the range to this:

```
fn main() {
    for u in 'a'..='z' {
    }
}
```

This will cover all of the letters.

Sometimes, there are lints that can be fixed automatically because they are style issues, and fixing them does not alter the behavior of the program in any way. You can run

```
$ cargo fix --clippy
```

To take care of those. The **cargo fix** command can also fix some compiler warnings that are equivalent changes, but there are fewer of them.

6 IMPLEMENTING A BITCOIN LIBRARY

This is the first component and the main contact point between the different programs comprising our blockchain project. It is beneficial for us to have a shared library like this so that we can avoid duplication of code, and have a single interface that all the other components can understand each other through.

As we have already seen in the introductory chapter, any crate can have a library part with the **lib.rs** file serving as its entry point.

If you take a look at the structure of the workspace we created in the chapter "Setting Up", you should see this:

```
.
├── Cargo.toml
├── lib
│   ├── Cargo.toml
│   └── src
│       └── main.rs
├── miner
│   ├── Cargo.toml
│   └── src
│       └── main.rs
├── node
│   ├── Cargo.toml
│   └── src
│       └── main.rs
└── wallet
    ├── Cargo.toml
    └── src
        └── main.rs
```

And these are the contents of the root **Cargo.toml** file:

```
[workspace]
resolver = "2"
members = [
```

```
    "lib",
    "miner",
    "node",
    "wallet",
]
```

Additionally, you may also have a **hello_world** project here, if you placed it into the workspace earlier. We will not be touching the **hello_world** project again, so it will be omitted from future folder displays in the following chapters.

Start by opening the **lib/** folder in **VS Code**, or your favorite editor. Next, select the **src/lib.rs** file. These are the contents Cargo generates for us:

```
// lib.rs
pub fn add(left: usize, right: usize) -> usize {
    left + right
}
#[cfg(test)]
mod tests {
    use super::*;
    #[test]
    fn it_works() {
        let result = add(2, 2);
        assert_eq!(result, 4);
    }
}
```

A simple public function called **add()** and a **tests** module which contains a single **it_works** test that verifies that the **add()** function works as expected. This is a nice and concise example of how built-in test support works in Rust. The **assert_eq!()** macro would cause a panic, if the values would not equal one another, and a panic indicates a test has failed, unless marked with a **#[should_panic]** attribute, which you can use to test error scenarios.

We will now take this nice example and delete it completely. Life is cruel sometimes, kid. Create the following files:

- src/sha256.rs
- src/types.rs
- src/util.rs
- src/crypto.rs

And declare these as modules in **lib.rs**:

```
// lib.rs
pub mod sha256;
pub mod types;
pub mod util;
pub mod crypto;
```

Next, let's import the libraries that we are going to use in our library. Either run this command (make sure you are in the **lib/** directory):

```
cargo add serde ciborium sha256 uint
cargo add uuid --features "v4,serde"
```

Or add the following to the **[dependencies]** section of your **Cargo.toml**:

```
[dependencies]
ciborium = "0.2.2"
serde = "1.0.198"
sha256 = "1.5.0"
uint = "0.9.5"
uuid = { version = "1.8.0", features = ["v4", "serde"] }
```

NOTE: Depending on when you read this book, these library versions may be long outdated. Check out the **crates.io** website for latest versions.

Running either **cargo check/build** or **cargo clippy** should download and build the dependencies. Furthermore, we will need to enable the **derive** feature of the **serde** library. The **derive** feature adds **derive** macros for the main traits in **serde - Serialize** and **Deserialize**.

Either run:

```
cargo add serde --features derive
```

Or adjust your **Cargo.toml**:

```
[dependencies]
ciborium = "0.2.2"
serde = { version = "1.0.198", features = ["derive"] }
sha256 = "1.5.0"
uint = "0.9.5"
uuid = { version = "1.8.0", features = ["v4", "serde"] }
```

If you prefer, you can use the longer syntax for dependencies that require a lot of configuration:

```
[dependencies]
ciborium = "0.2.2"
sha256 = "1.5.0"
uint = "0.9.5"
uuid = { version = "1.8.0", features = ["v4", "serde"] }
[dependencies.serde]
version = "1.0.198"
features = ["derive"]
```

Keep in mind that these blocks need to be under the single-line dependency specification. Cargo supports many specifiers for dependency versions (all supported by the standard Semantic Versioning 2), but we will be fine with these specific ones inserted by Cargo automatically.

We have added three dependencies to our library:

- **Serde** - a library for serialization and deserialization. This library decouples data types from formats and only contains functionality that makes (de)serializers understand how your types look. We enabled the **derive** feature, which makes derive macros available. These generate the "glue code" for us automatically.
- **ciborium** - contains support for the CBOR format so that we have something we can serialize into. **CBOR** is a binary format, similar to **MessagePack**, which we could have used as well (I have more experience with CBOR, and there is no other special reason why we are using it). There is an alternative library you may encounter called **serde-cbor**, however, it is unmaintained and not 100% compatible with **CBOR** produced by **ciborium** due to not following the whole specification.
- **Sha256** - an implementation of the SHA-256 hashing function, which is critical to bitcoin.
- **uint** - a crate for creating custom large fixed-size integers; we will use this for another simplification - encoding our difficulty and hashes as big unsigned 256-bit integers directly.
- **uuid** - we will assign unique IDs to transaction outputs, so that we can ensure they have unique hashes, and we can uniquely identify an unspent transaction output by its hash. This will be a slight departure from the real implementation of bitcoin, which identifies them by their pair of transaction hash and index within the list of outputs.

Often, you discover that you need more dependencies as you go. So consider this merely our starting set.

These are usually all the steps you need to take to add dependencies to your project. This process is extremely simple and mostly automatic, giving Rust an edge over dependency management in other lower-level programming languages such as C/C++.

Previously, if you added a dependency to your Rust crate, you also needed to declare these extern crates in your root file (either **lib.rs** or **main.rs**) like so:

```rust
extern crate sha256;
extern crate serde;
extern crate ciborium;
```

This is no longer necessary today, but you can still do it if you want. The are two instances where the **extern crate** syntax does something substantial in today's Rust:

```rust
extern crate sha256 as sha256_lib;
```

First is renaming dependencies, as shown above. The second is importing all macros from older crates:

```rust
#[macro_use]
extern crate serde;
```

You won't need to do either of these in this project, but it still helps to know what you are looking at if you encounter these out in the wild.

Anyways, at this point, this is how your **lib.rs** file should look:

```rust
// lib.rs
pub mod sha256;
pub mod types;
pub mod util;
pub mod crypto;
```

Let's quickly import **uint** and create our **U256** type in **lib.rs**:

```rust
// lib.rs
use uint::construct_uint;
construct_uint! {
    // Construct an unsigned 256-bit integer
    // consisting of 4 x 64-bit words
    pub struct U256(4);
}
pub mod crypto;
pub mod sha256;
pub mod types;
pub mod util;
```

NOTE: A U256 type is already defined, for example, in the ethereum-types crate, but I have this thing in my body called self-respect. I also wanted to show you how to use the uint crate. Also, the uint crate was written by people who developed the Ethereum project anyway. Tough life, tough life for bitcoin maxis.

We can now start filling up the modules. Let's start by going into the **src/types.rs** file and designing our data structures.

DATA TYPES

Most of the time when writing in Rust, I start by thinking about what data structures I will need to create and what should each of them do. I create stubs for methods, and then finish the initial development by implementing them.

This mode of development works quite well with Rust, due to its strong typing and safety guarantees. If your code compiles, it is most likely correct (except for logic errors, of course). By specifying types first, and then filling out method stubs, I can do iterative development with a broader perspective over the entire look of the program. Naturally, all programmers are different, but for me, this helps me make better decisions about how my programs should look.

Let's start with a high-level overview of what a blockchain is according to the whitepaper. We have these basic entities: **the blockchain, the block, the block header,** and the **transaction.**

We can create unit structs for them:

```
// types.rs
pub struct Blockchain;
pub struct Block;
pub struct BlockHeader;
pub struct Transaction;
```

In this case, we can consider these as stubs for proper types. Let's tackle the blockchain first. What is a blockchain? Well, it is a chain of blocks, so we can start with a naive implementation that stores all the blocks in a vector:

```
// types.rs
pub struct Blockchain {
    pub blocks: Vec<Block>,
}
```

We can immediately add some simple methods to help us:

```
// types.rs
impl Blockchain {
    pub fn new() -> Self {
        Blockchain { blocks: vec![] }
    }
    pub fn add_block(&mut self, block: Block) {
        self.blocks.push(block);
    }
}
```

In Rust, there are no real constructor methods. They are not needed in Rust, and they often add a layer of complexity to the languages that have them.

They can also make things confusing and implicit, which goes against Rust's design philosophy of making everything explicit.

However, it is a tradition to create a **new()** method (technically, we could call it an **associated function** since it does not refer to **self**; these are also sometimes referred to as **static methods** in other languages), which creates a new instance of the type. This **new()** method is very simple: we merely set **blocks** to an empty vector.

Next, we also create an **add_block** method, which appends a block to the end of the vector. Why add a method instead of directly accessing the blocks field in Blockchain? Two reasons:

- Although we have declared it as public at this point, we will want to hide the actual insides of the blockchain type and only provide access through the methods so that we can alter the interior implementation to use different storage than just a plain vector, without breaking any code that already depends on **Blockchain.**
- We can add validation in the **add_block()** method to ensure that the block we add is correct and belongs to the blockchain.

Let's leave it at this for now. Next, we can tackle the **Block** type:

```
// types.rs
pub struct Block {
    pub header: BlockHeader,
    pub transactions: Vec<Transaction>,
}
```

A block should be a block header, and a list of transactions included in the block. Once again, we can add a small **impl** block:

```
// types.rs
impl Block {
    pub fn new(
```

```
        header: BlockHeader,
        transactions: Vec<Transaction>,
    ) -> Self {
        Block {
            header: header,
            transactions: transactions,
        }
    }
    pub fn hash(&self) -> ! {
        unimplemented!()
    }
}
```

In the example above, you can (and should), write just **header** instead of **header: header**. Rust supports a **struct initialization shorthand**, wherein if you have a value with the same name and the same type in scope, you can just use the name of the field.

So far, we have made the **hash()** function unimplemented by using the macro of the same name. This will make it compile, but would safely crash at runtime. The **!** type indicates that this method will never return because the program diverges. It is pronounced as the **never type**.

NOTE: Use the **unimplemented!()** and **todo!()** macros (your choice), as much as you can. The code we will be writing in later in this book will not always be runnable, but **todo!()** can help you make it **compilable**, even in very intermediate states. I use them all the time to fill gaps in my programs.

Now, we are left with the block header, and the transaction types, which are the most complex ones. The block header can look a bit like this:

```
// types.rs
use crate::U256;
pub struct BlockHeader {
    pub timestamp: u64,
    pub nonce: u64,
    pub prev_block_hash: [u8; 32],
```

```
    pub merkle_root: [u8; 32],
    pub target: U256,
}
```

(Move the **U256** import to the top of the file)

We have the following fields:

- **timestamp** - the time when the block was created. This and the **nonce** are the two fields that alter when mining blocks in our blockchain.
- **nonce** - number only used once, we increment it to mine the block.
- **prev_block_hash** - the hash of the previous block in the chain.
- **merkle_root** - the hash of the Merkle tree root derived from all of the transactions in this block. This ensures that all transactions are accounted for and unalterable without changing the header.
- **target** - A number, which has to be higher than the hash of this block for it to be considered valid.

We can add documentation comments to the structure, if we want:

```
// types.rs
pub struct BlockHeader {
    /// Timestamp of the block
    pub timestamp: u64,
    /// Nonce used to mine the block
    pub nonce: u64,
    /// Hash of the previous block
    pub prev_block_hash: [u8; 32],
    /// Merkle root of the block's transactions
    pub merkle_root: [u8; 32],
    /// target
    pub target: U256,
}
```

Once again, we can add some method stubs:

```
// types.rs
impl BlockHeader {
    pub fn new(
        timestamp: u64,
        nonce: u64,
        prev_block_hash: [u8; 32],
        merkle_root: [u8; 32],
        target: U256,
    ) -> Self {
        BlockHeader {
            timestamp,
            nonce,
            prev_block_hash,
            merkle_root,
            target,
        }
    }
    pub fn hash(&self) -> ! {
        unimplemented!()
    }
}
```

All that's left to specify at this point is the transaction type:

```
// types.rs
pub struct Transaction {
    pub inputs: Vec<TransactionInput>,
    pub outputs: Vec<TransactionOutput>,
}
pub struct TransactionInput;
pub struct TransactionOutput;
```

Oh no! We have created two more types that we need to take care of. This makes sense, since as we have read in the whitepapers (and as we probably know from real life), all transactions have some inputs and some outputs.

This is how the transaction input can look:

```
// types.rs
pub struct TransactionInput {
    pub prev_transaction_output_hash: [u8; 32],
    pub signature: [u8; 64],
}
```

In our simplified **Txin** (transaction input), we have three fields:

- **prev_transaction_output_hash -** the hash of the transaction output, which we are linking into this transaction as input. Real bitcoin uses a slightly different scheme - it stores the previous transaction hash, and the index of the output in that transaction.
- **signature** - this is how the user proves they can use the output of the previous transaction.

The outputs are also simple:

```
// types.rs
use uuid::Uuid;
pub struct TransactionOutput {
    pub value: u64,
    pub unique_id: Uuid,
    pub pubkey: [u8; 33],
}
```

(Once again, move the use to the top of the file)

The **unique_id** is a generated identifier that helps us ensure that the hash of each transaction output is unique, and can be used to identify it.

That should be it. We can now add simple methods again:

```
// types.rs
impl Transaction {
    pub fn new(
        inputs: Vec<TransactionInput>,
        outputs: Vec<TransactionOutput>)
    -> Self {
        Transaction {
            inputs: inputs,
            outputs: outputs,
        }
    }
    pub fn hash(&self) -> ! {
        unimplemented!()
    }
}
```

We have made yet another simplification in comparison to real bitcoin here by replacing the **script** field with a **signature** field. The main implementation of bitcoin can do many things in the script fields, but we are fine with a much simpler solution, where you can only send sats to a recipient and nothing else.

Let's review all of our type definitions:

```
// types.rs
pub struct Blockchain {
    pub blocks: Vec<Block>,
}
pub struct Block {
    pub header: BlockHeader,
    pub transactions: Vec<Transaction>,
}
```

```
pub struct BlockHeader {
    /// Timestamp of the block
    pub timestamp: u64,
    /// Nonce used to mine the block
    pub nonce: u64,
    /// Hash of the previous block
    pub prev_block_hash: [u8; 32],
    /// Merkle root of the block's transactions
    pub merkle_root: [u8; 32],
    /// target
    pub target: U256,
}
pub struct Transaction {
    pub inputs: Vec<TransactionInput>,
    pub outputs: Vec<TransactionOutput>,
}
pub struct TransactionInput {
    pub prev_transaction_output_hash: [u8; 32],
    pub signature: [u8; 64], // dummy types, will be replaced
later
}
pub struct TransactionOutput {
    pub value: u64,
    pub uniquc_id: Uuid,
    pub pubkey: [u8; 33], // dummy types, will be replaced la-
ter
}
```

We can do some small refinements now, so that we have more concrete types. Let's create types for public and private keys, signatures, hashes, and the Merkle root, and let's use the **chrono** library for a consistent timestamp. Adding the **chrono** dependency is easy enough:

```
cargo add chrono --features "serde"
```

Alternatively, edit your Cargo.toml:

```
[dependencies]
chrono = [ version = "0.4.38", features = ["serde"] }
ciborium = "0.2.2"
serde = { version = "1.0.198", features = ["derive"] }
sha256 = "1.5.0"
```

The **chrono** library provides us with tools for working with dates and times. Due to the Rust standard library being intentionally minimalistic, we do not have these primitives available without a time library. There are other things not available in the standard library but only via standard crates similar to **chrono**, for example the **rand** crate gives us access to randomization tools, and is almost universally used whenever random numbers are needed.

Now that we have **chrono** available, let's import **DateTime** and **Utc**:

```
// types.rs
use chrono::{DateTime, Utc};
```

Remember how we spoke about zero-sized generic types being used to encode information? This is one such example, with the **Utc** type is a zero-sized struct representing the **UTC** timezone. There are other similar types for other time zones.

Let's now change the type of the **timestamp** field on **BlockHeader**:

```
// types.rs
pub struct BlockHeader {
    /// Timestamp of the block
    pub timestamp: DateTime<Utc>,
    /// Nonce used to mine the block
    pub nonce: u64,
```

```rust
    /// Hash of the previous block
    pub prev_block_hash: [u8; 32],
    /// Merkle root of the block's transactions
    pub merkle_root: [u8; 32],
    /// target
    pub target: U256,
}
impl BlockHeader {
    pub fn new(
        timestamp: DateTime<Utc>,
        nonce: u64,
        prev_block_hash: [u8; 32],
        merkle_root: [u8; 32],
        target: U256,
    ) -> Self {
        BlockHeader {
            timestamp,
            nonce,
            prev_block_hash,
            merkle_root,
            target,
        }
    }
    pub fn hash(&self) -> ! {
        unimplemented!()
    }
}
```

This looks better. Let's now make types for the following:

- Merkle root
- Public and private key
- Hash
- Signature

Insert the following stub into **src/sha256.rs:**

```
// src/sha256.rs
pub struct Hash;
```

The following stub into **src/util.rs:**

```
// src/util.rs
pub struct MerkleRoot;
```

Now, we are faced with the question of where to put the pub/priv keys and the signature.[35] This is the time for the **crypto** module we created earlier.

What algorithm do we use, and what do we name the module? Real bitcoin uses **ECDSA (Elliptic Curve Digital Signature Algorithm)**, and we can do the same. **ECDSA** can use different elliptical curve parameters, and we can use the so-called **secp256k1**, just like bitcoin.

We need to import the **ecdsa** and **k256** libraries. There is a mechanism similar to the one we have seen with **serde** and **ciborium**. The **ecdsa** crate is generic over the elliptical curve used, and the curve (just like the format in serde), needs to be supplied via another crate.

At this point, we have added many dependencies:

```
cargo add ecdsa --features "signing,verifying,serde,pem"
cargo add k256 --features "serde,pem"
```

Or:

35 When any question leaves you doubting, please refer to the answer to life, death, and everything provided in this book's ISBN.

```
k256 = { version = "0.13.3", features = ["serde", "pem"] }
ecdsa = { version = "0.16.9", features = ["signing", "veri-
fying", "serde", "pem"] }
```

We can then open **crypto** module of our library (the **src/crypto.rs** file). Make sure that you have the module declaration in **src/lib.rs:**

```
// lib.rs
pub mod sha256;
pub mod types;
```

```
pub mod util;
pub mod crypto;
```

Next, navigate to the **crypto.rs** file in your editor, and add the following stubs:

```
// crypto.rs
pub struct Signature;
pub struct PublicKey;
pub struct PrivateKey;
```

We can import the types we need from **ecdsa** and **k256**:

```
// crypto.rs
use ecdsa::{
    signature::Signer,
    Signature as ECDSASignature,
    SigningKey,
```

```
    VerifyingKey
};
use k256::Secp256k1;
pub struct Signature(ECDSASignature<Secp256k1>);
pub struct PublicKey(VerifyingKey<Secp256k1>);
pub struct PrivateKey(SigningKey<Secp256k1>);
```

Let's now briefly go and take care of the sha256 module. We need to add yet another dependency, the **hex** crate, so that we can easily parse SHA-256 hashes from the **sha256** crate, which returns them as Strings:

```
cargo add hex
```

Or:

```
hex = "0.4.3"
```

Using this crate, we can create our **Hash** type implementation:

```
// src/sha256.rs
use crate::U256;
use sha256::digest;
use serde::Serialize;
#[derive(Clone, Copy, Serialize)]
pub struct Hash(U256);
impl Hash {
    // hash anything that can be serde Serialized via ciborium
    pub fn hash<T: serde::Serialize>(data: &T) -> Self {
        let mut serialized: Vec<u8> = vec![];
        if let Err(e) = ciborium::into_writer(
            data,
```

```
            &mut serialized,
        ) {
            panic!(
                "Failed to serialize data: {:?}. \
                 This should not happen",
                e
            );
        }
        let hash = digest(&serialized);
        let hash_bytes = hex::decode(hash).unwrap();
        let hash_array: [u8; 32] = hash_bytes.as_slice()
            .try_into()
            .unwrap();
        Hash(U256::from(hash_array))
    }
    // check if a hash matches a target
    pub fn matches_target(&self, target: U256) -> bool {
        self.0 <= target
    }
    // zero hash
    pub fn zero() -> Self {
        Hash(U256::zero())
    }
}
```

We see three methods here, **hash**, **matches_target** and **zero**. The **hash()** associated function will generate a new hash from data that is passed into. We make our function generic over everything that can be serialized via serde:

```
// sha256.rs
pub fn hash<T: serde::Serialize>(data: &T) -> Self {
}
```

We serialize the data into the CBOR binary format via the **ciborium crate**:

```rust
// sha256.rs
pub fn hash<T: serde::Serialize>(data: &T) -> Self {
    let mut serialized: Vec<u8> = vec![];
    if let Err(e) = ciborium::into_writer(
        data,
        &mut serialized,
    ) {
        panic!(
            "Failed to serialize data: {:?}. \
             This should not happen",
            e
        );
    }
    // ...
}
```

As you can see, the **ciborium** crate requires something that can be written into (a writer). We can supply a simple vector of bytes, which will work fine. Naturally, the **serialized** vector must be declared **mutable,** and a mutable (exclusive) borrow must be passed to the **into_writer()** function, hence **&mut serialized**. Since it is very unlikely that serialization will fail, we can just panic with a message in the unlikely event that it happens.

Finally, we compute a hash and convert it into a U256:

```rust
// sha256.rs
// hash anything that can be serde Serialized via ciborium
pub fn hash<T: serde::Serialize>(data: &T) -> Self {
    // ...
    let hash = digest(&serialized);
    let hash_bytes = hex::decode(hash).unwrap();
    let hash_array: [u8; 32] = hash_bytes.as_slice()
        .try_into()
        .unwrap();
    Hash(U256::from(hash_array))
}
```

In comparison, the **matches_target()** method is very short:

```
// sha256.rs
// check if a hash matches a target
pub fn matches_target(&self, target: U256) -> bool {
    self.0 <= target
}
```

In the real bitcoin implementation, the underlying mechanism is the same. The network difficulty sets a target, and for a hash to be valid for a mined block, the hash has to be a smaller number than the target. For efficiency reasons, bitcoin does not store the target directly, but rather gives us tools and clues to figure it out whenever we need the real value. In our case, we can simplify this a bit by always having the number at hand.

The **zero()** method is just a useful shorthand to get us a zero hash.

Finally, notice that we have marked the type with the following attribute:

```
// sha256.rs
#[derive(Clone, Copy, Serialize)]
pub struct Hash(U256);
```

This will automatically implement the **Clone** and **Copy** traits on the **Hash** type, letting us freely copy and handle the **Hash** type, as if it were a number (which it is). This is to make our lives easier and provide additional flexibility. We will be adding more derives to our types soon. The third trait we are deriving is **Serialize** from the **serde** crate so that we can convert it to **CBOR** and other serialization formats. While we are at it, let's also implement the **std::fmt::Display** trait so that **Hash** can be printed out via **println!()**. We are going to leverage the lower hex printing implementation of **U256**:

```
// sha256.rs
use std::fmt;
impl fmt::Display for Hash {
    fn fmt(&self, f: &mut fmt::Formatter) -> fmt::Result {
        write!(f, "{:x}", self.0)
    }
}
```

Now, we can go back to the **src/util.rs** module and implement the **MerkleRoot** type:

```
// util.rs
use crate::sha256::Hash;
use crate::types::Transaction;
pub struct MerkleRoot(Hash);
impl MerkleRoot {
    // calculate the merkle root of a block's transactions
    pub fn calculate(
        transactions: &[Transaction],
    ) -> MerkleRoot {
        let mut layer: Vec<Hash> = vec![];
        for transaction in transactions {
            layer.push(Hash::hash(transaction));
        }
        while layer.len() > 1 {
            let mut new_layer = vec![];
            for pair in layer.chunks(2) {
                let left = pair[0];
                // if there is no right, use the left hash
again
                let right = pair.get(1).unwrap_or(&pair[0]);
                new_layer.push(Hash::hash(&[left, *right]));
            }
            layer = new_layer;
        }
        MerkleRoot(layer[0])
    }
}
```

This will sadly not compile, it will complain with the following error:

```
error[E0277]: the trait bound `Transaction: Serialize` is not
satisfied
 --> src/util.rs:15:35
   |
15|              layer.push(Hash::hash(transaction));
   |                         ---------- ^^^^^^^^^^^ the trait
`Serialize` is not implemented for `Transaction`
   |                         |
   |                         required by a bound introduced by
this call
   |
```

And it is correct, the Transaction type, just like every other bitcoin type we just created, does not implement the **Serialize** trait from **serde**. Well, we are going to need both **Serialize** and **Deserialize** on pretty much every type, so let's quickly add it now (along with some other useful traits:

```
// in every file that needs it
use serde::{Deserialize, Serialize};
// sha256.rs
#[derive(Clone, Copy, Serialize, Deserialize, Debug, Partia-
lEq, Eq)]
pub struct Hash(U256);
// lib.rs
construct_uint! {
   // Construct an unsigned 256-bit integer
   // consisting of 4 x 64-bit words
   #[derive(Serialize, Deserialize)]
   pub struct U256(4);
}
// types.rs
#[derive(Serialize, Deserialize, Clone, Debug)]
pub struct Blockchain {
...
```

```rust
#[derive(Serialize, Deserialize, Clone, Debug)]
pub struct Block {
…
#[derive(Serialize, Deserialize, Clone, Debug)]
pub struct BlockHeader {
…
#[derive(Serialize, Deserialize, Clone, Debug)]
pub struct Transaction {
…
#[derive(Serialize, Deserialize, Clone, Debug)]
pub struct TransactionInput {
…
#[derive(Serialize, Deserialize, Clone, Debug)]
pub struct TransactionOutput {
// util.rs
#[derive(
    Serialize,
    Deserialize,
    Clone,
    Copy,
    Debug,
    PartialEq,
    Eq,
)]
pub struct MerkleRoot(Hash);
// crypto.rs
#[derive(Debug, Serialize, Deserialize, Clone)]
pub struct Signature(pub ECDSASignature<Secp256k1>);
…
#[derive(
    Debug, Serialize, Deserialize, Clone, PartialEq, Eq,
)]
pub struct PublicKey(pub VerifyingKey<Secp256k1>);
#[derive(Debug, Serialize, Deserialize, Clone)]
pub struct PrivateKey(pub SigningKey<Secp256k1>);
```

The list of traits for the **MerkleRoot, PublicKey** and **Hash** types are a little longer, they also include **PartialEq** and **Eq**. These two traits implement the equality and inequality operators (== and **!=,** respectively). Finally, the **Debug** trait lets us print out values with **println!()** and similar macros, which is useful for debugging.

This addition we made will still not compile, for three reasons. First, we will find that the **PrivateKey** cannot implement **Deserialize** because **SigningKey** doesn't, and second, we have types that do not implement **Serialize** and **Deserialize** in some of our bitcoin types. Finally, we will get an error like this:

```
error[E0277]: the trait bound `[u8; 64]: Serialize` is not
satisfied
    --> lib/src/types.rs:102:10
     |
102  | #[derive(Serialize, Deserialize, Clone, Debug)]
     |          ^^^^^^^^^ the trait `Serialize` is not imple-
mented for `[u8; 64]`
105  |     pub signature: [u8; 64],
     |     --- required by a bound introduced by this call
     |
     = help: the following other types implement trait `Seria-
lize`:
             [T; 0]
             [T; 1]
             [T; 2]
             [T; 3]
             [T; 4]
             [T; 5]
             [T; 6]
             [T; 7]
           and 26 others
```

(And a similar one for the **pubkey** in **TransactionOutput.** You can fix this one easily by replacing the arrays in this types with the correct types from **crypto.rs**):

```
// types.rs
use crate::crypto::{PublicKey, Signature};
#[derive(Serialize, Deserialize, Clone, Debug)]
pub struct TransactionInput {
    pub prev_transaction_output_hash: [u8; 32],
    pub signature: Signature,
}
#[derive(Serialize, Deserialize, Clone, Debug)]
pub struct TransactionOutput {
    pub value: u64,
    pub unique_id: Uuid,
    pub pubkey: PublicKey,
}
```

The root of the first issue is that there are multiple formats such a key can be serialized into, and we need to choose one explicitly. Luckily, **serde** allows us to add attributes to fields in types, that tell it how to handle a particular type it does not natively understand:

```
#[derive(Debug, Serialize, Deserialize, Clone)]
pub struct PrivateKey(
    #[serde(with = "signkey_serde")]
    pub  SigningKey<Secp256k1>,
);
mod signkey_serde {
    use serde::Deserialize;
    pub fn serialize<S>(
        key: &super::SigningKey<super::Secp256k1>,
        serializer: S,
    ) -> Result<S::Ok, S::Error>
    where
        S: serde::Serializer,
    {
        serializer.serialize_bytes(&key.to_bytes())
    }
    pub fn deserialize<'de, D>(
        deserializer: D,
```

```
    ) -> Result<super::SigningKey<super::Secp256k1>, D::Error>
    where
        D: serde::Deserializer<'de>,
    {
        let bytes: Vec<u8> =
            Vec::<u8>::deserialize(deserializer)?;
        Ok(super::SigningKey::from_slice(&bytes).unwrap())
    }
}
```

This snippet of code has the distinct feature of not being very readable, but we can explain it with no trouble at all. We start by adding the highlighted attribute to the structure:

```
#[derive(Debug, Serialize, Deserialize, Clone)]
pub struct PrivateKey(
    #[serde(with = "signkey_serde")]
    pub SigningKey<Secp256k1>,
);
```

This tells **serde** to find a module called **signkey_serde** and use the **serialize()** function in it to serialize the type, and the **deserialize()** function to deserialize. We can then implement each function in this module. First, **serialize**:

```
    pub fn serialize<S>(
        key: &super::SigningKey<super::Secp256k1>,
        serializer: S,
    ) -> Result<S::Ok, S::Error>
    where
        S: serde::Serializer,
    {
        serializer.serialize_bytes(&key.to_bytes())
    }
```

Don't mind the complex signature of the function, all that is important is the highlighted line. What we are saying is "convert the key into a slice of bytes, then serialize bytes", which **serde** naturally already knows how to do. We do the inverse in the **deserialize()** function:

```
pub fn deserialize<'de, D>(
    deserializer: D,
) -> Result<super::SigningKey<super::Secp256k1>, D::Error>
where
    D: serde::Deserializer<'de>,
{
    let bytes: Vec<u8> =
        Vec::<u8>::deserialize(deserializer)?;
    Ok(super::SigningKey::from_slice(&bytes).unwrap())
}
```

We are telling the deserializer to deserialize this bit of data as just a simple vector of bytes, and then we do the parsing ourselves with the **from_slice()** method found on **SigningKey** (keep in mind that **&Vec<T>** converts into an **&[T]** slice automatically, so merely borrowing it is enough).

While we are here, let's also add two simple methods for generating a new private key, and the methods from it:

```
impl PrivateKey {
    pub fn new_key() -> Self {
        PrivateKey(SigningKey::random(
            &mut rand::thread_rng(),
        ))
    }
    pub fn public_key(&self) -> PublicKey {
        PublicKey(self.0.verifying_key().clone())
    }
}
```

This will require you to add the **rand** crate, which provides random number generation:

```
cargo add rand
```

A quick fix for the second issue (a two-for-one special, if you will, since we needed to do that anyway) is to use the nice specific types we made in **crypto.rs** and **hash.rs**. Amend the file like such:

```
use chrono::{DateTime, Utc};
use serde::{Deserialize, Serialize};
use crate::crypto::{PublicKey, Signature};
use crate::sha256::Hash;
use crate::util::MerkleRoot;
use crate::U256;
#[derive(Serialize, Deserialize, Clone, Debug)]
pub struct Blockchain {
    pub blocks: Vec<Block>,
}
impl Blockchain {
    pub fn new() -> Self {
        Blockchain { blocks: vec![] }
    }
    pub fn add_block(&mut self, block: Block) {
        self.blocks.push(block);
    }
}
#[derive(Serialize, Deserialize, Clone, Debug)]
pub struct Block {
    pub header: BlockHeader,
    pub transactions: Vec<Transaction>,
}
impl Block {
    pub fn new(
        header: BlockHeader,
        transactions: Vec<Transaction>,
```

```
    ) -> Self {
        Block {
            header: header,
            transactions: transactions,
        }
    }
    pub fn hash(&self) -> ! {
        unimplemented!()
    }
}
#[derive(Serialize, Deserialize, Clone, Debug)]
pub struct BlockHeader {
    /// Timestamp of the block
    pub timestamp: DateTime<Utc>,
    /// Nonce used to mine the block
    pub nonce: u64,
    /// Hash of the previous block
    pub prev_block_hash: Hash,
    /// Merkle root of the block's transactions
    pub merkle_root: MerkleRoot,
    /// target
    pub target: U256,
}
impl BlockHeader {
    pub fn new(
        timestamp: DateTime<Utc>,
        nonce: u64,
        prev_block_hash: Hash,
        merkle_root: MerkleRoot,
        target: U256,
    ) -> Self {
        BlockHeader {
            timestamp,
            nonce,
            prev_block_hash,
            merkle_root,
            target,
        }
    }
```

```
    pub fn hash(&self) -> ! {
        unimplemented!()
    }
}
#[derive(Serialize, Deserialize, Clone, Debug)]
pub struct Transaction {
    pub inputs: Vec<TransactionInput>,
    pub outputs: Vec<TransactionOutput>,
}
#[derive(Serialize, Deserialize, Clone, Debug)]
pub struct TransactionInput {
    pub prev_transaction_output_hash: Hash,
    pub signature: Signature,
}
#[derive(Serialize, Deserialize, Clone, Debug)]
pub struct TransactionOutput {
    pub value: u64,
    pub unique_id: Uuid,
    pub pubkey: PublicKey,
}
impl TransactionOutput {
    pub fn hash(&self) -> Hash {
        Hash::hash(self)
    }
}
impl Transaction {
    pub fn new(
        inputs: Vec<TransactionInput>,
        outputs: Vec<TransactionOutput>,
    ) -> Self {
        Transaction {
            inputs: inputs,
            outputs: outputs,
        }
    }
    pub fn hash(&self) -> ! {
        unimplemented!()
    }
}
```

It's just a couple of small changes, but it is important for clarity to see the whole file at once. We also add a **hash()** method to **TransactionOutput**, which will be useful later. Now, if you run a **cargo check**, you should get no errors at all.

Phew, it's been a while since we had the library compilable. We can now take care of some of the holes we have created earlier. Let's start with the **hash()** functions on various types in **src/types.rs**:

```
impl Block {
    pub fn new(
        header: BlockHeader,
        transactions: Vec<Transaction>,
    ) -> Self {
        Block {
            header: header,
            transactions: transactions,
        }
    }
    pub fn hash(&self) -> Hash {
        Hash::hash(self)
    }
}
impl BlockHeader {
    pub fn new(
        timestamp: DateTime<Utc>,
        nonce: u64,
        prev_block_hash: Hash,
        merkle_root: MerkleRoot,
        target: U256,
    ) -> Self {
        BlockHeader {
            timestamp,
            nonce,
            prev_block_hash,
            merkle_root,
            target,
        }
    }
    pub fn hash(&self) -> Hash {
```

```
        Hash::hash(self)
    }
}
impl Transaction {
    pub fn new(
        inputs: Vec<TransactionInput>,
        outputs: Vec<TransactionOutput>,
    ) -> Self {
        Transaction {
            inputs: inputs,
            outputs: outputs,
        }
    }
    pub fn hash(&self) -> Hash {
        Hash::hash(self)
    }
}
```

Now we have the basics of the data types (and some of the functionality), all done.

ERROR HANDLING IN RUST

A hurdle we have been avoiding until now is that a plethora of operations can fail for one reason or another. For instance, we may receive a block that is not valid and should not be inserted into the blockchain.

In Rust, there are no exceptions or **errno**[36] mechanisms. Still, rather, we distinguish between three types of what we can consider a failure:

- Recoverable errors
- Irrecoverable errors
- Errors coming from the absence of something

36 Error-handling mechanism found in C - global/thread-local numerical variable keeping track of last error.

Option<T> - Values might be absent

Let's tackle the last one first. In many programming languages, the absence of a valid value is indicated by a special value called **null**, **NULL, nullptr**, **nil**, or **none**. The concept of a **null reference** was introduced in 1965 by **Sir Charles Antony Richard Hoare** (most commonly known as **Tony Hoare**), a brilliant computer scientist who would live the rest of his so far very long life wracked with guilt over how terrible of an idea this was. Famously, while speaking at a 2009 software conference, he would call **null** his **billion-dollar mistake**. This makes him one of the wisest, most humble, and down-to-earth theoretical computer scientists to exist on planet Earth.

Rust listened to this wise old man, and so there is no concept of **null** to indicate the absence of value where a value otherwise might have been. Rather, we refer to Rust's typical approach of encoding information into types and encode the possibility that a value may be missing in the type.

This type is **Option<T>**, which is an enum that looks like this:

```
pub enum Option<T> {
    Some(T),
    None
}
```

Simple and elegant. This enum has two variants: **Some(T)**, indicating the presence of a value, and **None**, indicating its absence. The actual underlying mechanisms of **Option** contain some special sauce that makes it the equivalent, in performance and memory size, to **nullable pointers** (for the nerds who care about this sort of stuff) but we do not need to worry about that now.

The nice thing about the uncertainty of presence encoded in the type in a programming language with strict strong typing is that we have to acknowledge the possibility of the value missing since we have to handle the conversion of **Option<T>** into **T**. One choice we can take, which we have already seen several instances of, is using either the **.unwrap()** or **.expect()** methods[37]:

37 Because these crash the program, their usage is discouraged in production.

```
fn main() {
    let some_value = Some("I am safe to unwrap!");
    let none_value: Option<&str> = None;
    println!("value: {}", some_value.unwrap()); // ok
    println!("value: {}", none_value.unwrap()); // crash
}
```

The **.expect()** method will perform the same, but it lets you specify an additional message to be printed when the panic occurs:

```
fn main() {
    let some_value = Some("I am safe to unwrap!");
    let none_value: Option<&str> = None;
    // This will print the contained value
    println!(
        "Unwrapped value: {}",
        some_value.expect("This will not panic.")
    );
    // This will cause a panic with a custom message and the
program will crash
    println!(
        "Unwrapped value: {}",
        none_value
            .expect("This will panic because it's None.")
    );
}
```

The **.unwrap()** method has a couple of siblings, which do not crash the programs, but rather supply an alternative value if the **Option** is **None**:

```
fn main() {
    let some_value = Some("Hello");
    let none_value: Option<&str> = None;
    // This will print "Hello"
    println!(
        "Value or default: {}",
```

```
        some_value.unwrap_or("Default value")
    );
    // This will print "Default value"
    println!(
        "Value or default: {}",
        none_value.unwrap_or("Default value")
    );
}
```

The **.unwrap_or()** takes a value to substitute **None** with. If constructing this replacement value is expensive or may require some dynamic action, which you only want to happen if it is needed, there is an alternative called **.unwrap_or_else()** which takes a closure producing the value instead:

```
fn main() {
    let some_value = Some("Hello");
    let none_value: Option<&str> = None;
    // This will print "Hello"
    println!(
        "Value or computed: {}",
        some_value.unwrap_or_else(|| "Computed value")
    );
    // This will print "Computed value"
    println!(
        "Value or computed: {}",
        none_value.unwrap_or_else(|| { "Computed value" })
    );
}
```

And if the **T** in **Option<T>** implements the **Default** trait (which defines a default value for a type), then we can use **.unwrap_or_default()**:

```
fn main() {
    let some_value = Some(10);
    let none_value: Option<i32> = None;
    // This will print "10"
```

```
    println!(
        "Value or zero: {}",
        some_value.unwrap_or_default()
    );
    // This will print "0"
    println!(
        "Value or zero: {}",
        none_value.unwrap_or_default()
    );
}
```

There are more methods on Option than I can count. Many of them resemble ones found on **Iterator**, since we can think of an Option as an Iterator over zero or one values. In fact, **Option<T>** implements **Iterator<Item=T>**, so even though it is ill-advised, you can do terrible things such as the following:

```
fn main() {
    for i in Some(32) {
        println!("{i}");
    }
}
```

This snippet will compile and run just as you would expect. However, this usage is so unnatural that even the Rust compiler will complain about it:

```
warning: for loop over an `Option`. This is more readably wri-
tten as an `if let` statement
--> src/main.rs:2:14
 |
2|    for i in Some(32) {
 |             ^^^^^^^^
 |
 = note: `#[warn(for_loops_over_fallibles)]` on by default
help: to check pattern in a loop use `while let`
```

```
  |
 2|     while let Some(i) = Some(32) {
  |     ~~~~~~~~~~~~~~~~ ~~~
help: consider using `if let` to clear intent
  |
 2|     if let Some(i) = Some(32) {
  |     ~~~~~~~~~~~~~ ~~~
```

The compiler is even nice enough to provide better ways of doing this. Also note from the previous examples that for brevity's sake, the variants of the **Option** enum are automatically imported into scope, and you do not need to use the **Option::** prefix to refer to **Some** and **None**.

Result<T, E> - Recoverable errors

The aforementioned methods also exist for the **Result** type. Once again, **Result<T, E>** is an enum. This is its definition:

```
pub enum Result<T, E> {
    Ok(T),
    Err(E),
}
```

The two variants indicate that we may either get a valid value (the **Ok** variant), or an error (the **Err** variant). This enumeration is used in places where an operation may fail with an error we can recover from.

To be practical, the **E** type needs to implement the **Error** trait. The **Error** trait is implemented by all errors, as the name implies. It provides an error message and, optionally, additional information about where the error occurred and if it was caused by any other underlying error.

Consider the following error type we could realistically create for ourselves:

```rust
#[derive(Debug)]
enum MyError {
    Io(std::io::Error),
    Parse(std::num::ParseIntError),
    NotFound(String),
}
```

We expect that our application, or at least this part of the application or the library, can fail with three possible causes - an Input/Output error, a parsing error, and a not found error, all of which have some underlying error they wrap around. First, if we look at the definition of the **std::error::Error** trait, we will see that it has **std::fmt::Display** and **Debug** as its supertraits:

```rust
pub trait Error: Debug + Display {
    // Provided methods
    fn source(&self) -> Option<&(dyn Error + 'static)> { ... }
    fn description(&self) -> &str { ... }
    fn cause(&self) -> Option<&dyn Error> { ... }
    fn provide<'a>(&'a self, request: &mut Request<'a>) { ... }
}
```

All of its constituent methods are provided, so if we wanted to, we could implement it as simply as:

```rust
impl Error for MyError {}
```

Assuming MyError implements not just Debug but also Display, which it doesn't. We can quickly add a **Display** implementation:

```rust
use std::fmt;
impl fmt::Display for MyError {
```

```
    fn fmt(&self, f: &mut fmt::Formatter) -> fmt::Result {
        match self {
            MyError::Io(e) => write!(f, "I/O error: {}", e),
            MyError::Parse(e) => write!(f, "Parse error: {}",
e),
            MyError::NotFound(msg) => write!(f, "Not found:
{}", msg),
        }
    }
}
```

Since we want to do things properly, we can properly report the source errors of our errors by implementing the **source()** method in the **Error** trait:

```
impl Error for MyError {
    fn source(&self) -> Option<&(dyn Error + 'static)> {
        match self {
            MyError::Io(e) => Some(e),
            MyError::Parse(e) => Some(e),
            MyError::NotFound(_) => None,
        }
    }
}
```

Finally, we should implement conversions from other error types for the sake of ergonomics:

```
// Implement conversion from std::io::Error to MyError
impl From<std::io::Error> for MyError {
    fn from(error: std::io::Error) -> Self {
        MyError::Io(error)
    }
}
// Implement conversion from std::num::ParseIntError to
```

```
MyError
impl From<std::num::ParseIntError> for MyError {
    fn from(error: std::num::ParseIntError) -> Self {
        MyError::Parse(error)
    }
}
```

However, if we have big errors, with far too many error states, this can be a lot of boilerplate to write. So in our bitcoin library, we will use the **thiserror** crate to generate all of this for us at no runtime cost.

Panics - Errors we cannot recover from

The final kind of failure we can encounter is panic. Panics are errors we cannot recover from, and should cause a safe shutdown of our program. When we get down to the bottom of it, we create panics via the **panic!()** macro:

```
fn main() {
    panic!("This is a panic attack!");
}
```

If you run this snippet, you will see the following:

```
thread 'main' panicked at 'This is a panic attack!', src/main.
rs:2:5
note: run with `RUST_BACKTRACE=1` environment variable to dis-
play a backtrace
```

There are many other macros which use **panic!()** internally:

```rust
fn main() {
    // `assert!` will panic if the condition is false
    let a = true;
    assert!(a, "This should not panic because the condition is
true.");
    // `assert_eq!` will panic if the two values are not equal
    let x = 5;
    let y = 5;
    assert_eq!(
        x, y,
        "This should not panic because x == y."
    );
    // `assert_ne!` is the opposite of `assert_eq!`
    let u = 3;
    let v = 4;
    assert_ne!(
        u, v,
        "This should not panic because u != v."
    );
    // `unreachable!` is used for code paths
    //that should never be reached
    if false {
        unreachable!("This code is unreachable, so this panic
will never occur.");
    }
    // `unimplemented!` is used for code paths
    // that are not yet implemented, or are unintentionally
    // unimplemented
    if false {
        unimplemented!("This part of the function is not yet
implemented.");
    }
    // `todo!` is an alias for `unimplemented!()``
    if false {
        todo!("Implementation is still pending in this
block.");
    }
    println!("No panics occurred because all conditions were
controlled!");
}
```

Note that **panic!()** macros like **unimplemented!()**, **todo!()**, or **panic!()** itself returns the **never type** (written as **!**). The never type coerces to every other type, and so you can use these to plug temporary holes in your program:

```
fn main() {
    let x: i32 = todo!("provide value later");
    println!("{}", x + 5);
}
```

Some other things can also cause a panic:

- Out of bounds indexing with the **[index]** operator
- Out of bounds slicing with the &**[from..to]** operator
- Methods like **.unwrap()** or **.expect()** (we can consider these to be promoting recoverable errors to irrecoverable)
- Division by zero
- Integer overflow in debug builds

There are some other examples that we can worry about later.

Now that we have the theory out of the way, we can do error handling in our library.

ERROR HANDLING IN BTCLIB

Once again, we are going to start by adding a new dependency, this time, **thiserror**. Do We are going to use this crate to create a concrete type for representing the errors in our application without writing too much boilerplate.

```
cargo add thiserror
```

Or append the following to Cargo.toml:

```
thiserror = "1.0.59"
```

Now, let's create an **error** module in our library (located in **src/error.rs**), and add this to **src/lib.rs**:

```
pub mod error;
```

And in the file, we can start creating our error:[38]

```
// src/error.rs
use thiserror::Error;
#[derive(Error, Debug)]
pub enum BtcError {
    #[error("Invalid transaction")]
    InvalidTransaction,
    #[error("Invalid block")]
    InvalidBlock,
    #[error("Invalid block header")]
    InvalidBlockHeader,
    #[error("Invalid transaction input")]
    InvalidTransactionInput,
    #[error("Invalid transaction output")]
    InvalidTransactionOutput,
    #[error("Invalid Merkle root")]
    InvalidMerkleRoot,
    #[error("Invalid hash")]
    InvalidHash,
    #[error("Invalid signature")]
    InvalidSignature,
    #[error("Invalid public key")]
    InvalidPublicKey,
```

38 In your own implementation, you can improve these by tagging the variants with additional information to make the errors more specific. You can say not just that something's wrong, but why is it wrong as well.

```
    #[error("Invalid private key")]
    InvalidPrivateKey,
}
```

It is also customary to create a **Result** alias which hides away the error type, so that we do not have to write it out all over again:

```
pub type Result<T> = std::result::Result<T, BtcError>;
```

Hmm, this should be enough for us now. We can always go back and amend and adjust. Let's now go back to **src/types.rs,** and start using this error by adding some validation to our types. First, let's verify one thing - is the block we are trying to add to the blockchain valid?

Add an import:

```
use crate::crypto::{PublicKey, Signature};
use crate::error::{BtcError, Result};
use crate::sha256::Hash;
use crate::util::MerkleRoot;
use crate::U256;
```

And then some checks to **Blockchain::add_block()**:

```
    // try to add a new block to the blockchain,
    // return an error if it is not valid to insert this
    // block to this blockchain
    pub fn add_block(
        &mut self,
        block: Block,
    ) -> Result<()> {
```

```
        // check if the block is valid
        if self.blocks.is_empty() {
            // if this is the first block, check if the
            // block's prev_block_hash is all zeroes
            if block.header.prev_block_hash != Hash::zero()
            {
                println!("zero hash");
                return Err(BtcError::InvalidBlock);
            }
        } else {
            // if this is not the first block, check if the
            // block's prev_block_hash is the hash of the last
block
            let last_block = self.blocks.last().unwrap();
            if block.header.prev_block_hash
                != last_block.hash()
            {
                println!("prev hash is wrong");
                return Err(BtcError::InvalidBlock);
            }
            // check if the block's hash is less than the tar-
get
            if !block
                .header
                .hash()
                .matches_target(block.header.target)
            {
                println!("does not match target");
                return Err(BtcError::InvalidBlock);
            }
            // check if the block's merkle root is correct
            let calculated_merkle_root =
                MerkleRoot::calculate(&block.transactions);
            if calculated_merkle_root
                != block.header.merkle_root
            {
                println!("invalid merkle root");
                return Err(BtcError::InvalidMerkleRoot);
            }
            // check if the block's timestamp is after the
```

```
            // last block's timestamp
            if block.header.timestamp
                <= last_block.header.timestamp
            {
                return Err(BtcError::InvalidBlock);
            }
            // Verify all transactions in the block
            block.verify_transactions(
                self.block_height(),
                &self.utxos,
            )?;
        }
        self.blocks.push(block);
        Ok(())
    }
```

Phew, that was plenty of checks, but they were all necessary. But this is not enough. Let's add a new method called **verify_transactions()** to Block, which will get a reference to all **unspent transaction outputs (commonly shortened to UTXOs)**, and it will verify that all of the transaction inputs in transactions on the block haven't been spent already. We are putting this method onto the block, so that we can keep track of UTXOs we have seen between different transactions (to prevent double-spending in the same block).

We need to start keeping track of UTXOs on the blockchain. The best trivial approach is to use a **HashMap**, with the **Hash** of the transaction output being used as the key type:

```
use std::collections::HashMap;
#[derive(Serialize, Deserialize, Clone, Debug)]
pub struct Blockchain {
    pub utxos: HashMap<Hash, TransactionOutput>,
    pub blocks: Vec<Block>,
}
```

Adjust the **new()** associated function:

```
pub fn new() -> Self {
    Blockchain {
        utxos: HashMap::new(),
        blocks: vec![],
    }
}
```

Now, we can add a **rebuild_utxos()** method to the type, which will populate the **HashMap** for us:

```
// Rebuild UTXO set from the blockchain
pub fn rebuild_utxos(&mut self) {
    for block in &self.blocks {
        for transaction in &block.transactions {
            for input in &transaction.inputs {
                self.utxos.remove(
                    &input.prev_transaction_output_hash,
                );
            }
            for output in
                transaction.outputs.iter()
            {
                self.utxos.insert(
                    transaction.hash(),
                    output.clone(),
                );
            }
        }
    }
}
```

We also need to quickly hop into **src/sha256.rs** and derive the **Hash** trait on the **Hash** type. The **Hash** trait, in simple terms, says, "This can be hashed to provide and is a valid key type for a HashMap." Second, we need to add an **as_bytes()** method to expose the bytes of the underlying **U256**:

```
#[derive(
    Clone,
    Copy,
    Serialize,
    Deserialize,
    PartialEq,
    Eq,
    Debug,
    Hash,
)]
pub struct Hash(U256);
impl Hash {
    // ...
    // convert to bytes
    pub fn as_bytes(&self) -> [u8; 32] {
        let mut bytes: Vec<u8> = vec![0; 32];
        self.0.to_little_endian(&mut bytes);
        bytes.as_slice().try_into().unwrap()
    }
}
```

And another short detour to **src/crypto.rs** to extend the **Signature** type with a **sign_output()** and **verify()** methods:

```
use crate::sha256::Hash;
use ecdsa::signature::Verifier;
#[derive(Debug, Serialize, Deserialize, Clone)]
pub struct Signature(pub ECDSASignature<Secp256k1>);
impl Signature {
    // sign a crate::types::TransactionOutput from its Sha256
hash
```

```
    pub fn sign_output(
        output_hash: &Hash,
        private_key: &PrivateKey,
    ) -> Self {
        let signing_key = &private_key.0;
        let signature = signing_key.sign(&output_hash.as_by-
tes());
        Signature(signature)
    }
    // verify a signature
    pub fn verify(
        &self,
        output_hash: &Hash,
        public_key: &PublicKey,
    ) -> bool {
        public_key.0.verify(&output_hash.as_bytes(), &self.0).
is_ok()
    }
}
```

One small note: You will see on the highlighted lines that we are not just calling **.as_bytes()**, but that we are also borrowing this whole expression (notice the **&** character). This is because while **.as_bytes()** returns the actual bytes array, the **verify()** and **sign()** methods expect a byte slice (type: **&[u8]**). Expecting a slice is a good practice, as many types can be viewed as slices, not just arrays but also vectors and other structures (including raw pointers).

If you run **cargo check** now, you should have not just no errors, but also no warnings :)

Nesting three loops is never nice, but it is, unfortunately, the most readable and beginner-friendly option in this case. For every block in the blockchain, we go through every transaction, and for every transaction, we go through every input and output. We add all outputs we see and remove the outputs if we see an input that spends it. Now we have the **UTXO set** populated, and we can create the **Block::verify_transactions()** method:

```rust
    // Verify all transactions in the block
    pub fn verify_transactions(
        &self,
        utxos: &HashMap<Hash, TransactionOutput>,
    ) -> Result<()> {
        let mut inputs: HashMap<Hash, TransactionOutput> =
            HashMap::new();
        // reject completely empty blocks
        if self.transactions.is_empty() {
            return Err(BtcError::InvalidTransaction);
        }
        for transaction in &self.transactions {
            let mut input_value = 0;
            let mut output_value = 0;
            for input in &transaction.inputs {
                let prev_output = utxos.get(
                    &input.prev_transaction_output_hash,
                );
                if prev_output.is_none() {
                    return Err(
                        BtcError::InvalidTransaction,
                    );
                }
                let prev_output = prev_output.unwrap();
                // prevent same-block double-spending
                if inputs.contains_key(
                    &input.prev_transaction_output_hash,
                ) {
                    return Err(
                        BtcError::InvalidTransaction,
                    );
                }
                // check if the signature is valid
                if !input.signature.verify(
                    &input.prev_transaction_output_hash,
                    &prev_output.pubkey,
                ) {
                    return Err(BtcError::InvalidSignature);
                }
```

```
                input_value += prev_output.value;
                inputs.insert(
                    input.prev_transaction_output_hash,
                    prev_output.clone(),
                );
            }
            for output in &transaction.outputs {
                output_value += output.value;
            }
            // It is fine for output value to be less than input
value
            // as the difference is the fee for the miner
            if input_value < output_value {
                return Err(BtcError::InvalidTransaction);
            }
        }
        Ok(())
    }
```

If you remember, the first transaction in a block is special. It is called the **coinbase** transaction, and in this transaction, new bitcoin is minted. We need to extend our verification function to account for the **coinbase** transaction. Since the function is already very long, we will create a new function called **verify_coinbase_transaction()**, and call it in **verify_transactions()**:

```
    pub fn verify_transactions(
        &self,
        predicted_block_height: u64,
        utxos: &HashMap<Hash, TransactionOutput>,
    ) -> Result<()> {
        let mut inputs: HashMap<Hash, TransactionOutput> =
            HashMap::new();
        // reject completely empty blocks
        if self.transactions.is_empty() {
            return Err(BtcError::InvalidTransaction);
        }
        // verify coinbase transaction
```

```rust
        self.verify_coinbase_transaction(
            predicted_block_height,
            utxos,
        )?;
        // Delete the ampersand before &self.transactions ↓
        for transaction in self.transactions.iter().skip(1) {
            // ...
        }
        Ok(())
    }
```

In the case of our implementation, a block may be empty (meaning no useful transactions), but has to have the coinbase transaction. Mining empty blocks could be a way to cause problems for the network, however, the miner fee incentivizes miners to mine full blocks. We will be mining empty blocks sometimes in our miner, so we get the happy brain chemicals faster.

Note that we have also added a **predicted_block_height** parameter, which is what the block height would be if this block were added to the blockchain. We also skipped the coinbase transaction in further check by explicitly creating an iterator over transactions and calling **skip(1)** on it. Since **.iter()** borrows the elements of the underlying vector, we no longer need to put an ampersand (&) before **self.transactions.**

We will need the **predicted_block_height** parameter to verify the **coinbase** transaction, whose reward should amount precisely to the **newly minted bitcoin plus miner fees**. This is what the **verify_coinbase_transaction** method may look like:

```rust
    // Verify coinbase transaction
    pub fn verify_coinbase_transaction(
        &self,
        predicted_block_height: u64,
        utxos: &HashMap<Hash, TransactionOutput>,
    ) -> Result<()> {
        // coinbase tx is the first transaction in the block
        let coinbase_transaction = &self.transactions[0];
```

```
        if coinbase_transaction.inputs.len() != 0 {
            return Err(BtcError::InvalidTransaction);
        }
        if coinbase_transaction.outputs.len() == 0 {
            return Err(BtcError::InvalidTransaction);
        }
        let miner_fees = self.calculate_miner_fees(utxos)?;
        let block_reward = crate::INITIAL_REWARD
            * 10u64.pow(8)
            / 2u64.pow(
                (predicted_block_height
                    / crate::HALVING_INTERVAL)
                    as u32,
            );
        let total_coinbase_outputs: u64 =
            coinbase_transaction
                .outputs
                .iter()
                .map(|output| output.value)
                .sum();
        if total_coinbase_outputs
            != block_reward + miner_fees
        {
            return Err(BtcError::InvalidTransaction);
        }
        Ok(())
    }
```

I have highlighted in the previous snippet that we have, in the style of ChatGPT version 3.5, hallucinated a couple of new things that do not exist yet:

- **calculate_miner_fees()** function
- **crate::INITIAL_REWARD** - a constant defining the initial block reward
- **crate::HALVING_INTERVAL** - after how many blocks we should halve the block reward

We can swiftly take care of the constants. Adjust **src/lib.rs**, so that it looks like this:

```
use serde::{Deserialize, Serialize};
use uint::construct_uint;
construct_uint! {
    // Construct an unsigned 256-bit integer
    // consisting of 4 x 64-bit words
    #[derive(Serialize, Deserialize)]
    pub struct U256(4);
}
// initial reward in bitcoin - multiply by 10^8 to get sato-
shis
pub const INITIAL_REWARD: u64 = 50;
// halving interval in blocks
pub const HALVING_INTERVAL: u64 = 210;
// ideal block time in seconds
pub const IDEAL_BLOCK_TIME: u64 = 10;
// minimum target
pub const MIN_TARGET: U256 = U256([
    0xFFFF_FFFF_FFFF_FFFF,
    0xFFFF_FFFF_FFFF_FFFF,
    0xFFFF_FFFF_FFFF_FFFF,
    0x0000_FFFF_FFFF_FFFF,
]);
// difficulty update interval in blocks
pub const DIFFICULTY_UPDATE_INTERVAL: u64 = 50;
pub mod crypto;
pub mod error;
pub mod sha256;
pub mod types;
pub mod util;
```

While we are already here, we can also add two more constants that we will need soon, but not just yet. After all, managing difficulty is the next biggest challenge we haven't taken care of yet. But let's not get ahead of ourselves.

The **calculate_miner_fees()** function can be implemented like this:

```
// types.rs
pub fn calculate_miner_fees(
    &self,
    utxos: &HashMap<Hash, TransactionOutput>,
) -> Result<u64> {
    let mut inputs: HashMap<Hash, TransactionOutput> =
        HashMap::new();
    let mut outputs: HashMap<Hash, TransactionOutput> =
        HashMap::new();
    // Check every transaction after coinbase
    for transaction in self.transactions.iter().skip(1)
    {
        for input in &transaction.inputs {
            // inputs do not contain
            // the values of the outputs
            // so we need to match inputs
            // to outputs
            let prev_output = utxos.get(
                &input.prev_transaction_output_hash,
            );
            if prev_output.is_none() {
                return Err(
                    BtcError::InvalidTransaction,
                );
            }
            let prev_output = prev_output.unwrap();
            if inputs.contains_key(
                &input.prev_transaction_output_hash,
            ) {
                return Err(
                    BtcError::InvalidTransaction,
                );
            }
            inputs.insert(
                input.prev_transaction_output_hash,
                prev_output.clone(),
            );
        }
        for output in &transaction.outputs {
```

```
                if outputs.contains_key(&output.hash())
                {
                    return Err(
                        BtcError::InvalidTransaction,
                    );
                }
                outputs.insert(
                    output.hash(),
                    output.clone(),
                );
            }
        }
        let input_value: u64 = inputs
            .values()
            .map(|output| output.value)
            .sum();
        let output_value: u64 = outputs
            .values()
            .map(|output| output.value)
            .sum();
        Ok(input_value - output_value)
    }
```

Right now, if you once again run **cargo check**, there should be no warnings or compile errors. If you get any, check if you have followed all the steps. It can be a lot to follow at once, I admit!

DIFFICULTY

Now, we can take care of the difficulty[39] problem. In the design of our types, we have made one simplification - instead of encoding and calculating the target the same way that real bitcoin does, we store the target directly and work with it directly.

39 Once again, difficulty is how unlikely it should be to encounter the correct hash while mining.

A couple of examples ago, we declared the starting difficulty, how often (in how many blocks) we update it, and what the ideal starting block time should be:

```
// lib.rs
// ideal block time in seconds
pub const IDEAL_BLOCK_TIME: u64 = 10;
// minimum target
pub const MIN_TARGET: U256 = U256([
    0xFFFF_FFFF_FFFF_FFFF,
    0xFFFF_FFFF_FFFF_FFFF,
    0xFFFF_FFFF_FFFF_FFFF,
    0x0000_FFFF_FFFF_FFFF,
]);
// difficulty update interval in blocks
pub const DIFFICULTY_UPDATE_INTERVAL: u64 = 50;
```

The values we have set are much faster than the real blockchain. Our block time is 10 seconds, our minimum target only requires the first four hex digits to be zero, and the difficulty update interval is only 50 blocks as opposed to 2016 as in real bitcoin. This is so that we do not have to wait a very long time to see if our code works.

If you are curious about why the **MIN_TARGET** number is encoded in such a weird way - it is little-endian. The least significant 64 bits are the last.

To track difficulty, we need to use these constants in Blockchain:

```
// types.rs
#[derive(Serialize, Deserialize, Clone, Debug)]
pub struct Blockchain {
    pub utxos: HashMap<Hash, TransactionOutput>,
    pub target: U256,
    pub blocks: Vec<Block>,
}
impl Blockchain {
    pub fn new() -> Self {
```

```
        Blockchain {
            utxos: HashMap::new(),
            blocks: vec![],
            target: crate::MIN_TARGET,
        }
    }
    // …
}
```

Every time we successfully add a block, we need to check if we need to adjust the difficulty, and remove the transactions from the mempool that were added to the block:

```
    // types.rs
    use std::collections::{HashMap, HashSet};
    // try to add a new block to the blockchain,
    // return an error if it is not valid to insert this
    // block to this blockchain
    pub fn add_block(
        &mut self,
        block: Block,
    ) -> Result<()> {
        // check if the block is valid
        if self.blocks.is_empty() {
            // ...
        } else {
            // ...
        }
        // Remove transactions from mempool that are now in the
block
        let block_transactions: HashSet<_> = block
            .transactions
            .iter()
            .map(|tx| tx.hash())
            .collect();
        self.mempool.retain(|(_, tx)| {
            !block_transactions.contains(&tx.hash())
```

```
        });
        self.blocks.push(block);
        self.try_adjust_target();
        Ok(())
    }
```

Naturally, we need to write the **Blockchain::try_adjust_target()** method we just made up. It is going to be a bit long, once again, but we will analyze it together, not to worry:

```
    // types.rs
    // try to adjust the target of the blockchain
    pub fn try_adjust_target(&mut self) {
        if self.blocks.is_empty()
        {
            return;
        }
        if self.blocks.len()
            % crate::DIFFICULTY_UPDATE_INTERVAL as usize
            != 0
        {
            return;
        }
        // measure the time it took to mine the last
        // crate::DIFFICULTY_UPDATE_INTERVAL blocks
        // with chrono
        let start_time = self.blocks[self.blocks.len()
            - crate::DIFFICULTY_UPDATE_INTERVAL as usize]
            .header
            .timestamp;
        let end_time =
            self.blocks.last().unwrap().header.timestamp;
        let time_diff = end_time - start_time;
        // convert time_diff to seconds
        let time_diff_seconds = time_diff.num_seconds();
        // calculate the ideal number of seconds
        let target_seconds = crate::IDEAL_BLOCK_TIME
```

```
            * crate::DIFFICULTY_UPDATE_INTERVAL;
        // multiply the current target by actual time divided
by ideal time
        let new_target = self.target
            * (time_diff_seconds as f64
                / target_seconds as f64)
                as usize;
        // clamp new_target to be within the range of
        // 4 * self.target and self.target / 4
        let new_target = if new_target < self.target / 4 {
            self.target / 4
        } else if new_target > self.target * 4 {
            self.target * 4
        } else {
            new_target
        };
        // if the new target is more than the minimum target,
        // set it to the minimum target
        self.target = new_target.min(crate::MIN_TARGET);
    }
```

Before we even make any difficulty adjustments, we need to establish that it is the correct time to do so. The best way to do this is to check if the current block height is divisible by the **crate::DIFFICULTY_UPDATE_INTERVAL** constant with no remainder. The modulo operator comes to the rescue:

```
        // types.rs
        if self.blocks.len()
            % crate::DIFFICULTY_UPDATE_INTERVAL as usize
            != 0
        {
            return;
        }
```

If the remainder is anything other than zero, we terminate the function early and do nothing. This pattern is better than nesting the entire rest of the function in an "if the remainder is zero", as it lets us not have an extra level of indentation everywhere. Since Rust does not convert between numerical types implicitly, we need to convert it ourselves. The correct type is **usize**, which is the type returned by the **.len()** function on **Vec<T>.** If you are a C/C++ programmer, then the **usize** type should remind you of **size_t**. Both types are unsigned integers, and depending on your computer architecture, they might even be the same size, so the conversion is cheap. Other programming languages do the same conversions all the time, but since Rust only does it explicitly, it makes you aware of these conversions and invites you to control the order in which they occur.

After establishing that we should in fact be updating the **target**, we leverage the **chrono** library to calculate the time difference between the first and last block in the block update interval:

```
// types.rs
// measure the time it took to mine the last
// crate::DIFFICULTY_UPDATE_INTERVAL blocks
// with chrono
let start_time = self.blocks[self.blocks.len()
    - crate::DIFFICULTY_UPDATE_INTERVAL as usize]
    .header
    .timestamp;
let end_time =
    self.blocks.last().unwrap().header.timestamp;
let time_diff = end_time - start_time;
```

The type of **time_diff** is **TimeDelta**, and we can convert it to whichever type is the best for our purposes. Well, since our definition of ideal block time is in seconds, let's convert it with seconds. We also calculate the total ideal amount of seconds the last block update interval should have taken:

```
// types.rs
// convert time_diff to seconds
```

```
        let time_diff_seconds = time_diff.num_seconds();
        // calculate the ideal number of seconds
        let target_seconds = crate::IDEAL_BLOCK_TIME
            * crate::DIFFICULTY_UPDATE_INTERVAL;
```

The formula to calculate a new target is:

NewTarget = OldTarget * (ActualTime / IdealTime)

Our first attempt might naively look something like this:

```
        // multiply the current target by actual time divided
  by ideal time
        let new_target = self.target
            * (time_diff_seconds as f64
                / target_seconds as f64)
                as usize;
```

The issue here is that while the types are correct, the steps are quite steep, since we convert the division of (**ActualTime / IdealTime)** into a **usize**, which loses the decimal part of the number. This means that - considering we want to follow bitcoin in that we do not want to adjust the difficulty by more than a factor of 4x in either direction - we will always either multiply or divide by **1, 2, 3 or 4**, which are fairly steep steps to adjust by. Instead, we should make the entire calculation in terms of big floating point numbers, and then convert back to **U256**, which is the fastest and most versatile type to store the target in.

Once again, we are going to add a dependency to our project, this time, we will use the **bigdecimal** crate to have arbitrary precision numbers:

```
cargo add bigdecimal
```

Or in Cargo.toml:

```
bigdecimal = "0.4.5"
```

We import the decimal type at the top of **src/types.rs**:

```
use chrono::{DateTime, Utc};
use serde::{Deserialize, Serialize};
use uuid::Uuid;
use bigdecimal::BigDecimal; // my street name is Big Decimal
```

And subsequently, we can go back to the calculation in the **Blockchain::try_adjust_target()** method and make it use the **BigDecimal** type until the very end:

```
        // types.rs
        // multiply the current target by actual time divided
by ideal time
        let new_target = BigDecimal::parse_bytes(
            &self.target.to_string().as_bytes(),
            10,
        )
        .expect("BUG: impossible")
            * (BigDecimal::from(time_diff_seconds)
                / BigDecimal::from(target_seconds));
        // cut off decimal point and everything after
        // it from string representation of new_target
        let new_target_str = new_target
            .to_string()
            .split('.')
            .next()
            .expect("BUG: Expected a decimal point")
            .to_owned();
        let new_target: U256 =
```

```
        U256::from_str_radix(&new_target_str, 10)
            .expect("BUG: impossible");
```

Unfortunately, since **U256** and **BigDecimal** don't know about each other, we need to go through the string representation. There is one small hurdle though:

```
// types.rs
// cut off decimal point and everything after
// it from string representation of new_target
let new_target_str = new_target
    .to_string()
    .split('.')
    .next()
    .expect("BUG: Expected a decimal point")
    .to_owned();
```

U256, being an integer type, expects that there will be no decimal point in the string representation, so we need to cut it off. It took a bit of work, but now we have a far smoother calculation of difficulty adjustments. All that we need to do is now clamp it so that we do not increase or decrease the target by more than a factor of 4x:

```
// types.rs
// clamp new_target to be within the range of
// 4 * self.target and self.target / 4
let new_target = if new_target < self.target / 4 {
    self.target / 4
} else if new_target > self.target * 4 {
    self.target * 4
} else {
    new_target
};
```

And finally, we need to ensure that we do not decrease the target below minimum target:

```
        // if the new target is more than the minimum target,
        // set it to the minimum target
        self.target = new_target.min(crate::MIN_TARGET);
```

That's it for our difficulty adjustment for now. Once again, if you check the program now, you should be getting no warnings and no compilation errors whatsoever.

MINING

Let's reorient ourselves back to the **BlockHeader** structure. Let's create a simple function that does mining for us. Since we know the target the block's hash should fall under, and we have a function on **Hash** that can compare it for us (**Hash::matches_target()**), we can make a simple mining method on the **BlockHeader** structure called **mine()**. This function will rotate the **nonce** and, if it runs out of the **nonce**, update the **timestamp**:

```
// types.rs
pub fn mine(&mut self, steps: usize) -> bool {
    // if the block already matches target, return early
    if self.hash().matches_target(self.target) {
        return true;
    }
    for _ in 0..steps {
        if let Some(new_nonce) =
            self.nonce.checked_add(1)
        {
            self.nonce = new_nonce;
        } else {
            self.nonce = 0;
            self.timestamp = Utc::now()
        }
```

```
            if self.hash().matches_target(self.target) {
                return true;
            }
        }
        false
    }
```

In comparison to the previous examples we made, this one is very simple. The reason why we only do a finite number of steps at a time is because we may want to interrupt the mining if we receive an update from the network that we should work on a new block (because a new block has been found in the meantime).

BLOCKCHAIN METHODS

The nature of bitcoin is that we have a network of nodes that share information between each other in order to maintain a single source of truth - the blockchain itself. Currently, the methods we have created on our **Blockchain** type are only enough if we ever plan to have just one node, which defeats the purpose of a blockchain. We need to add a couple of methods that will help us share the blockchain.

First, let's improve our design by making our fields private and creating methods that expose them:

```
// types.rs
#[derive(Serialize, Deserialize, Clone, Debug)]
pub struct Blockchain {
   utxos: HashMap<Hash, TransactionOutput>,
   target: U256,
   blocks: Vec<Block>,
}
```

Notice how we removed the **pub** keyword from every field. The new methods will be:

```
// types.rs
// utxos
pub fn utxos(&self) -> &HashMap<Hash, TransactionOutput> {
    &self.utxos
}
// target
pub fn target(&self) -> U256 {
    self.target
}
// blocks
pub fn blocks(&self) -> impl Iterator<Item = &Block> {
    self.blocks.iter()
}
```

This is considered to be a better design, as it lets you change the underlying implementation of the storage. It could be quite impractical to store the entire blockchain in RAM, and using some on-disk storage (or outright hooking up the project to some database), could be an improvement you may want to make in your implementation. We should also expose block height as a method:

```
// types.rs
// block height
pub fn block_height(&self) -> u64 {
    self.blocks.len() as u64
}
```

It is left as an exercise to the reader to go, and use this method in places where we previously needed block height.

Another critical aspect that is missing in our Blockchain is the **mempool**. The **mempool** is a list of transactions that have been sent to the network and haven't been processed yet. These are the ones that are put into new blocks and mined by miners. Miners are incentivized to assemble blocks from transactions that have the highest fees first, so we can make our mempool helpful by pre-sorting it by fee size.

We can make our mempool very simple, by using another vector:

```
// types.rs
#[derive(Serialize, Deserialize, Clone, Debug)]
pub struct Blockchain {
    utxos: HashMap<Hash, TransactionOutput>,
    target: U256,
    blocks: Vec<Block>,
    #[serde(default, skip_serializing)]
    mempool: Vec<Transaction>,
}
impl Blockchain {
    pub fn new() -> Self {
        Blockchain {
            utxos: HashMap::new(),
            blocks: vec![],
            target: crate::MIN_TARGET,
            mempool: vec![],
        }
    }
    // mempool
    pub fn mempool(
        &self,
    ) -> &[Transaction] { // later, we will also need to keep
track of time
        &self.mempool
    }
    // ...
}
```

Now we need to teach the blockchain to receive and add transactions to the mempool, consider this **Blockchain::add_to_mempool()** method:

```
    // types.rs
    // add a transaction to mempool
    pub fn add_to_mempool(&mut self, transaction: Transaction)
{
        self.mempool.push(transaction);
        // sort by miner fee
        self.mempool.sort_by_key(|transaction| {
            let all_inputs = transaction
                .inputs
                .iter()
                .map(|input| {
                    self.utxos
                        .get(&input.prev_transaction_output_
hash)
                        .expect("BUG: impossible")
                        .value
                })
                .sum::<u64>();
            let all_outputs: u64 = transaction
                .outputs
                .iter()
                .map(|output| output.value)
                .sum();
            let miner_fee = all_inputs - all_outputs;
            miner_fee
        });
    }
```

We should also do some verification of the transaction, as we just accept it now as it is, but it may, in fact, be malformed. This would make that **BUG: impossible** actually possible (The seemingly impossible bugs are the worst kind of bugs!). This means we also need to do some error handling in case the transaction is not valid:

- Outputs should be less or equal to inputs (the difference between the two is the miner fee)
- All inputs must have a known UTXO

- All inputs must be unique (no double-spending within a single transaction)

We can modify the method in the following way:

```
// types.rs
use std::collections::HashSet; // move this to the top
// add a transaction to mempool
pub fn add_to_mempool(
    &mut self,
    transaction: Transaction,
) -> Result<()> {
    // validate transaction before insertion
    // all inputs must match known UTXOs, and must be
unique
    let mut known_inputs = HashSet::new();
    for input in &transaction.inputs {
        if !self.utxos.contains_key(
            &input.prev_transaction_output_hash,
        ) {
            return Err(BtcError::InvalidTransaction);
        }
        if known_inputs.contains(
            &input.prev_transaction_output_hash,
        ) {
            return Err(BtcError::InvalidTransaction);
        }
        known_inputs
            .insert(input.prev_transaction_output_hash);
    }
    // all inputs must be lower than all outputs
    let all_inputs = transaction
        .inputs
        .iter()
        .map(|input| {
            self.utxos
                .get(
                    &input.prev_transaction_output_hash,
                )
```

```rust
                    .expect("BUG: impossible")
                    .value
            })
            .sum::<u64>();
        let all_outputs = transaction
            .outputs
            .iter()
            .map(|output| output.value)
            .sum();
        if all_inputs < all_outputs {
            return Err(BtcError::InvalidTransaction);
        }
        self.mempool.push(transaction);
        // sort by miner fee
        self.mempool.sort_by_key(|transaction| {
            // ...
        });
        Ok(())
    }
```

Don't forget that little **Ok(())** at the end of the function. We need this because we changed the return type of the function. At this stage, the library should compile correctly.

There is yet another security issue we must take care of: So far, it is still possible to add multiple transactions to the mempool that reference the same unspent transaction outputs. Furthermore, transactions in the mempool will stay stuck there until the node is restarted (at which point, other nodes would share the same transactions with the node again).

Therefore we need a mechanism to detect this type of double-spending, to discard old unprocessed transactions, and to replace transactions with newer transactions that reference the same inputs (which will prevent a potential double-spending problem). To do this, we will need to make two adjustments:

- Track the time when a particular transaction was inserted into the mempool, and dump it if it has been there for too long.

- Mark UTXOs that are being referenced by a transaction in mempool, and find and remove the old transaction that marks those UTXOs.

For the second task, we just need to add a mark to each UTXO:

```
// types.rs
#[derive(Serialize, Deserialize, Clone, Debug)]
pub struct Blockchain {
    utxos: HashMap<Hash, (bool, TransactionOutput)>,
    target: U256,
    blocks: Vec<Block>,
    #[serde(default, skip_serializing)]
    mempool: Vec<Transaction>,
}
```

This will break a couple of places, so we need to make some adjustments. First, in **add_to_mempool()**:

```
    // types.rs
    // add a transaction to mempool
    pub fn add_to_mempool(
        &mut self,
        transaction: Transaction,
    ) -> Result<()> {
        // ...
        let all_inputs = transaction
            .inputs
            .iter()
            .map(|input| {
                self.utxos
                    .get(
                        &input.prev_transaction_output_hash,
                    )
                    .expect("BUG: impossible")
                    .1 // < - - - Look here
                    .value
```

```
        })
        .sum::<u64>();
    // ...
    // sort by miner fee
    self.mempool.sort_by_key(|transaction| {
        let all_inputs = transaction
            .inputs
            .iter()
            .map(|input| {
                self.utxos
                    .get(&input.prev_transaction_output_
hash)
                    .expect("BUG: impossible")
                    .1 // < - - - Look here
                    .value
            })
            .sum::<u64>();
            // ...
    });
}
```

Note that this is just adding **.1** to get the second field of the tuple. The next place we need to fix is the **utxos()** method:

```
// types.rs

// utxos
pub fn utxos(
    &self,
) -> &HashMap<Hash, (bool, TransactionOutput)>
{
    &self.utxos
}
```

Here, we are just fixing the return type to account for the boolean value we use to mark the UTXOs as "primed for spending by a transaction in mempool". Then, we must hop over to **Block** and update the functions that verify transactions with a list of UTXOs:

```
// types.rs
// Verify all transactions in the block
pub fn verify_transactions(
    &self,
    predicted_block_height: u64,
    utxos: &HashMap<Hash, (bool, TransactionOutput)>,
) -> Result<()> {
    let mut inputs: HashMap<Hash, TransactionOutput> =
        HashMap::new();
    // reject completely empty blocks
    if self.transactions.is_empty() {
        return Err(BtcError::InvalidTransaction);
    }
    // verify coinbase transaction
    self.verify_coinbase_transaction(
        predicted_block_height,
        utxos,
    )?;
    for transaction in self.transactions.iter().skip(1)
    {
        let mut input_value = 0;
        let mut output_value = 0;
        for input in &transaction.inputs {
            let prev_output = utxos
                .get(
                    &input.prev_transaction_output_hash,
                )
                .map(|(_, output)| output);
            // ...
        }
        // ...
    }
}
```

The beginning of **calculate_miner_fees():**

```
// types.rs
pub fn calculate_miner_fees(
    &self,
    utxos: &HashMap<Hash, (bool, TransactionOutput)>,
) -> Result<u64> {
    let mut inputs: HashMap<Hash, TransactionOutput> =
        HashMap::new();
    let mut outputs: HashMap<Hash, TransactionOutput> =
        HashMap::new();
    // Check every transaction after coinbase
    for transaction in self.transactions.iter().skip(1)
    {
        for input in &transaction.inputs {
            let prev_output = utxos
                .get(
                    &input.prev_transaction_output_hash,
                )
                .map(|(_, output)| output);
```

And the signature of **verify_coinbase_transaction():**

```
// types.rs

// Verify coinbase transaction
pub fn verify_coinbase_transaction(
    &self,
    predicted_block_height: u64,
    utxos: &HashMap<Hash, (bool, TransactionOutput)>,
) -> Result<()> {
```

Finally, we need to jump back to **Blockchain** and fix **rebuild_utxos()** to insert new transactions with the mark included:

```
// types.rs
// Rebuild UTXO set from the blockchain
pub fn rebuild_utxos(&mut self) {
    for block in &self.blocks {
        for transaction in &block.transactions {
            for input in &transaction.inputs {
                self.utxos.remove(
                    &input.prev_transaction_output_hash,
                );
            }
            for output in transaction.outputs.iter() {
                self.utxos.insert(
                    output.hash(),
                    (false, output.clone()),
                );
            }
        }
    }
}
```

Check if the library compiles now. It should, and it should be without warnings.

We insert the mark set to false, since new UTXOs cannot already be reserved by a transaction in the mempool. Now, we can change **add_to_mempool()** to detect and remove overlapping transactions:

```
// types.rs
// add a transaction to mempool
pub fn add_to_mempool(
    &mut self,
    transaction: Transaction,
) -> Result<()> {
    // validate transaction before insertion
    // all inputs must match known UTXOs, and must be
unique
    let mut known_inputs = HashSet::new();
    for input in &transaction.inputs {
```

```
            // ...
        }
        // check if any of the utxos have the bool mark set to
true
        // and if so, find the transaction that references them
        // in mempool, remove it, and set all the utxos it refe-
rences
        // to false
        for input in &transaction.inputs {
            if let Some((true, _)) = self
                .utxos
                .get(&input.prev_transaction_output_hash)
            {
                // find the transaction that references the
UTXO
                // we are trying to reference
                let referencing_transaction = self.mempool
                .iter()
                .enumerate()
                .find(
                    |(_, transaction)| {
                        transaction
                            .outputs
                            .iter()
                            .any(|output| {
                                output.hash()
                                    == input.prev_transacti-
on_output_hash
                            })
                    },
                );
                // If we have found one, unmark all of its
UTXOs
                if let Some((
                    idx,
                    referencing_transaction,
                )) = referencing_transaction
                {
                    for input in
```

```
                        &referencing_transaction.inputs
                    {
                        // set all utxos from this transaction
to false
                        self.utxos
                            .entry(input.prev_transaction_out-
put_hash)
                            .and_modify(|(marked, _)| {
                                *marked = false;
                            });
                    }
                    // remove the transaction from the mempool
                    self.mempool.remove(idx);
                } else {
                    // if, somehow, there is no matching
transaction,
                    // set this utxo to false
                    self.utxos
                        .entry(input.prev_transaction_output_
hash)
                        .and_modify(|(marked, _)| {
                            *marked = false;
                        });
                }
            }
        }
        // ...
    }
```

Note that we are making a bit of a simplification. In two conflicting transactions, real Bitcoin would remove the one with the smaller fee (which is great for ergonomics - you can't get your transaction through fast enough -> you increase the fee). You should be able to implement this pretty easily if you'd like to :)

Let's analyze the snippet we have inserted into the function. First, we are iterating through all of the transaction inputs, and trying to find their matching UTXO:

```
        for input in &transaction.inputs {
            if let Some((true, _)) = self
                .utxos
                .get(&input.prev_transaction_output_hash)
            {
                // ...
            }
        }
```

Here, we are using pattern matching with the **if-let** control structure. This **if**'s body will only be executed if the tuple we find in utxos has **true** in the first field, meaning this UTXO has already been marked by another transaction. Next, we need to find the transaction that references the UTXO:

```
                // find the transaction that references the
UTXO
                // we are trying to reference
                let referencing_transaction = self.mempool
                .iter()
                .enumerate()
                .find(
                    |(_, transaction)| {
                        transaction
                            .outputs
                            .iter()
                            .any(|output| {
                                output.hash()
                                == input.prev_transaction_out-
put_hash
                            })
                    },
                );
```

The type of this variable is **Option<(usize, &Transaction)>** due to the fact that we have inserted **.enumerate()** into this iterator chain. This method()

includes the index of each element with it, and we need it, so that we can remove the offending transaction from the mempool without having to go through it again. We now need to handle the possibility, that we may not find the correct transaction (this shouldn't happen, but let's be safe):

```
            // If we have found one, unmark all of its
UTXOs
            if let Some((
                idx,
                referencing_transaction,
            )) = referencing_transaction
            {
                // ...
            } else {
                // ...
            }
```

If the **if-let** matches, we go through every **UTXO** and unmark it, then finally remove the transaction from the mempool (this is in the **if** block):

```
                for input in
                    &referencing_transaction.inputs
                {
                    // set all utxos from this transaction
to false
                    self.utxos
                        .entry(input.prev_transaction_out-
put_hash)
                        .and_modify(|(marked, _)| {
                            *marked = false;
                        });
                }
                // remove the transaction from the mempool
                self.mempool.remove(idx);
```

In the other case, where there is no transaction found, we will simply unmark the **UTXO** whose matching mempool transaction we were trying to find (this is in the **else** block):

```
                    // if, somehow, there is no matching
transaction,
                    // set this utxo to false
                    self.utxos
                        .entry(input.prev_transaction_output_
hash)
                        .and_modify(|(marked, _)| {
                            *marked = false;
                        });
```

Notice how, while pattern-matching in the closure on the highlighted lines, we are replacing the second parameter with an _ (underscore), this is Rust's syntax for ignoring a particular value. We only care about the **marked** status, and do not need to modify the actual **UTXO** at all.

Now, we can implement the second half of the puzzle, the automatic removal of old transactions in mempool. To do this, we need to start tracking the time that these were inserted into the mempool. But first, we need to decide how long transactions should last. In the real bitcoin implementation and its nodes, the **time-based eviction policy** is typically **72 hours**. That is too long for us, so we can shorten it to **600 seconds**. To provide additional context - real bitcoin also evicts lowest-fee transactions if the mempool gets too big. Not setting a limit on the size of the mempool is a security risk, as a malicious agent could crash our application by adding thousands upon thousands of fraudulent transactions into the mempool until we run out of RAM.

Tracking submission time is easy enough, we just stick a **DateTime<Utc>** to every transaction in the **mempool**, similar to how we did it with the **bool** mark on the **UTXOs**. First, we adjust the **Blockchain** struct like this:

```
#[derive(Serialize, Deserialize, Clone, Debug)]
pub struct Blockchain {
    utxos: HashMap<Hash, (bool, TransactionOutput)>,
    target: U256,
    blocks: Vec<Block>,
    #[serde(default, skip_serializing)]
    mempool: Vec<(DateTime<Utc>, Transaction)>,
}
```

Once again, if you try to run **cargo check**, the Rust compiler will get very angry with you. This is good, in more dynamic languages such as JavaScript, you could possibly go without having any idea of all the places you need to fix until you run your application and it crashes in your hands in every possible spot. And sometimes, it might be very rare to encounter those spots. But this is not a critique of JavaScript, and there are tools even for JS and other dynamic languages that help lessen the severity of this issue. All of the compilation errors we are getting now are still in the **src/types.rs** file, so we can fix them one by one and fix all of them. First, in **add_to_mempool()**:

```
        // types.rs
        // find the transaction that references the UTXO
        // we are trying to reference
        let referencing_transaction = self.mempool
            .iter()
            .enumerate()
            .find(
                |(_, (_, transaction))| {
                    transaction
                        .outputs
                        .iter()
                        .any(|output| {
                            output.hash()
                              == input.prev_transaction_out-
put_hash
                        })
                },
        );
```

Here, we destructure the tuple at the spot I marked. We do not care about the timestamp in **add_to_mempool()** so we can safely ignore it with the **underscore** character. Seeing, finding and fixing these issues really highlights how useful a tool **rust-analyzer** is. **Rust-analyzer's** inlay hints show us the resolved types of the variables, and we could see that before this change we had **|(_: usize, transact on: &(DateTime<Utc>, Transaction))|**, and we were able to change it to **|(_: usize, (_: &DateTime<Utc>, transaction: &Transaction))|**.

Note that there is a bit of magic going on in that Rust is perfectly willing to transpose a reference to a tuple to a tuple of references. This makes it far more ergonomic. Subtly transposing references and reducing multiple references into one (it is called **auto-deref**) is pretty much the only implicit magic that **Rust** is willing to do. Considering that none of these change the semantics of your program at all, these are pretty safe things to do automatically to provide an extra degree of ergonomics.

Next spot we need to fix is only a couple of lines below, and it is very similar:

```
                // types.rs
                // If we have found one, unmark all of its
UTXOs
                if let Some((
                    idx,
                    (_, referencing_transaction),
                )) = referencing_transaction
                {
                    // ...
                }
```

It is precisely the same situation as above. The next complaint is still in **add_to_mempool()**. To preserve some space, I will only include the context that's around it:

```
        // types.rs
        if all_inputs < all_outputs {
            return Err(BtcError::InvalidTransaction);
```

```
    }
    self.mempool.push((Utc::now(), transaction));
    // sort by miner fee
    self.mempool.sort_by_key(|transaction| {
        // ...
    });
    Ok(())
```

This is just adding the timestamp when inserting the transaction into the mempool. The final two issues are very similar to the first two issues, and they are found in the **sort by miner fee** statement that we have snipped out of the previous example for the sake of brevity. Here they are with the fixes highlighted:

```
    // types.rs

    // sort by miner fee
    self.mempool.sort_by_key(|(_, transaction)| {
        // ...
    });
```

Lastly for **add_to_mempool()**, we need to make sure that we mark the UTXOs we have used in the transaction we have just created. This is the whole function with the added portion highlighted:

```
// types.rs

// add a transaction to mempool
pub fn add_to_mempool(
    &mut self,
    transaction: Transaction,
) -> Result<()> {
    // validate transaction before insertion
    // all inputs must match known UTXOs, and must be
```

```
unique
        let mut known_inputs = HashSet::new();
        for input in &transaction.inputs {
            if !self.utxos.contains_key(
                &input.prev_transaction_output_hash,
            ) {
                println!("UTXO not found");
                dbg!(&self.utxos);
                return Err(BtcError::InvalidTransaction);
            }
            if known_inputs
                .contains(&input.prev_transaction_output_hash)
            {
                println!("duplicate input");
                return Err(BtcError::InvalidTransaction);
            }
            known_inputs
                .insert(input.prev_transaction_output_hash);
        }
        // check if any of the utxos have the bool mark set to
true
        // and if so, find the transaction that references
them
        // in mempool, remove it, and set all the utxos it refe-
rences
        // to false
        for input in &transaction.inputs {
            if let Some((true, _)) = self
                .utxos
                .get(&input.prev_transaction_output_hash)
            {
                // find the transaction that references the
UTXO
                // we are trying to reference
                let referencing_transaction = self.mempool
            .iter()
            .enumerate()
            .find(
                |(_, (_, transaction))| {
```

```
                transaction
                    .outputs
                    .iter()
                    .any(|output| {
                        output.hash()
                         == input.prev_transaction_out-
put_hash
                    })
            },
        );
            // If we have found one, unmark all of its
UTXOs
            if let Some((
                idx,
                (_, referencing_transaction),
            )) = referencing_transaction
            {
                for input in &referencing_transaction.
inputs
                {
                 // set all utxos from this transaction to
false
                    self.utxos
                    .entry(input.prev_transaction_out-
put_hash)
                    .and_modify(|(marked, _)| {
                        *marked = false;
                    });
                }
                // remove the transaction from the mempool
                self.mempool.remove(idx);
            } else {
               // if, somehow, there is no matching
transaction,
                // set this utxo to false
                self.utxos
                    .entry(
```

```
                        input.prev_transaction_output_hash,
                    )
                    .and_modify(|(marked, _)| {
                        *marked = false;
                    });
            }
        }
    }
    // all inputs must be lower than all outputs
    let all_inputs = transaction
        .inputs
        .iter()
        .map(|input| {
            self.utxos
                .get(&input.prev_transaction_output_hash)
                .expect("BUG: impossible")
                .1
                .value
        })
        .sum::<u64>();
    let all_outputs = transaction
        .outputs
        .iter()
        .map(|output| output.value)
        .sum();
    if all_inputs < all_outputs {
        print!("inputs are lower than outputs");
        return Err(BtcError::InvalidTransaction);
    }
    // Mark the UTXOs as used
    for input in &transaction.inputs {
        self.utxos
            .entry(input.prev_transaction_output_hash)
            .and_modify(|(marked, _)| {
                *marked = true;
            });
    }
    // push the transaction to the mempool
    self.mempool.push((Utc::now(), transaction));
```

```
    // sort by miner fee
    self.mempool.sort_by_key(|(_, transaction)| {
        let all_inputs = transaction
            .inputs
            .iter()
            .map(|input| {
                self.utxos
                    .get(&input.prev_transaction_output_
hash)
                    .expect("BUG: impossible")
                    .1
                    .value
            })
            .sum::<u64>();
        let all_outputs: u64 = transaction
            .outputs
            .iter()
            .map(|output| output.value)
            .sum();
        let miner_fee = all_inputs - all_outputs;
        miner_fee
    });
    Ok(())
}
```

Finally, we need to adjust the **mempool()** function itself:

```
// types.rs

// mempool
pub fn mempool(&self) -> &[(DateTime<Utc>, Transaction)] {
    &self.mempool
}
```

That should be it. If you run **cargo check** now, the command should succeed and you should get no errors at all. The final piece of this puzzle is adding the method to **Blockchain** which cleans up the **mempool**. First, let's add another constant to **src/lib.rs**:

```
// lib.rs
// initial reward in bitcoin - multiply by 10^8 to get sato-
shis
pub const INITIAL_REWARD: u64 = 50;
// halving interval in blocks
pub const HALVING_INTERVAL: u64 = 210;
// ideal block time in seconds
pub const IDEAL_BLOCK_TIME: u64 = 10;
// minimum target
pub const MIN_TARGET: U256 = U256([
    0xFFFF_FFFF_FFFF_FFFF,
    0xFFFF_FFFF_FFFF_FFFF,
    0xFFFF_FFFF_FFFF_FFFF,
    0x0000_FFFF_FFFF_FFFF,
]);
// difficulty update interval in blocks
pub const DIFFICULTY_UPDATE_INTERVAL: u64 = 50;
// maximum mempool transaction age in seconds
pub const MAX_MEMPOOL_TRANSACTION_AGE: u64 = 600;
```

Now, let's add a **cleanup_mempool()** function to **Blockchain**:

```
    // types.rs
    // Cleanup mempool - remove transactions older than
    // MAX_MEMPOOL_TRANSACTION_AGE
    pub fn cleanup_mempool(&mut self) {
        let now = Utc::now();
        let mut utxo_hashes_to_unmark: Vec<Hash> = vec![];
        self.mempool.retain(|(timestamp, transaction)| {
            if now - *timestamp
                > chrono::Duration::seconds(
                    crate::MAX_MEMPOOL_TRANSACTION_AGE
```

```rust
                as i64,
            )
        {
            // push all utxos to unmark to the vector
            // so we can unmark them later
            utxo_hashes_to_unmark
                .extend(transaction.inputs.iter().map(
                |input| {
                    input.prev_transaction_output_hash
                },
            ));
            false
        } else {
            true
        }
    });
    // unmark all of the UTXOs
    for hash in utxo_hashes_to_unmark {
        self.utxos.entry(hash).and_modify(
            |(marked, _)| {
                *marked = false;
            },
        );
    }
}
```

Once again, let's break it down into individual steps. First, we get the current time, and create an empty vector where we will store the hashes of the UTXOs we want to unmark because their transaction will be removed:

```rust
// types.rs
let now = Utc::now();
let mut utxo_hashes_to_unmark: Vec<Hash> = vec![];
```

Then we use the **.retain()** method on **Vec**. This method will retain all of the elements that match the predicate (meaning that the closure must return **true** if we want to keep that element):

```
// types.rs
self.mempool.retain(|(timestamp, transaction)| {
    if now - *timestamp
        > chrono::Duration::seconds(
            crate::MAX_MEMPOOL_TRANSACTION_AGE
                as i64,
        )
    {
        // ...
        false
    } else {
        true
    }
});
```

Inside the **if** block, we will be doing a little hack, which typically is not done in the **.retain()** method's predicate, and that is copying the hashes of the UTXOs referenced by this transaction into the vector we have prepared earlier:

```
// types.rs
if now - *timestamp
    > chrono::Duration::seconds(
        crate::MAX_MEMPOOL_TRANSACTION_AGE
            as i64,
    )
{
    // push all utxos to unmark to the vector
    // so we can unmark them later
    utxo_hashes_to_unmark
        .extend(transaction.inputs.iter().map(
        |input| {
            input.prev_transaction_output_hash
```

```
                },
            ));
            false
        } else {
            true
        }
```

The **extend()** method drains an iterator, adding all of the elements it produces into the vector. This is a really handy method, just make sure you never put an infinite iterator there, as that might take a while for it to successfully crash the program, or your computer. Finally, we unmark all of the **UTXO**s we have collected from the removed transactions:

```
// types.rs
// unmark all of the UTXOs
for hash in utxo_hashes_to_unmark {
    self.utxos.entry(hash).and_modify(
        |(marked, _)| {
            *marked = false;
        },
    );
}
```

That's it for the mempool cleanup.

SPLITTING UP THE BIG FILE

If your situation is the same as mine, your **src/types.rs** will have about 650-ish lines, give or take a couple depending on your formatting preferences. While this is still maintainable and there are many projects with much longer source files, we can practice breaking down this big file into submodules and re-exporting their items.

In Rust, there two modes of creating submodules:

- A folder with a **mod.rs** file and files or folders for its submodules in it
- A file named **module_name.rs** with **module_name/** folder and files or folders for its submodules in the folder

The second option was added to Rust more recently, and since we already have a **src/types.rs** file, we can practice this one now.

Do the following steps:
1. Create a **types/** folder

2. In it, create the following files:

- blockchain.rs
- block.rs
- transaction.rs

3. Declare these modules privately (without the **pub** keyword) in the **src/types.rs** file

If you have performed these steps correctly, your file structure in this folder should look a bit like this:

```
.
|-- Cargo.lock
|-- Cargo.toml
|-- rustfmt.toml
`-- src
    |-- crypto.rs
    |-- error.rs
    |-- lib.rs
    |-- sha256.rs
    |-- types
    |   |-- block.rs
    |   |-- blockchain.rs
    |   `-- transaction.rs
    |-- types.rs
    `-- util.rs
```

You will also have a large **target/** folder with many files in it, of course, but that is not important now. If you want to reduce the size of your **target/** folder, run **cargo clean**. Note that this will require a full rebuild next time you run any **cargo check/build/run** command.

And if you did the third step correctly, you should have the following new lines in your **src/types.rs**:

```
// types.rs
mod block;
mod blockchain;
mod transaction;
```

Now, let's do some cutting. Place everything related to the **Block** and **BlockHeader** structures into **src/types/block.rs**. You will also need to include the imports needed by this part of the program. If you have done it correctly, your **src/types/block.rs** file should look like this:

```
// types/block.rs
use chrono::{DateTime, Utc};
use serde::{Deserialize, Serialize};
use super::{Transaction, TransactionOutput};
use crate::error::{BtcError, Result};
use crate::sha256::Hash;
use crate::util::MerkleRoot;
use crate::U256;
use std::collections::HashMap;
#[derive(Serialize, Deserialize, Clone, Debug)]
pub struct Block {
    // ...
}
impl Block {
    // ...
}
#[derive(Serialize, Deserialize, Clone, Debug)]
pub struct BlockHeader {
```

```
    // ...
}
impl BlockHeader {
    // ...
}
```

You will get some unused warnings, but it should be fine. Notice the highlighted import statement, this is how you import items from the parent module of your own. Next, let's split off transaction items into **src/types/transaction.rs:**

```
// types/transaction.rs
use serde::{Deserialize, Serialize};
use uuid::Uuid;
use crate::crypto::{PublicKey, Signature};
use crate::sha256::Hash;
#[derive(Serialize, Deserialize, Clone, Debug)]
pub struct Transaction {
    // ...
}
#[derive(Serialize, Deserialize, Clone, Debug)]
pub struct TransactionInput {
    // ...
}
#[derive(Serialize, Deserialize, Clone, Debug)]
pub struct TransactionOutput {
    // ...
}
impl TransactionOutput {
    // ...
}
impl Transaction {
    // ...
}
```

There we go. Finally, let's move **Blockchain** and its methods to **src/types/blockchain.rs**:

```
// types/blockchain.rs
use bigdecimal::BigDecimal;
use chrono::{DateTime, Utc};
use serde::{Deserialize, Serialize};
use super::{Block, Transaction, TransactionOutput};
use crate::error::{BtcError, Result};
use crate::sha256::Hash;
use crate::util::MerkleRoot;
use crate::U256;
use std::collections::{HashMap, HashSet};
#[derive(Serialize, Deserialize, Clone, Debug)]
pub struct Blockchain {
    // ...
}
impl Blockchain {
    // ...
}
```

Once again, take notice of the highlighted import statement. Now that we have split off all of the pieces into separate modules, the **src/types.rs** file will be very short. After removing the unused imports, this will be all that is left:

```
// types.rs
mod block;
mod blockchain;
mod transaction;
```

To make the library compile again, we need to add a couple of **pub use** statements. This statement works as both an import and a re-export. From the outside (and from the submodules' perspective, too) it will look as if all of the types from the submodules were defined in **src/types.rs** instead:

```
// types.rs
mod block;
mod blockchain;
mod transaction;
pub use block::{Block, BlockHeader};
pub use blockchain::Blockchain;
pub use transaction::{
    Transaction, TransactionInput, TransactionOutput,
};
```

If there are any leftover unused imports, remove them now :)

That's it for the cleanup. Congratulations on keeping up with the difficult work so far. Once this library is complete, we will have the majority of the work done. :)

SERIALIZATION INTO AND DESERIALIZATION OUT OF FILES

Now that we cleaned up this crate a little, let's add functionality to export and import some of these structures to and from files. We are going to leverage the power of Rust traits by creating a **Saveable** trait, which will have a **save()** and **load()** function that serializes the structure into a generic writer or deserializes out of a generic reader, and that will let us create a unified interface for sending bytes into files or over network.

This functionality is a bit of a utility, so we can put it in the **src/util.rs** module. To begin with, we can define the **Saveable trait**:

```
// util.rs
use std::io::{Read, Write, Result as IoResult};
pub trait Saveable {
    fn load<I: Read>(&self, reader: I);
    fn save<O: Write>(&self, writer: O);
}
```

Move the newly added **use** statement to the top of the file, as it belongs with the other ones. We can now extend the trait with **save_to_file()** and **load_from_file()** trait methods:

```
// util.rs
use std::fs::File;
use std::io::{Read, Result as IoResult, Write};
use std::path::Path;
pub trait Saveable
where
    Self: Sized,
{
    fn load<I: Read>(reader: I) -> IoResult<Self>;
    fn save<O: Write>(&self, writer: O) -> IoResult<()>;
    fn save_to_file<P: AsRef<Path>>(
        &self,
        path: P,
    ) -> IoResult<()> {
        let file = File::create(&path)?;
        self.save(file)
    }
    fn load_from_file<P: AsRef<Path>>(
        path: P,
    ) -> IoResult<Self> {
        let file = File::open(&path)?;
        Self::load(file)
    }
}
```

A couple of notes:

- We added the **Self: Sized** `where` clause. This trait bound is required because not all types have a size known at compile time (for example, **&str** has a known size, it is the size of a fat pointer[40], but the underlying **str** does not have a size known at compile-time, since it refers to the real bytes of

40 A pointer that includes additional data alongside the memory address, typically size information or bounds for the underlying data. Trait objects have their virtual methods table pointer as this metadata. Since you can imagine a fat pointer as a well defined struct - e.g. pointer and usize, or pointer and pointer, it is sized.

the string). Here, we needed it because of the requirement of **Result<T, E>** that both **T** and **E** are **Sized**.

- Because we only need the **self.save()** and **self.load()** methods to be able to implement **save_to_file()**, we can give them default implementations in the traits, and none of our implementors will need to implement these again.
- The two new methods take **P: AsRef<Path>** as a generic parameter for the path variable instead of taking the **Path** type directly, and that tells us that we can use anything convertible into a path, which includes a **&str** string slice.

The last point lets us do the following:

```
// util.rs
something_saveable.save_to_file("some_file.cbor")
```

Which is short, sweet and readable as opposed to:

```
// util.rs
something_saveable.save_to_file(Path::new("some_file.cbor"))
```

The final piece for this section is implementing this trait on **Blockchain**, **Block** and **Transaction**. By random choice, let's start with the transaction one in **src/types/transaction.rs**:

```
// types/transaction.rs
// add this to the imports at the top of the file
use crate::util::Saveable;
use std::io::{
    Error as IoError, ErrorKind as IoErrorKind, Read,
    Result as IoResult, Write,
};
// save and load expecting CBOR from ciborium as format
```

```
impl Saveable for Transaction {
    fn load<I: Read>(reader: I) -> IoResult<Self> {
        ciborium::de::from_reader(reader).map_err(|_| {
            IoError::new(
                IoErrorKind::InvalidData,
                "Failed to deserialize Transaction",
            )
        })
    }
    fn save<O: Write>(&self, writer: O) -> IoResult<()> {
        ciborium::ser::into_writer(self, writer).map_err(
            |_| {
                IoError::new(
                    IoErrorKind::InvalidData,
                    "Failed to serialize Transaction",
                )
            },
        )
    }
}
```

The ones for **Blockchain** and **Block** will be almost identical, just slightly different errors, and the type name replaced with the appropriate one. For **Blockchain** in **src/types/blockchain.rs**:

```
// types/blockchain.rs
// add this to the imports at the top of the file
use crate::util::Saveable;
use std::io::{
   Error as IoError, ErrorKind as IoErrorKind, Read,
   Result as IoResult, Write,
};
// save and load expecting CBOR from ciborium as format
impl Saveable for Blockchain {
   fn load<I: Read>(reader: I) -> IoResult<Self> {
       ciborium::de::from_reader(reader).map_err(|_| {
           IoError::new(
```

```
                IoErrorKind::InvalidData,
                "Failed to deserialize Blockchain",
            )
        })
    }
    fn save<O: Write>(&self, writer: O) -> IoResult<()> {
        ciborium::ser::into_writer(self, writer).map_err(
            |_| {
                IoError::new(
                    IoErrorKind::InvalidData,
                    "Failed to serialize Blockchain",
                )
            },
        )
    }
}
```

And for **Block** in **src/types/block.rs**:

```
// types/block.rs
// add this to the imports at the top of the file
use crate::util::Saveable;
use std::io::{
    Error as IoError, ErrorKind as IoErrorKind, Read,
    Result as IoResult, Write,
};
// save and load expecting CBOR from ciborium as format
impl Saveable for Block {
    fn load<I: Read>(reader: I) -> IoResult<Self> {
        ciborium::de::from_reader(reader).map_err(|_| {
            IoError::new(
                IoErrorKind::InvalidData,
                "Failed to deserialize Block",
            )
        })
    }
```

```
    fn save<O: Write>(&self, writer: O) -> IoResult<()> {
        ciborium::ser::into_writer(self, writer).map_err(
            |_| {
                IoError::new(
                    IoErrorKind::InvalidData,
                    "Failed to serialize Block",
                )
            },
        )
    }
}
```

That's it, all that awaits us now in this chapter is developing the utility binaries that will help us with the Miner and other parts of the program.

UTILITY BINARIES

Before we say goodbye to library development, we need to create what we promised in the introductory chapters - utility binaries to help us with development. Let's create the following ones to help us test the next part of our project, the simple CPU miner:

- Block generator
- Transaction generator
- Block printer
- Transaction printer

We only need a bit of testing data, so we can make them very simple. While we have already mentioned that the entry point for Rust binaries in a crate is the **src/main.rs** file, there is another option - the **src/bin/{name}.rs** files. These are useful for when your project has either multiple binaries on the same level, or one main binary and several other smaller binaries. Our case is the first case, since this is still a library.

Start by creating the following files (still in the **lib/** folder):

- **src/bin/block_gen.rs**
- **src/bin/tx_gen.rs**
- **src/bin/block_print.rs**
- **src/bin/tx_print.rs**

Now, our project technically has binaries, but the Rust compiler will still complain because these files lack a **main()** function. Let's make two dummy ones, just so that we can try running them with Cargo:

```
// bin/tx_gen.rs
fn main() {
    println!("Hello from transaction generator!");
}
// bin/block_gen.rs
fn main() {
    println!("Hello from block generator!");
}
```

It is left as an exercise for the reader to make identical **main()** functions for the other two programs.

If you run **cargo run** now, it will complain with the following message:

```
error: `cargo run` could not determine which binary to run.
Use the `--bin` option to specify a binary, or the `default-
-run` manifest key.
available binaries: block_gen, tx_gen
```

Well, we can do what Cargo wants, and try running the transaction generator, for example:

```
$ cargo run --bin tx_gen
    Finished dev [unoptimized + debuginfo] target(s) in 0.04s
```

```
   Running `target/debug/tx_gen`
Hello from transaction generator!
```

There we go. We will make our testing programs as simple as possible, so all of them will only take a single argument, the **name of the file** to either read or write to. Let's start with the printing programs, as they are going to be very simple, and almost identical to one another.

First, the **block printer**. We will start by reading the second argument (since the first one is the name of the program):

```
// bin/block_print.rs
use btclib::types::Block;
use btclib::util::Saveable;
use std::env;
use std::process::exit;
fn main() {
    let path = if let Some(arg) = env::args().nth(1) {
        arg
    } else {
        eprintln!("Usage: block_print <block_file>");
        exit(1);
    };
}
```

Depending on how you called the **lib** part of the project, you may get the following error:

```
error[E0433]: failed to resolve: use of undeclared crate or
module `btclib`
--> lib/src/bin/block_print.rs:1:5
 |
1 | use btclib::types::Block;
 |     ^^^^^^ use of undeclared crate or module `btclib`
```

```
error[E0433]: failed to resolve: use of undeclared crate or
module `btclib`
--> lib/src/bin/block_print.rs:2:5
  |
2 | use btclib::util::Saveable;
  |     ^^^^^^ use of undeclared crate or module `btclib`
warning: unused variable: `path`
--> lib/src/bin/block_print.rs:8:9
  |
8 |     let path = if let Some(arg) = env::args().nth(1) {
  |         ^^^^ help: if this is intentional, prefix it with
an underscore: `_path`
  |
 = note: `#[warn(unused_variables)]` on by default
For more information about this error, try `rustc --explain
E0433`.
warning: `lib` (bin "block_print") generated 1 warning
error: could not compile `lib` (bin "block_print") due to 2
previous errors; 1 warning emitted
```

You can fix this by either changing the **use** statements to refer to **lib::**, or rename the **lib** in **Cargo.toml**:

```
[package]
name = "btclib"
version = "0.1.0"
edition = "2021"
```

We are already going to add the **Block** type and the **Saveable** trait, as they are everything we need from our **btclib**. The next step is to open the file and load the **Block** from it:

```
// bin/block_print.rs
use btclib::types::Block;
```

```rust
use btclib::util::Saveable;
use std::env;
use std::fs::File;
use std::process::exit;
fn main() {
    let path = if let Some(arg) = env::args().nth(1) {
        arg
    } else {
        eprintln!("Usage: block_print <block_file>");
        exit(1);
    };
    if let Ok(file) = File::open(path) {
        let block = Block::load(file)
            .expect("Failed to load block");
        println!("{:#?}", block);
    }
}
```

That's it. That's the entire program. One done, three more to go. The **tx_print** program is almost the same:

```rust
// bin/tx_print.rs
use btclib::types::Transaction;
use btclib::util::Saveable;
use std::env;
use std::fs::File;
use std::process::exit;
fn main() {
    let path = if let Some(arg) = env::args().nth(1) {
        arg
    } else {
        eprintln!("Usage: tx_print <tx_file>");
        exit(1);
    };
    if let Ok(file) = File::open(path) {
        let tx = Transaction::load(file)
            .expect("Failed to load transaction");
```

```
        println!("{:#?}", tx);
    }
}
```

The lines that are different between these two programs are highlighted. Having a robust library really makes our programs quite simple, doesn't it? The program for generating blocks is also simple, but it will require a lot of imports:

```
// bin/block_gen.rs
use btclib::crypto::PrivateKey;
use btclib::sha256::Hash;
use btclib::types::{
    Block, BlockHeader, Transaction, TransactionOutput,
};
use btclib::util::{MerkleRoot, Saveable};
use chrono::Utc;
use uuid::Uuid;
use std::env;
use std::process::exit;
```

And the implementation of the **main()** function for this program can be this:

```
// bin/block_gen.rs
fn main() {
    let path = if let Some(arg) = env::args().nth(1) {
        arg
    } else {
        eprintln!("Usage: block_gen <block_file>");
        exit(1);
    };
    let private_key = PrivateKey::new_key();
    let transactions = vec![Transaction::new(
        vec![],
```

```
        vec![TransactionOutput {
            unique_id: Uuid::new_v4(),
            value: btclib::INITIAL_REWARD * 10u64.pow(8),
            pubkey: private_key.public_key(),
        }],
    )];
    let merkle_root = MerkleRoot::calculate(&transactions);
    let block = Block::new(
        BlockHeader::new(
            Utc::now(),
            0,
            Hash::zero(),
            merkle_root,
            btclib::MIN_TARGET,
        ),
        transactions,
    );
    block.save_to_file(path).expect("Failed to save block");
}
```

First, we once again retrieve the path from the first argument:

```
// bin/block_gen.rs
let path = if let Some(arg) = env::args().nth(1) {
    arg
} else {
    eprintln!("Usage: block_gen <block_file>");
    exit(1);
};
```

Then, we generate a new private key. We will need this key to generate a public key from the private key which will serve as the owner of the newly minted bitcoin in the coinbase transaction:

```rust
// bin/block_gen.rs
let private_key = PrivateKey::new_key();
let transactions = vec![Transaction::new(
    vec![],
    vec![TransactionOutput {
        unique_id: Uuid::new_v4(),
        value: btclib::INITIAL_REWARD * 10u64.pow(8),
        pubkey: private_key.public_key(),
    }],
)];
```

In this utility, we are essentially creating a genesis block - only a coinbase transaction, no previous block, initial reward and minimum target. This is how that block looks:

```rust
// bin/block_gen.rs
let merkle_root = MerkleRoot::calculate(&transactions);
let block = Block::new(
    BlockHeader::new(
        Utc::now(),
        0,
        Hash::zero(),
        merkle_root,
        btclib::MIN_TARGET,
    ),
    transactions,
);
```

And all that is left is to save it to the correct location:

```rust
// bin/block_gen.rs
block.save_to_file(path).expect("Failed to save block");
```

At this point, we have three out of the four utilities we planned to implement. The final library, the transaction generator located in **src/bin/tx_gen.rs**. Here it goes:

```
// bin/tx_gen.rs
use btclib::crypto::PrivateKey;
use btclib::types::{Transaction, TransactionOutput};
use btclib::util::Saveable;
use uuid::Uuid;
use std::env;
use std::process::exit;
fn main() {
    let path = if let Some(arg) = env::args().nth(1) {
        arg
    } else {
        eprintln!("Usage: tx_gen <tx_file>");
        exit(1);
    };
    let private_key = PrivateKey::new_key();
    let transaction = Transaction::new(
        vec![],
        vec![TransactionOutput {
            unique_id: Uuid::new_v4(),
            value: btclib::INITIAL_REWARD * 10u64.pow(8),
            pubkey: private_key.public_key(),
        }],
    );
    transaction
        .save_to_file(path)
        .expect("Failed to save transaction");
}
```

Congratulations on getting this far. Writing this library was the hardest part of this project. Now, we have gotten over the biggest hill, and can enjoy writing the rest of the blockchain implementation. As a small reward for your hard work, please enjoy this doodle of a frog I made:

Also consider having a nice cup of good coffee, tea, gin, or whatever your beverage of choice[41] is, before getting to the next part of the project - writing a simple CPU miner. Finally, make sure you try running the programs you just created. For example:

```
cargo run --bin tx_gen tx.cbor
cargo run --bin tx_print tx.cbor
```

Prints out the following on my computer:

```
Transaction {
  inputs: [],
```

41 The existence of Javascript makes me drink. I can demolish Gin and tonics like you wouldn't believe.

```
outputs: [
    TransactionOutput {
        value: 5000000000,
        unique_id: 42dc7889-20fa-4fc7-ba13-a1db8c8ffd86,
        pubkey: PublicKey(
            VerifyingKey {
                inner: PublicKey {
                    point: AffinePoint {
                        x: FieldElement(
                            FieldElementImpl {
                                value: FieldElement5x52(
                                    [
                                        1580850141496799,
                                        542666622657044,
                                        3723734510971934,
                                        3207064064113201,
                                        142606895145726,
                                    ],
                                ),
                                magnitude: 1,
                                normalized: true,
                            },
                        ),
                        y: FieldElement(
                            FieldElementImpl {
                                value: FieldElement5x52(
                                    [
                                        1870844964934659,
                                        442470295413054,
                                        980791626273540,
                                        3755959221253978,
                                        25491951452455,
                                    ],
                                ),
                                magnitude: 1,
                                normalized: true,
                            },
                        ),
                        infinity: 0,
```

```
                                    },
                                },
                            },
                        ),
                    },
                ],
            }
```

Unfortunately, the representation of the public key here is not the nice string one you may be used to, but rather how the library internally represents it. But you win some, you lose some, that's just how life is. After you have some rest (or immediately, if you are fired up), let's implement our miner.

7

CREATING A CPU MINER

This is going to be a fairly short chapter. We have already implemented some of the mining functionality before as a method on the **BlockHeader** type. Now, all we have to do is create a program which accepts a block template, mines it and prints out the header it successfully found (along with the original header, so that we have something to compare to).

At this point, we have no node to test networking against, so our miner will not do networking at all. At this stage, we will come back to it when we have the node up and running. This is a real chicken-and-egg problem, but I think we have been able to sidestep it nicely.

First, we will need to completely switch gears and navigate to our **miner** crate. Open the **miner/** folder in your editor, and navigate to its **Cargo.toml** file. First, we will add a dependency on **btclib:**

```
[dependencies]
btclib = { path = "../lib" }
```

The library is now available in the **miner** crate. Let's summarize what the miner needs to do:

- Read CLI arguments
- Read block template file from the path specified by the first CLI argument
- Mine the block (in increments specified by the second CLI parameter, so that you can choose smaller increments if your computer is slow)
- Print out the original block and its hash
- Print out the mined block and its hash
- Exit

That sounds simple enough. Let's start working on it.

We have already seen how to read command-line arguments a couple of times already. In the future, we will use a library that does CLI parsing for us, and is much smarter and more flexible than we could ever make our own small solution here, but still, our requirements are fairly minimal for now. This old-fashioned way will suffice:

```rust
// main.rs
use std::env;
use std::process::exit;
fn main() {
    // parse block path and steps count from the
    // first and second argument respectively
    let (path, steps) = if let (Some(arg), Some(arg2)) =
        (env::args().nth(1), env::args().nth(2))
    {
        (arg, arg2)
    } else {
        eprintln!("Usage: miner <block_file> <steps>");
        exit(1);
    };
    // parse steps count
    let steps: usize = if let Ok(s @ 1..=usize::MAX) =
        steps.parse()
    {
        s
    } else {
        eprintln!("<steps> should be a positive integer");
        exit(1);
    };
}
```

Now, let's load the block and make a copy of it, so that we can compare the original and the mined one (insert this after the **steps** variable):

```rust
// main.rs
use btclib::types::Block;    // <-
use btclib::util::Saveable; // add to the top of the file
    // load block from file
    let og_block = Block::load_from_file(path)
        .expect("Failed to load block");
    let mut block = og_block.clone();
```

Then we mine the block:

```
// main.rs
while !block.header.mine(steps) {
    println!("mining...");
}
```

And print its information:

```
// main.rs

// print original block and its hash
println!("original: {:#?}", og_block);
println!("hash: {}", og_block.header.hash());
// print mined block and its hash
println!("final: {:#?}", block);
println!("hash: {}", block.header.hash());
```

If you generate a block with **block_gen** and mine it with **miner** (which will most likely find the correct nonce very quickly, considering how high we set our **MIN_TARGET**), you should see the following two lines in the output (for you, both the number and the hash will be different):

```
// ...
nonce: 25032354,
// ...
hash: 000000462237a74ea853d3a3d81c112e215c8029bced286cc6485ed-
0fa9ee022
```

This is from an experiment where I lowered the **MIN_TARGET**. As you can see, it took a little over 25 million tries to find the correct hash. While that took about a minute on my crappy one million year old Lenovo ThinkPad[42], ASICs would find it several orders of magnitude faster. You can try that too by generating a new testing block. How to do that is left as an exercise to the reader, however, I will hint that you have two options - either change or extend **block_gen** to not use the **MIN_TARGET** constant, or change the constant in **src/lib.rs** of **btclib**. However make sure you don't leave the **MIN_TARGET** set too low for when we will be testing target adjustment.

NETWORKING

We are now unfortunately reaching a very painful part of network software development. The fact that it needs to do some networking. And we need to design the protocol for it. Given how simple our blockchain is meant to be, we can largely depend on what we already have, and what we already know.

Our situation is significantly simplified to the current real bitcoin in that we do not have pools. We want to have miners talking to nodes directly, and so we only need to handle the following three cases:

- Miner talks to Node
- Node talks to another Node
- Wallet talks to Node

In the first case, this is what is going to happen:

- Miner talks to node so that it can assemble a block template (the node provides information such as the current difficulty)
- Node talks to miner to confirm the validity of its requests and provide the data
- Miner talks to the node so it can submit a mined block
- Node talks to miner the confirm the validity of the block

In the second case:

- Node talks to another node to share transactions newly added to mempool

42 I love this machine. It was going to be either a ThinkPad obsession or wearing programmer socks, and I, trust me, DO NOT look good in thigh-highs.

- Node talks to another node to share newly added blocks
- Node talks to another node to share which nodes it knows about

When a node starts running, it has no mempool. We can add functionality to request another node's all the lack of a mempool. Note that since we **don't trust, (but rather) verify**, we still need to verify the validity of transactions incoming from other nodes (because what if these other nodes were malicious actors? I am a malicious actor. You should have seen me on Minecraft servers in 2012). Furthermore, we may run into a situation where we receive a block with some transactions that we did not have in the mempool. This is not an issue and we should not reject such a block, but we should still verify that these are in fact valid transactions and no double-spending is occurring.

And finally, the wallet <-> node communication goes like this:

- Wallet queries the node for the UTXOs that belong to it
- The node sends over the information
- The wallet assembles transactions and sends them to the node
- The node verifies them and adds them to the mempool, sending confirmation back to the wallet

The simplest way we can implement networking is to use TCP (so we do not have to worry about data integrity), and use **length-prefixed encoding**. This means that we will serialize each message into a binary format (in our case **CBOR** since we are already using it), then measure its size in bytes, and for each message, we will first send the size of the message, then the message itself. The other side will then know how many bytes exactly it should expect to receive, and we can optionally complain if that is not the case. One issue that we need to keep in mind is that our protocol will not necessarily be backward and forward-compatible. We would have to make the protocol smarter in order to do that, and introduce some versioning and version-negotiation mechanisms. A good tool for such functionality would be **gRPC** with **Protocol Buffers**, but that is an additional complexity that we will not be introducing in this book. However, if you want, this is a great improvement you can make to the project.

But first, what messages? We can think of a number of messages from the communication we have described above. And to represent the messages, we can use a **Rust enum**.

This **Message** type will be shared between all of our components, and so the correct place is in the **btclib** library. Therefore, after taking a very short detour from the library, we came back to it again.

In its **src/lib.rs**, create a **network** module:

```
// lib.rs
pub mod crypto;
pub mod error;
pub mod network;
pub mod sha256;
pub mod types;
pub mod util;
```

(also create the **src/network.rs** file)

In this module, we define a **Message** enum which covers all of the possible messages we have discussed until now. It can look like this:

```
// network.rs
use serde::{Deserialize, Serialize};
use crate::crypto::PublicKey;
use crate::types::{Block, Transaction, TransactionOutput};
#[derive(Debug, Clone, Deserialize, Serialize)]
pub enum Message {
    /// Fetch all UTXOs belonging to a public key
    FetchUTXOs(PublicKey),
    /// UTXOs belonging to a public key. Bool determines if
marked
    UTXOs(Vec<(TransactionOutput, bool)>),
    /// Send a transaction to the network
    SubmitTransaction(Transaction),
    /// Broadcast a new transaction to other nodes
    NewTransaction(Transaction),
    /// Ask the node to prepare the optimal block template
    /// with the coinbase transaction paying the specified
```

```
    /// public key
    FetchTemplate(PublicKey),
    /// The template
    Template(Block),
    /// Ask the node to validate a block template.
    /// This is to prevent the node from mining an invalid
    /// block (e.g. if one has been found in the meantime,
    /// or if transactions have been removed from the mempool)
    ValidateTemplate(Block),
    /// If template is valid
    TemplateValidity(bool),
    /// Submit a mined block to a node
    SubmitTemplate(Block),
    /// Ask a node to report all the other nodes it knows
    /// about
    DiscoverNodes,
    /// This is the response to DiscoverNodes
    NodeList(Vec<String>),
    /// Ask a node whats the highest block it knows about
    /// in comparison to the local blockchain
    AskDifference(u32),
    /// This is the response to AskDifference
    Difference(i32),
    /// Ask a node to send a block with the specified height
    FetchBlock(usize),
    /// Broadcast a new block to other nodes
    NewBlock(Block),
}
```

Now, we need to create a small implementation that will do the conversions between bytes and deserialized data. Start by adding the following imports:

```
// network.rs
use std::io::{Error as IoError, Read, Write};
```

And then we can create the following implementation:

```rust
// network.rs
// We are going to use length-prefixed encoding for message
// And we are going to use ciborium (CBOR) for serialization
impl Message {
    pub fn encode(
        &self,
    ) -> Result<Vec<u8>, ciborium::ser::Error<IoError>>
    {
        let mut bytes = Vec::new();
        ciborium::into_writer(self, &mut bytes)?;
        Ok(bytes)
    }
    pub fn decode(
        data: &[u8],
    ) -> Result<Self, ciborium::de::Error<IoError>> {
        ciborium::from_reader(data)
    }
    pub fn send(
        &self,
        stream: &mut impl Write,
    ) -> Result<(), ciborium::ser::Error<IoError>> {
        let bytes = self.encode()?;
        let len = bytes.len() as u64;
        stream.write_all(&len.to_be_bytes())?;
        stream.write_all(&bytes)?;
        Ok(())
    }
    pub fn receive(
        stream: &mut impl Read,
    ) -> Result<Self, ciborium::de::Error<IoError>> {
        let mut len_bytes = [0u8; 8];
        stream.read_exact(&mut len_bytes)?;
        let len = u64::from_be_bytes(len_bytes) as usize;
        let mut data = vec![0u8; len];
        stream.read_exact(&mut data)?;
        Self::decode(&data)
    }
}
```

We can leverage generics to allow sending and receiving messages over anything we want that implements **Read** and **Write** (the two traits that govern whether we can write or read bytes to something).

Now that we have this type available, we can go back to the miner, and implement networking in it.

Miner that can talk to a node - Asynchronous Rust

Since it will take a while before we have a node ready that can appropriately respond to a miner, it may be a good idea to backup the offline miner that you have now, so you still have something you can run and test things with (if you need to). You can either copy and rename it and make it a new member of the Rust workspace, or move it to a sub-binary (under **src/bin/{name}.rs**) in the current crate.

This is the part where we encounter the wonders of asynchronous programming in Rust. If you have done parallel programming before, you may already know that system threads are expensive. Threads are expensive, it's not a good idea to spin up many threads, since it takes up resources and context-switching takes time. Writing multi-threaded sync code is best suited to a small number of expensive computational tasks, or alternatively, writing low-level OS code allows you to schedule tasks precisely and gives you a great amount of control. Using threads directly might also be preferred in **real-time computing**.

For many applications, we need a practical way to avoid spawning many threads. A thread pool alleviates the issue partially, but you still spin-up threads, and it's not easy to manage a multi-threaded application. Furthermore, what if you only have one thread available?

This is where concurrent programming comes in. **Concurrent programming** is a general term for an approach which allows having **more than one task in progress at once**. The difference between **concurrent**, **parallel** and **distributed programming** is that in concurrent programming, all tasks can run on one thread (and a mechanism exists for switching between them) in parallel programming, tasks run *simultaneously*, whereas distributed programming uses multiple processes, often each running on a separate machine.

There are a number of mechanisms that facilitate concurrent programming (apart from using threads), for example event-driven programming, coroutines, or actor architecture. It is possible to utilize all of these in Rust by way of specialized libraries, however, Rust has native support for only one approach -> asynchronous **programming**.

If you‘ve been involved with other Rust materials, you might have seen the keywords **async/await** mentioned, these are the ones we use for asynchronous programming.

Futures and promises

The Rust async model revolves around the abstract concept of a **Future**, also called a ***promise***. You might have heard about the ***Promise*** type from Javascript, which is very similar to Rust's **Future**.

A Future is the promise that at some point in the future, a value of a given type will be available.

In Rust, **Future** is a trait, there is nothing stopping you from implementing it on your own custom type, although you are unlikely to want to do that unless you are writing low-level async libraries. Most of the time, you will use the trait as a handy-dandy way to abstract from the anonymous type Rust generates for each future, similar to how the **Fn** traits, which we have mentioned earlier, abstract away anonymous types of **closures**. Here is how you can create a future in Rust:

```
async fn give_me_a_number() -> usize {
    20090103
}
fn main() {
    let x = give_me_a_number();
}
```

The **async** keyword serves to provide a tiny bit of syntactic sugar. Under the hood, the function definition is transformed to this:

```rust
use std::future::Future;
fn give_me_a_number() -> impl Future<Output=usize> {
    async {
        20090103
    }
}
```

Rust futures and async code exhibit some behavior that you might not be used to when coming from other languages.

Rust Futures are inert (lazy)

Creating a future will not run its code, it is lazy-evaluated and the future won't start until it's first polled, or, in other words, .awaited.[43]

Consider the following example:

```rust
async fn foobar() {
    println!("Back to the future");
}
fn main() {
    println!("Hello");
    let x = foobar();
    println!("What's your favorite movie?");
}
```

If you try running this example (for example in Rust playground), you can see that we will never get the answer we so desire. This future was never polled or awaited, so the code never got executed. We can fix this easily by using the **futures** crate:

43 This is the difference between Rust's Futures and Javascript's Promises.

```rust
async fn foobar() {
    println!("Back to the future B-)");
}
fn main() {
    println!("Hello");
    let x = foobar();
    println!("What's your favorite movie?");
    futures::executor::block_on(x);
}
```

Now you should see the message. As you can tell by the two Back to The Future mentions, my favorite movie is, in fact, American Psycho.[44]

The **futures** crate provides the most basic tools for working with asynchronous code, and it is highly recommended you check it out. It is an official crate, but it is not built in.

In the previous example, we used something called an executor. An executor is a tool for running asynchronous code. We can't just declare **main()** as async, since that posits the problem of what would execute the **Future** it would become Rust does not have a built-in or default executor, and users are encouraged to use different implementations depending on their particular use case, whether it be single-threaded or multi-threaded. This allows for a great degree of flexibility.

Some crates, such as **tokio** also provide macros in the form of attributes for declaring an async main(). This also results in syntactic sugar, and an executor is spun up behind the scenes, but the specifics of that are beyond the scope of this text.

The term executor is also sometimes confused with the terms **reactor** and **runtime**. A **reactor** is a means of providing subscription mechanisms for events like IO, inter-process communication and timers. Executors only handle scheduling and execution of tasks. The term **runtime** describes **reactors** bundled with **executors**. You will find **reactors** in places where the program is supposed to interact with the outside world or interact with things which

44 Now let's see Paul Allen's trait bound.

may not be ready yet. In most async libraries, the common reactors are types for files and file manipulation, and all sorts of sockets. A future to sleep in the task (in the case of tokio, that would be **tokio::time::sleep**) may also be considered a reactor (it reacts to a time duration elapsing).

No built-in runtime

As just mentioned, Rust does not come with any built-in runtime. The most commonly used are:

- **tokio**
- **futures** (very primitive)
- **async_std**
- **smol**
- **bastion** (facilitates distributed programming)

At the time of this writing, **tokio** has the largest market share and is the most common **async** framework.[45]

I also have the most experience with it, followed by **smol**, which is very similar to **tokio**, but much smaller and simpler (with some costs to performance and features available).

Bastion is also a very interesting project, as it transforms your single-process application into a distributed, multi-process one. However, playing around with **bastion** is sadly beyond the scope of this book. But check it out, if you have the time for it!

Note that **mixing executors and async frameworks is generally a very bad idea**. Compatibility between the major worlds of Rust async (**tokio-based** and **async_std-based**) is often accidental, and cannot be depended on. It may also lead to panics at runtime.

45 You like tokio? Its early work was a little too new wave for my taste. But when async/await support came out in Rust 1.39, I think it really came into its own, functionally and ergonomically. The whole runtime has a clear, crisp approach, and a new sheen of open source professionalism that really gives the library a big boost. It's been compared to goroutines, but I think tokio has a far more bitter, cynical sense of humor.

TOKIO IN MINER

Let's start by introducing tokio to the miner crate:

```
cargo add tokio --features full
```

Or alternatively in Cargo.toml:

```
tokio = { version = "1.37.0", features = ["full"] }
```

The full feature set enables everything we need from Tokio to be able to develop a full-fledged application. For the sake of convenience, Tokio contains types that are very similar to the ones found in the standard library. As mentioned before, before we can do meaningful async stuff, we need to instantiate an asynchronous executor. Luckily, Tokio comes with a macro that makes it easy for us. Let's adjust the **src/main.rs** of the miner to the following:

```
// main.rs
use btclib::crypto::PublicKey;
use btclib::network::Message;
use btclib::util::Saveable;
use std::env;
use std::process::exit;
```

```
use tokio::net::TcpStream;
fn usage() -> ! {
    eprintln!(
        "Usage: {} <address> <public_key_file>",
        env::args().next().unwrap()
    );
    exit(1);
```

```
}
#[tokio::main]
async fn main() {
    let address = match env::args().nth(1) {
        Some(address) => address,
        None => usage(),
    };
    let public_key_file = match env::args().nth(2) {
        Some(public_key_file) => public_key_file,
        None => usage(),
    };
    let Ok(public_key) =
        PublicKey::load_from_file(&public_key_file)
    else {
        eprintln!(
            "Error reading public key from file {}",
            public_key_file
        );
        exit(1);
    };
    println!(
        "Connecting to {address} to mine with {public_key:?}",
    );
}
```

Note: The way we are printing the public_key here is not very nice. We are relying on the **Debug** trait, which just spits out what the Rust struct looks like. Can you implement a better way to print the key?

This example will not work because we have not implemented **Saveable** for public and private keys. We can do that quickly, and we can also create a **key_gen** util in **btclib.** First, in the **src/crypto.rs** file, we start by adding this:

```
// crypto.rs (in lib/)
// add imports to the top of the file
use spki::EncodePublicKey;
use std::io::{
```

```
    Error as IoError, ErrorKind as IoErrorKind, Read,
    Result as IoResult, Write,
};
use crate::util::Saveable;
impl Saveable for PrivateKey {
    fn load<I: Read>(reader: I) -> IoResult<Self> {
        ciborium::de::from_reader(reader).map_err(|_| {
            IoError::new(
                IoErrorKind::InvalidData,
                "Failed to deserialize PrivateKey",
            )
        })
    }
    fn save<O: Write>(&self, writer: O) -> IoResult<()> {
        ciborium::ser::into_writer(self, writer).map_err(
            |_| {
                IoError::new(
                    IoErrorKind::InvalidData,
                    "Failed to serialize PrivateKey",
                )
            },
        )?;
        Ok(())
    }
}
// save and load as PEM
impl Saveable for PublicKey {
    fn load<I: Read>(mut reader: I) -> IoResult<Self> {
        // read PEM-encoded public key into string
        let mut buf = String::new();
        reader.read_to_string(&mut buf)?;
        // decode the public key from PEM
        let public_key = buf.parse().map_err(|_| {
            IoError::new(
                IoErrorKind::InvalidData,
                "Failed to parse PublicKey",
            )
        })?;
        Ok(PublicKey(public_key))
```

```
    }
    fn save<O: Write>(
        &self,
        mut writer: O,
    ) -> IoResult<()> {
        let s = self
            .0
            .to_public_key_pem(Default::default())
            .map_err(|_| {
                IoError::new(
                    IoErrorKind::InvalidData,
                    "Failed to serialize PublicKey",
                )
            })?;
        writer.write_all(s.as_bytes())?;
        Ok(())
    }
}
```

You will need to add **spki** with the feature **pem** to your dependencies. And in **src/bin/key_gen.rs**:

```
// bin/key_gen.rs (in lib/)
use std::env;
use btclib::crypto::PrivateKey;
use btclib::util::Saveable;
fn main() {
    let name =
        env::args().nth(1).expect("Please provide a name");
    let private_key = PrivateKey::new_key();
    let public_key = private_key.public_key();
    let public_key_file = name.clone() + ".pub.pem";
    let private_key_file = name + ".priv.cbor";
    private_key.save_to_file(&private_key_file).unwrap();
    public_key.save_to_file(&public_key_file).unwrap();
}
```

You can use this to generate a pair of keys to place in the miner folder for testing:

```
cargo run --bin key_gen ../miner/alice
```

And when testing in the **miner/** folder, you should now be able to run:

```
cargo run localhost:9000 alice.pub.pem
```

And get the following output:

```
Connecting to localhost:9000 to mine with PublicKey-
(VerifyingKey { inner: PublicKey { point: AffinePo-
int { x: FieldElement(FieldElementImpl { value: Fiel-
dElement5x52([3993487666568872, 3933745244468088,
3856475409397746, 1877239772270698, 151220799024004]), magni-
tude: 1, normalized: true }), y: FieldElement(FieldElementImpl
{ value: FieldElement5x52([2756904875665325, 1679013187998920,
3132537210701700, 1384962182096143, 206174890851037]), magni-
tude: 1, normalized: true }), infinity: 0 } } })
```

We can now try connecting to the node:

```
// main.rs
let mut stream = match TcpStream::connect(&address).await {
    Ok(stream) => stream,
    Err(e) => {
        eprintln!("Failed to connect to server: {}", e);
        exit(1);
    }
};
```

First, we must ask the node for work:

```
// main.rs
// Ask the node for work
println!("requesting work from {address}");
let message = Message::FetchTemplate(public_key);
message.send(&mut stream);
```

This will not work because we need our send method to accept **AsyncWrite** and not just **Write**. The **AsyncWrite** and **AsyncRead** traits are counterparts to **std::io**'s **Read** and **Write**. The easiest way to solve this is to add **send_async** and **receive_async** methods to **btclib's src/network.rs**:

```
// network.rs (in lib/)
// after running `cargo add tokio --features net` or adding it
manually
use tokio::io::{
    AsyncRead, AsyncReadExt, AsyncWrite, AsyncWriteExt,
};
impl Message {
    //...
    pub async fn send_async(
        &self,
        stream: &mut (impl AsyncWrite + Unpin),
    ) -> Result<(), ciborium::ser::Error<IoError>> {
        let bytes = self.encode()?;
        let len = bytes.len() as u64;
        stream.write_all(&len.to_be_bytes()).await?;
        stream.write_all(&bytes).await?;
        Ok(())
    }
    pub async fn receive_async(
        stream: &mut (impl AsyncRead + Unpin),
    ) -> Result<Self, ciborium::de::Error<IoError>> {
        let mut len_bytes = [0u8; 8];
        stream.read_exact(&mut len_bytes).await?;
```

```
        let len = u64::from_be_bytes(len_bytes) as usize;
        let mut data = vec![0u8; len];
        stream.read_exact(&mut data).await?;
        Self::decode(&data)
    }
}
```

You will also need to add **tokio** to the dependencies of **btclib**. We can now use the newly created methods to talk to the mining node. First, let's create stubs for our upcoming networking miner program:

```
// main.rs
use anyhow::{anyhow, Result};
use btclib::crypto::PublicKey;
use btclib::network::Message;
use btclib::types::Block;
use btclib::util::Saveable;
use clap::Parser;
use std::sync::{
    atomic::{AtomicBool, Ordering},
    Arc,
};
use std::thread;
use tokio::net::TcpStream;
use tokio::sync::Mutex;
use tokio::time::{interval, Duration};
#[derive(Parser)]
#[command(author, version, about, long_about = None)]
struct Cli {
    #[arg(short, long)]
    address: String,
    #[arg(short, long)]
    public_key_file: String,
}
struct Miner;
impl Miner {
    async fn new(
```

```
        address: String,
        public_key: PublicKey,
    ) -> Result<Self> {
        // ...
    }
    async fn run(&self) -> Result<()> {
        // ...
    }
    fn spawn_mining_thread(&self) -> thread::JoinHandle<()> {
        // ...
    }
    async fn fetch_and_validate_template(&self) -> Result<()> {
        // ...
    }
    async fn fetch_template(&self) -> Result<()> {
        // ...
    }
    async fn validate_template(&self) -> Result<()> {
        // ...
    }
    async fn submit_block(&self, block: Block) -> Result<()> {
        // ...
    }
}
#[tokio::main]
async fn main() -> Result<()> {
    let cli = Cli::parse();
    let public_key =
        PublicKey::load_from_file(&cli.public_key_file)
            .map_err(|e| {
                anyhow!("Error reading public key: {}", e)
            })?;
    let miner = Miner::new(cli.address, public_key).await?;
    miner.run().await
}
```

We have added a couple more dependencies, this is how the **Cargo.toml** file looks on my end:

```
[package]
name = "miner"
version = "0.1.0"
edition = "2021"
[dependencies]
anyhow = "1.0.86"
btclib = { path = "../lib" }
clap = { version = "4.5.8", features = ["derive"] }
flume = "0.11.0"
tokio = { version = "1.38.0", features = ["full"] }
```

Now, we need to fill out the implementation. In this approach to development, we are creating a central **Miner** structure, which manages the entire state of the application. In order to be effective, we will need to mine on a different thread, so that we do not block the tokio runtime. In order to be able to communicate with the hardware thread effectively, we need to use so-called channels.

Channels are a staple of multi-threaded programming in Rust. The standard library offers its own **mpsc** (**M**ultiple **P**roducer **S**ingle **C**onsumer) channel in the **std::sync::mpsc** module, however, we will not be using it, as it has a couple of shortcomings:

- It cannot receive or send messages asynchronously
- It is not multiple consumer (**mpmc**)

Finally, while correct and very portable, the channels in the standard library are not that fast in comparison to other offerings we can find on **crates.io**. This is where **flume** import comes into play. The **flume** library provides fast, async/sync hybrid **mpmc** channels. We will be storing two ends of this channel in the **Miner** struct. This is how it's going to look:

```
// main.rs
struct Miner {
    public_key: PublicKey,
    stream: Mutex<TcpStream>,
    current_template: Arc<std::sync::Mutex<Option<Block>>>,
    mining: Arc<AtomicBool>,
```

```rust
    mined_block_sender: flume::Sender<Block>,
    mined_block_receiver: flume::Receiver<Block>,
}
impl Miner {
    async fn new(
        address: String,
        public_key: PublicKey,
    ) -> Result<Self> {
        let stream = TcpStream::connect(&address).await?;
        let (mined_block_sender, mined_block_receiver) =
            flume::unbounded();
        Ok(Self {
            public_key,
            stream: Mutex::new(stream),
            current_template: Arc::new(std::sync::Mutex::new(
                None,
            )),
            mining: Arc::new(AtomicBool::new(false)),
            mined_block_sender,
            mined_block_receiver,
        })
    }
```

We need to wrap the **stream** and the **current_template** in a Mutex because we want Miner to be safely accessible from multiple threads / tokio tasks. Notice that there are two **Mutex** types at play. While **current_template** is wrapped in a standard library mutex, **stream** is wrapped in a tokio **Mutex** (see the import statement above).

The reason for this is that we cannot carry a standard library mutex lock across an **.await** point without preventing the Future from being **Send/Sync**. This is possible with the Tokio one. However, the Tokio one is slower, and naturally only accessible in async contexts.

We are also using at **AtomicBool**, instead of a regular bool, so that we do not have to make the **Miner** mutable. Let's tackle the **run()** method next:

```
// main.rs
async fn run(&self) -> Result<()> {
    self.spawn_mining_thread();
    let mut template_interval =
        interval(Duration::from_secs(5));
    loop {
        let receiver_clone =
            self.mined_block_receiver.clone();
        tokio::select! {
            _ = template_interval.tick() => {
                self.fetch_and_validate_template().await?;
            }
            Ok(mined_block) = receiver_clone.recv_async()
=> {
                self.submit_block(mined_block).await?;
            }
        }
    }
}
```

We start by spawning the mining thread, and then we loop over a tokio **select!()** macro. Tokio's **select!()** macro allows concurrent waiting on multiple asynchronous operations, executing the branch of the first operation that completes. It's useful for handling multiple events or timeouts efficiently in asynchronous Rust programs. If one of these futures completes, the other one is dropped.

Note that **select** is an established tool/pattern in asynchronous programming, and will be found in pretty much every asynchronous runtime, regardless of the programming language.

In the select, we are waiting on two futures:

- The first one is the ticking of a tokio **Interval**, every 5 seconds to be precise, which will fetch and/or validate the template.
- The second one is waiting to receive mined blocks from the hardware threads, so that they can be submitted to the network.

Let's take a look at how we can implement the mining thread, by filling out its appropriate method in the **Miner** structure. A simple way how we can do it is like this:

```
// main.rs
fn spawn_mining_thread(&self) -> thread::JoinHandle<()> {
    let template = self.current_template.clone();
    let mining = self.mining.clone();
    let sender = self.mined_block_sender.clone();
    thread::spawn(move || loop {
        if mining.load(Ordering::Relaxed) {
            if let Some(mut block) =
                template.lock().unwrap().clone()
            {
                println!(
                    "Mining block with target: {}",
                    block.header.target
                );
                if block.header.mine(2_000_000) {
                    println!(
                        "Block mined: {}",
                        block.hash()
                    );
                    sender.send(block).expect(
                        "Failed to send mined block",
                    );
                    mining.store(false, Ordering::Relaxed);
                }
            }
        }
        thread::yield_now();
    })
}
```

Thanks to our usage of the **Arc** type, and that the **Sender** is clonable, we can create copies, which are not actually copies, but rather second handles into the same piece of memory. Rust forces us to use these types through the liberal amount of compile errors it provides if you try to do multi-threading without them.

I am a bit of a cautious person, so we have also added a **thread::yield_now();** statement, to decrease its priority, just so we can make sure that other things get ago (assuming, e.g. a bizarre operating system that confines each process to a single core, never letting the process to actually run in parallel).

Let's take care of **fetch_and_validate_template()** now:

```
// main.rs
async fn fetch_and_validate_template(&self) -> Result<()> {
    if !self.mining.load(Ordering::Relaxed) {
        self.fetch_template().await?;
    } else {
        self.validate_template().await?;
    }
    Ok(())
}
```

A very simple function. If we are not mining, we fetch a template, if we are, we validate it. Note the highlighted line. When working with atomics, we need to specify the ordering of atomic operations we would like to use. This ranges from **Ordering::Relaxed** (which roughly translates to "please just be atomic bro"), to **Ordering::SeqCst** (which roughly translates to Gandalf - not the bitcoin one - screaming "YOU SHALL NOT PASS!!!!" - all atomic operations before this one stay before it, all after it stay after it). There are a couple more variants in the **Ordering** enum, but those are beyond the scope of this book.

Fetching a template is rather simple:

```
// main.rs
async fn fetch_template(&self) -> Result<()> {
    println!("Fetching new template");
    let message =
        Message::FetchTemplate(self.public_key.clone());
```

```
        let mut stream_lock = self.stream.lock().await;
        message.send_async(&mut *stream_lock).await?;
        drop(stream_lock);
        let mut stream_lock = self.stream.lock().await;
        match Message::receive_async(&mut *stream_lock).await?
{
            Message::Template(template) => {
                drop(stream_lock);
                println!("Received new template with target:
{}", template.header.target);
                *self.current_template.lock().unwrap() = Some(-
template);
                self.mining.store(true, Ordering::Relaxed);
                Ok(())
            }
            _ => Err(anyhow!("Unexpected message received when
fetching template")),
        }
    }
```

On the highlighted lines, you will see that I am quite paranoid about dropping the lock as soon as possible. This is a personal choice, I like to not have to worry about deadlocking my process, but it is likely that you can survive with just one lock for the entire function. Regardless, it is a good practice to not lock shared resources longer than absolutely necessary - you are preventing others from working.

Template validation looks very, very similar, however, it sends a different message, naturally:

```
    // main.rs
    async fn validate_template(&self) -> Result<()> {
        if let Some(template) =
            self.current_template.lock().unwrap().clone()
        {
            let message = Message::ValidateTemplate(template);
            let mut stream_lock = self.stream.lock().await;
```

```
        message.send_async(&mut *stream_lock).await?;
        drop(stream_lock);
        let mut stream_lock = self.stream.lock().await;
        match Message::receive_async(&mut *stream_lock).
await? {
            Message::TemplateValidity(valid) => {
                drop(stream_lock);
                if !valid {
                    println!("Current template is no longer va-
lid");
                    self.mining.store(false, Ordering::Re-
laxed);
                } else {
                    println!("Current template is still va-
lid");
                }
                Ok(())
            }
            _ => Err(anyhow!("Unexpected message received
when validating template")),
        }
    } else {
        Ok(())
    }
}
```

This leaves us with just one thing to take care of, the **submit_block()** method, the one that sends the block to the node we are connecting to:

```
// main.rs
async fn submit_block(&self, block: Block) -> Result<()> {
    println!("Submitting mined block");
    let message = Message::SubmitTemplate(block);
    let mut stream_lock = self.stream.lock().await;
    message.send_async(&mut *stream_lock).await?;
    self.mining.store(false, Ordering::Relaxed);
    Ok(())
}
```

Welp, and that's it, we have successfully created a miner :)
This is how the entire miner looks at this stage on my machine:

```
// main.rs
use anyhow::{anyhow, Result};
use btclib::crypto::PublicKey;
use btclib::network::Message;
use btclib::types::Block;
use btclib::util::Saveable;
use clap::Parser;
use std::sync::{
    atomic::{AtomicBool, Ordering},
    Arc,
};
use std::thread;
use tokio::net::TcpStream;
use tokio::sync::Mutex;
use tokio::time::{interval, Duration};
#[derive(Parser)]
#[command(author, version, about, long_about = None)]
struct Cli {
    #[arg(short, long)]
    address: String,
    #[arg(short, long)]
    public_key_file: String,
}
struct Miner {
    public_key: PublicKey,
    stream: Mutex<TcpStream>,
    current_template: Arc<std::sync::Mutex<Option<Block>>>,
    mining: Arc<AtomicBool>,
    mined_block_sender: flume::Sender<Block>,
    mined_block_receiver: flume::Receiver<Block>,
}
impl Miner {
    async fn new(
        address: String,
        public_key: PublicKey,
    ) -> Result<Self> {
```

```
        let stream = TcpStream::connect(&address).await?;
        let (mined_block_sender, mined_block_receiver) =
            flume::unbounded();
        Ok(Self {
            public_key,
            stream: Mutex::new(stream),
            current_template: Arc::new(std::sync::Mutex::new(
                None,
            )),
            mining: Arc::new(AtomicBool::new(false)),
            mined_block_sender,
            mined_block_receiver,
        })
    }
    async fn run(&self) -> Result<()> {
        self.spawn_mining_thread();
        let mut template_interval =
            interval(Duration::from_secs(5));
        loop {
            let receiver_clone =
                self.mined_block_receiver.clone();
            tokio::select! {
                _ = template_interval.tick() => {
                    self.fetch_and_validate_template().await?;
                }
                Ok(mined_block) = receiver_clone.recv_async()
=> {
                    self.submit_block(mined_block).await?;
                }
            }
        }
    }
    fn spawn_mining_thread(&self) -> thread::JoinHandle<()> {
        let template = self.current_template.clone();
        let mining = self.mining.clone();
        let sender = self.mined_block_sender.clone();
        thread::spawn(move || loop {
            if mining.load(Ordering::Relaxed) {
                if let Some(mut block) =
```

```
                    template.lock().unwrap().clone()
                {
                    println!(
                        "Mining block with target: {}",
                        block.header.target
                    );
                    if block.header.mine(2_000_000) {
                        println!(
                            "Block mined: {}",
                            block.hash()
                        );
                        sender.send(block).expect(
                            "Failed to send mined block",
                        );
                        mining.store(false, Ordering::Relaxed);
                    }
                }
            }
            thread::yield_now();
        })
    }
    async fn fetch_and_validate_template(&self) -> Result<()> {
        if !self.mining.load(Ordering::Relaxed) {
            self.fetch_template().await?;
        } else {
            self.validate_template().await?;
        }
        Ok(())
    }
    async fn fetch_template(&self) -> Result<()> {
        println!("Fetching new template");
        let message =
            Message::FetchTemplate(self.public_key.clone());
        let mut stream_lock = self.stream.lock().await;
        message.send_async(&mut *stream_lock).await?;
        drop(stream_lock);
        let mut stream_lock = self.stream.lock().await;
        match Message::receive_async(&mut *stream_lock).await?
{
```

```
            Message::Template(template) => {
                drop(stream_lock);
                println!("Received new template with target:
{}", template.header.target);
              *self.current_template.lock().unwrap() = Some(tem-
plate);
                self.mining.store(true, Ordering::Relaxed);
                Ok(())
            }
            _ => Err(anyhow!("Unexpected message received when
fetching template")),
        }
    }
    async fn validate_template(&self) -> Result<()> {
        if let Some(template) =
            self.current_template.lock().unwrap().clone()
        {
            let message = Message::ValidateTemplate(template);
            let mut stream_lock = self.stream.lock().await;
            message.send_async(&mut *stream_lock).await?;
            drop(stream_lock);
            let mut stream_lock = self.stream.lock().await;
            match Message::receive_async(&mut *stream_lock).
await? {
                Message::TemplateValidity(valid) => {
                    drop(stream_lock);
                    if !valid {
                      println!("Current template is no longer va-
lid");
                        self.mining.store(false, Ordering::Re-
laxed);
                    } else {
                        println!("Current template is still va-
lid");
                    }
                    Ok(())
                }
                _ => Err(anyhow!("Unexpected message received
when validating template")),
```

```
            }
        } else {
            Ok(())
        }
    }
    async fn submit_block(&self, block: Block) -> Result<()> {
        println!("Submitting mined block");
        let message = Message::SubmitTemplate(block);
        let mut stream_lock = self.stream.lock().await;
        message.send_async(&mut *stream_lock).await?;
        self.mining.store(false, Ordering::Relaxed);
        Ok(())
    }
}
#[tokio::main]
async fn main() -> Result<()> {
    let cli = Cli::parse();
    let public_key =
        PublicKey::load_from_file(&cli.public_key_file)
            .map_err(|e| {
                anyhow!("Error reading public key: {}", e)
            })?;
    let miner = Miner::new(cli.address, public_key).await?;
    miner.run().await
}
```

There are many improvements you could make (for example, multithreaded mining can be implemented, as we are only mining with a single CPU core at the moment). It would also be a good idea to be able to submit your block to multiple nodes. But congratulations! You are one step closer to your very own blockchain. Here's a doodle of a cat:

Whenever you are ready, proceed to the next chapter, where we will be building the bitcoin node.

8 BUILDING A BITCOIN NODE

In the previous chapters, we have already established what the node is supposed to be doing. Now, we can finally make it. But first, let's introduce a new additional restraint - the maximum amount of transactions allowed in a block. We can add this constant to **btclib's** crate root, the **src/lib.rs** file:

```
// lib.rs (in lib/)
// initial reward in bitcoin - multiply by 10^8 to get sato-
shis
pub const INITIAL_REWARD: u64 = 50;
// halving interval in blocks
pub const HALVING_INTERVAL: u64 = 210;
// ideal block time in seconds
pub const IDEAL_BLOCK_TIME: u64 = 10;
// minimum target
pub const MIN_TARGET: U256 = U256([
    0xFFFF_FFFF_FFFF_FFFF,
    0xFFFF_FFFF_FFFF_FFFF,
    0xFFFF_FFFF_FFFF_FFFF,
    0x0000_00FF_FFFF_FFFF,
]);
// difficulty update interval in blocks
pub const DIFFICULTY_UPDATE_INTERVAL: u64 = 50;
// maximum mempool transaction age in seconds
pub const MAX_MEMPOOL_TRANSACTION_AGE: u64 = 600;
// maximum amount of transactions allowed in a block
pub const BLOCK_TRANSACTION_CAP: usize = 20;
```

These are the constants we have so far. Now, navigate to the **node/** crate, and start adding dependencies. Once again, we will need **tokio**, and we will also make use of several other libraries. It would be quite long to add them one by one, so here is the **[dependencies]** section of my **Cargo.toml**:

```
[dependencies]
anyhow = "1.0.82"
argh = "0.1.12"
btclib = { version = "0.1.0", path = "../lib" }
```

```
chrono = "0.4.38"
dashmap = "5.5.3"
static_init = "1.0.3"
tokio = { version = "1.37.0", features = ["full"] }
uuid = { version = "1.8.0", features = ["v4"] }
```

Here are a couple of libraries you haven't seen yet:

- **Anyhow** - This library is often used together with **thiserror**. While **thiserror** provides a macro to create a concrete type covering all sorts of errors, **anyhow** provides a dynamic type (and a **Result<T>** alias that is using this type), which can be converted into from any **Error-**-implementing type. Often, **anyhow** is used in applications (in places where you care merely about the *presence* and *reporting* of an error), and **thiserror** in libraries (where you want to let your users make decisions based on the content of the errors).
- **argh** - This is a small library for handling command-line arguments. It works by deserializing command-line arguments into a structure based on attributes that you stick onto its definition. It is a more lightweight alternative to **clap**, which is *the CLI app* framework for Rust.
- **dashmap** - Provides a fast HashMap that is thread-safe and has interior mutability. **Interior mutability** is a functionality provided by some types that mutate data through a **&self** (shared) reference. This makes them very handy in read-only context. Types with interior mutability must handle correctness and data integrity internally, and their implementations often contain unsafe code, or they internally depend on other types providing interior mutability.
- **static_init** - One of the many Rust libraries for creating global variables for types that require allocations.

ORGANIZATION

We can start by declaring all of the imports we are going to use in the **main.rs** file of **node**:

```rust
// main.rs (in node/)
use argh::FromArgs;
use dashmap::DashMap;
use static_init::dynamic;
use anyhow::Result;
use tokio::net::{TcpListener, TcpStream};
use tokio::sync::RwLock;
use btclib::types::Blockchain;
use std::path::Path;
```

We will be moving some of our functionality to two submodules, poorly named **util** and **handler**, which will provide utility functions and handling for all possible **Message** variants respectively:

```rust
// main.rs (in node/)
mod handler;
mod util;
```

Node will use the **argh** library to define a CLI interface matching this structure:

```rust
// main.rs (in node/)
#[derive(FromArgs)]
/// A toy blockchain node
struct Args {
    #[argh(option, default = "9000")]
    /// port number
    port: u16,
    #[argh(
        option,
        default = "String::from(\"./blockchain.cbor\")"
    )]
    /// blockchain file location
    blockchain_file: String,
    #[argh(positional)]
```

```
    /// addresses of initial nodes
    nodes: Vec<String>,
}
```

If we create a minimalistic main function (we are going to use Tokio, so let's use it already), which looks like this:

```
// main.rs
#[tokio::main]
async fn main() -> Result<()> {
    // Parse command line arguments
    let args: Args = argh::from_env();
    Ok(())
}
```

And run **cargo run -- --help,** you will see that the **argh** library has generated a very handy help text. Here**:**

```
Usage: node [<nodes...>] [--port <port>] [--blockchain-file
<blockchain-file>]
A toy blockchain node
Positional Arguments:
  nodes             addresses of initial nodes
Options:
  --port            port number
  --blockchain-file blockchain file location
  --help            display usage information
```

We define three inputs our application expects:

- A port to listen to
- Path to store/load the blockchain from

- A list of other nodes to connect to and communicate with

Let's extract the three parameters from the CLI struct:

```
// main.rs
async fn main() -> Result<()> {
    // Parse command line arguments
    let args: Args = argh::from_env();
    // Access the parsed arguments
    let port = args.port;
    let blockchain_file = args.blockchain_file;
    let nodes = args.nodes;
}
```

NODE DISCOVERY

Now, before we do anything, we need to check if the blockchain exists. If not, we will see if we have any other nodes to connect to. If we have no other nodes to connect to, we will assume we are a seed node and start a new blockchain.

This is how you can verify that a file exists:

```
// main.rs
#[tokio::main]
async fn main() -> Result<()> {
    // Parse command line arguments
    let args: Args = argh::from_env();
    // Access the parsed arguments
    let port = args.port;
    let blockchain_file = args.blockchain_file;
    let nodes = args.nodes;
    // Check if the blockchain_file exists
    if Path::new(&blockchain_file).exists() {
        // ...
    } else {
        // ...
```

```
    }
    Ok(())
}
```

If the blockchain does indeed exist, we can simply load it. To make sure that the **main()** function is not absolutely massive, we will extract this bit of behavior into a discrete function in the **util** module:

```
// main.rs
#[tokio::main]
async fn main() -> Result<()> {
    // Parse command line arguments
    let args: Args = argh::from_env();
    // Access the parsed arguments
    let port = args.port;
    let blockchain_file = args.blockchain_file;
    let nodes = args.nodes;
    // Check if the blockchain_file exists
    if Path::new(&blockchain_file).exists() {
        util::load_blockchain(&blockchain_file).await?;
    } else {
    }
    Ok(())
}
```

This is how we can implement the **util::load_blockchain()** function. The list of imports here includes more than we need for this function, but we will need everything in the future, so don't mind the unused warnings for now:

```
// util.rs
use anyhow::{Context, Result};
use tokio::net::TcpStream;
use tokio::time;
use btclib::network::Message;
```

```rust
use btclib::types::Blockchain;
use btclib::util::Saveable;
pub async fn load_blockchain(
    blockchain_file: &str,
) -> Result<()> {
    println!("blockchain file exists, loading...");
    let new_blockchain =
        Blockchain::load_from_file(blockchain_file)?;
    println!("blockchain loaded");
    let mut blockchain = crate::BLOCKCHAIN.write().await;
    *blockchain = new_blockchain;
    println!("rebuilding utxos...");
    blockchain.rebuild_utxos();
    println!("utxos rebuilt");
    println!("checking if target needs to be adjusted...");
    println!("current target: {}", blockchain.target());
    blockchain.try_adjust_target();
    println!("new target: {}", blockchain.target());
    println!("initialization complete");
    Ok(())
}
```

As you can see, we need to do some additional initialization, just to be safe. We rebuild the **utxos** and we check if the target is set correctly. This will not compile because we are referencing a global variable at **crate::BLOCKCHAIN**. We can create it now back in **main.rs** with the **static_init** crate, along with the second one we are going need, a hashmap of known nodes and connections to them:

```rust
// main.rs
#[dynamic]
pub static BLOCKCHAIN: RwLock<Blockchain> =
    RwLock::new(Blockchain::new());
// Node pool
#[dynamic]
pub static NODES: DashMap<String, TcpStream> =
    DashMap::new();
```

The **DashMap** types works very similarly to the **HashMap** type, for almost everything we can consider the two to be interchangeable (except that even **.get_mut()** on **DashMap** uses &self). We need this because truly mutable **statics** (that is, global variables), are very unsafe, and can lead to memory corruption. Therefore, they cannot be used in safe Rust. **RwLock** and **Mutex** are types which also provide interior mutability and are suitable as wrappers for types that do not provide it. They provide synchronization mechanisms and ensure that if there is a **read-write** access, it is the only one. **RwLock** differentiates between **read-only** and **read-write** access, allowing many **.read()** handles, but only a solitary **.write()** handle (which cannot co-exist with any **.read()** handle). **Mutex** only provides mutable handles. Sometimes, a **Mutex** is faster, but we can expect many accesses which can be **read-only.**

FETCHING THE BLOCKCHAIN FROM OTHER NODES

In the event that the blockchain does not exist, the node should complain about it, and check if it knows any other nodes:

```
// main.rs
#[tokio::main]
async fn main() -> Result<()> {
    // Parse command line arguments
    let args: Args = argh::from_env();
    // Access the parsed arguments
    let port = args.port;
    let blockchain_file = args.blockchain_file;
    let nodes = args.nodes;
    // Check if the blockchain_file exists
    if Path::new(&blockchain_file).exists() {
        util::load_blockchain(&blockchain_file).await?;
    } else {
        println!("blockchain file does not exist!");
        if nodes.is_empty() {
            println!("no initial nodes provided, starting as a
seed node");
        } else {
        }
    }
```

```
    Ok(())
}
```

Since we already have an empty blockchain ready, we do not need to do any additional initialization. But there are a lot of things we need to do if there are nodes that we can download a copy of the blockchain from:

```
        // main.rs
        util::populate_connections(&nodes).await?;
        println!(
            "total amount of known nodes: {}",
            NODES.len()
        );
        if nodes.is_empty() {
            println!("no initial nodes provided, starting as a
seed node");
        } else {
            let (longest_name, longest_count) =
                util::find_longest_chain_node().await?;
            // request the blockchain from the node with the
longest blockchain
            util::download_blockchain(
                &longest_name,
                longest_count,
            )
            .await?;
            println!(
                "blockchain downloaded from {}",
                longest_name
            );
            // recalculate utxos
            {
                let mut blockchain =
                    BLOCKCHAIN.write().await;
                blockchain.rebuild_utxos();
            }
            // try to adjust difficulty
```

```
            {
                let mut blockchain =
                    BLOCKCHAIN.write().await;
                blockchain.try_adjust_target();
            }
        }
```

There are plenty of additional **util** functions in this snippet. Let's create them now. First, we need to populate the **NODES DashMap** with names and connections. It is not the perfect solution, but we can probe one level deeper, and ask every node we know for the node it knows. Since we are storing the node names in a hash map, we do not need to worry about deduplication at all. This is my implementation:

```
// main.rs
pub async fn populate_connections(
    nodes: &[String],
) -> Result<()> {
    println!("trying to connect to other nodes...");
    for node in nodes {
        println!("connecting to {}", node);
        let mut stream = TcpStream::connect(&node).await?;
        let message = Message::DiscoverNodes;
        message.send_async(&mut stream).await?;
        println!("sent DiscoverNodes to {}", node);
        let message =
            Message::receive_async(&mut stream).await?;
        match message {
            Message::NodeList(child_nodes) => {
                println!("received NodeList from {}", node);
                for child_node in child_nodes {
                    println!("adding node {}", child_node);
                    let new_stream =
                        TcpStream::connect(&child_node)
                            .await?;
                    crate::NODES
                        .insert(child_node, new_stream);
```

```
                }
            }
            _ => {
                println!(
                    "unexpected message from {}",
                    node
                );
            }
        }
        crate::NODES.insert(node.clone(), stream);
    }
    Ok(())
}
```

We open a new **TcpStream** connection to every node, send it a **DiscoverNodes** message, which will make it return a list of nodes in the **NodeList** message, and then we open a connection through every child node. All of these nodes are added one by one to the **NODES** dashmap. That's all we need from this function. The next one on the list is **util::find_longest_chain_node()**. This function asks all the other nodes to report how long their blockchain is, then downloads from the one that is the longest:

```
// main.rs
pub async fn find_longest_chain_node(
) -> Result<(String, u32)> {
    println!("finding nodes with the highest blockchain
length...");
    let mut longest_name = String::new();
    let mut longest_count = 0;
    let all_nodes = crate::NODES
        .iter()
        .map(|x| x.key().clone())
        .collect::<Vec<_>>();
    for node in all_nodes {
        println!("asking {} for blockchain length", node);
        let mut stream = crate::NODES
            .get_mut(&node)
```

```
            .context("no node")?;
        let message = Message::AskDifference(0);
        message.send_async(&mut *stream).await.unwrap();
        println!("sent AskDifference to {}", node);
        let message =
            Message::receive_async(&mut *stream).await?;
        match message {
            Message::Difference(count) => {
                println!(
                    "received Difference from {}",
                    node
                );
                if count > longest_count {
                    println!(
                        "new longest blockchain: \
                    {} blocks from {node}",
                        count
                    );
                    longest_count = count;
                    longest_name = node;
                }
            }
            e => {
                println!(
                    "unexpected message from {}: {:?}",
                    node, e
                );
            }
        }
    }
    Ok((longest_name, longest_count as u32))
}
```

Here, we have made another simplification. In practice, this could be a potential security problem, as an attack might create a bogus node with a very long blockchain and it would propagate from there. But this is a toy blockchain and creating a consensus mechanism would make this book longer than necessary (but it is one of the things you can try implementing!). The **AskDifference** message could be used to do that. We are not using it to its full power here, as we are only sending it with a "my height" of zero to get the nodes to report a total block height of their blockchains.

Once the longest blockchain among our friends is found, downloading it is a simple matter:

```
// main.rs
pub async fn download_blockchain(
    node: &str,
    count: u32,
) -> Result<()> {
    let mut stream = crate::NODES.get_mut(node).unwrap();
    for i in 0..count as usize {
        let message = Message::FetchBlock(i);
        message.send_async(&mut *stream).await?;
        let message =
            Message::receive_async(&mut *stream).await?;
        match message {
            Message::NewBlock(block) => {
                let mut blockchain =
                    crate::BLOCKCHAIN.write().await;
                blockchain.add_block(block)?;
            }
            _ => {
                println!(
                    "unexpected message from {}",
                    node
                );
            }
        }
    }
    Ok(())
}
```

This is another spot where an improvement could be made. Instead of making many small requests, we could add another message type that would return an entire chain of blocks. That's it for the helper functions in **utils.rs** for this bit. Let's go back to **main()**.

HANDLING REQUESTS

Now that we have established the entire blockchain, we can start listening for requests and messages from other nodes, miners and wallets:

```
// main.rs
// Start the TCP listener on 0.0.0.0:port
let addr = format!("0.0.0.0:{}", port);
let listener = TcpListener::bind(&addr).await?;
println!("Listening on {}", addr);
loop {
    let (socket, _) = listener.accept().await?;
    tokio::spawn(handler::handle_connection(socket));
}
```

The **handler::handle_connection()** function is the heart of our application, it's where we will handle every possible message type. But before we implement it message type by message type, there are some automatic tasks we must take care of:

```
// main.rs
// start a task to periodically cleanup the mempool
// normally, you would want to keep and join the handle
tokio::spawn(util::cleanup());
// and a task to periodically save the blockchain
tokio::spawn(util::save(blockchain_file.clone()));
```

Place these above the **loop {}** above (seeing as the loop is infinite unless broken, these statements would otherwise not ever be executed). Their implementation is very simple, we use the **Interval** type from **tokio's** time module, which lets us do things every once in a while:

```
// util.rs
pub async fn cleanup() {
    let mut interval =
        time::interval(time::Duration::from_secs(30));
    loop {
        interval.tick().await;
        println!(
            "cleaning the mempool from old transactions"
        );
        let mut blockchain =
            crate::BLOCKCHAIN.write().await;
        blockchain.cleanup_mempool();
    }
}
pub async fn save(name: String) {
    let mut interval =
        time::interval(time::Duration::from_secs(15));
    loop {
        interval.tick().await;
        println!("saving blockchain to drive...");
        let blockchain = crate::BLOCKCHAIN.read().await;
        blockchain.save_to_file(name.clone()).unwrap();
    }
}
```

The interval futures yield every time tokio polls them until the given duration of time has elapsed. Now, we can finally make the handler:

```
// handler.rs
use btclib::sha256::Hash;
use chrono::Utc;
use uuid::Uuid;
use tokio::net::TcpStream;
```

```
use btclib::network::Message;
use btclib::types::{
    Block, BlockHeader, Transaction, TransactionOutput,
};
use btclib::util::MerkleRoot;
pub async fn handle_connection(mut socket: TcpStream) {
    loop {
        // read a message from the socket
        let message = match Message::receive_async(&mut socket)
            .await
        {
            Ok(message) => message,
            Err(e) => {
                println!(
                    "invalid message from peer: {e}, closing
that connection"
                );
                return;
            }
        };

        use btclib::network::Message::*;
        match message {
            // ...
        }
    }
}
```

I'll be honest with ya, chief. In my setup, the **match message** statement has 250 lines. It's big, we need to handle every possible message. First, let's get rid of the ones we do not want to handle as a node:

```
        // handler.rs
        UTXOs(_) | Template(_) | Difference(_)
        | TemplateValidity(_) | NodeList(_) => {
            println!(
                "I am neither a miner nor a \
```

```
                    wallet! Goodbye"
        );
        return;
    }
```

These are messages that the node sends as a response to either a miner or the wallet. We should never receive them as the node, so we can just safely ignore them and terminate the connection by returning from the function. Next, we have a couple of simple messages that merely return some data without doing any modifications to it or filtering it excessively. First **FetchBlock**:

```
// handler.rs
FetchBlock(height) => {
    let blockchain =
        crate::BLOCKCHAIN.read().await;
    let Some(block) = blockchain
        .blocks()
        .nth(height as usize)
        .cloned()
    else {
        return;
    };
    let message = NewBlock(block);
    message
        .send_async(&mut socket)
        .await
        .unwrap();
}
```

DiscoverNodes (no filtering going on - we just send all the nodes we know):

```
// handler.rs
DiscoverNodes => {
    let nodes = crate::NODES
```

```
            .iter()
            .map(|x| x.key().clone())
            .collect::<Vec<_>>();
        let message = NodeList(nodes);
        message
            .send_async(&mut socket)
            .await
            .unwrap();
    }
```

AskDifference (read and subtract):

```
    AskDifference(height) => {
        let blockchain =
            crate::BLOCKCHAIN.read().await;
        let count = blockchain.block_height()
            as i32
            - height as i32;
        let message = Difference(count);
        message
            .send_async(&mut socket)
            .await
            .unwrap();
    }
```

Returning **UTXOs** for a particular public key is a bit more involved process, as we need to filter them out, and separate them from the tags marking them:

```
    // handler.rs
    FetchUTXOs(key) => {
        println!("received request to fetch UTXOs");
        let blockchain =
            crate::BLOCKCHAIN.read().await;
        let utxos = blockchain
```

```
                .utxos()
                .iter()
                .filter(|(_, (_, txout))| {
                    txout.pubkey == key
                })
                .map(|(_, (marked, txout))| {
                    (txout.clone(), *marked)
                })
                .collect::<Vec<_>>();
            let message = UTXOs(utxos);
            message
                .send_async(&mut socket)
                .await
                .unwrap();
        }
```

The **.cloned()** method on an iterator (or Option, or Result), clones the type inside, transforming an **Iterator<Item=&T>** into an **Iterator<Item=T>** assuming that **T** implements **Clone**. Receiving a new block is easy also, as we have implemented validation into the **Blockchain** type:

```
        // handler.rs
        NewBlock(block) => {
            let mut blockchain =
                crate::BLOCKCHAIN.write().await;
            println!("received new block");
            if blockchain.add_block(block).is_err() {
                println!("block rejected");
            }
        }
```

Same goes for when we receive a new transaction from another node:

```rust
// handler.rs
NewTransaction(tx) => {
    let mut blockchain =
        crate::BLOCKCHAIN.write().await;
    println!("received transaction from friend");
    if blockchain.add_to_mempool(tx).is_err() {
        println!("transaction rejected, closing
connection");
        return;
    }
}
```

We are making a simplification here in that we just add it to the mempool. It would be a nice idea to send it back to other nodes that may not have it. However, we would have to add a mechanism for preventing the network from creating notification loops. You can try implementing one, if you want.

Validating the template is fairly easy, we can say it is invalid if it is no longer pointing to the top of the blockchain with the previous block hash contained in it:

```rust
// handler.rs
ValidateTemplate(block_template) => {
    let blockchain =
        crate::BLOCKCHAIN.read().await;
    let status = block_template
        .header
        .prev_block_hash
        == blockchain
            .blocks()
            .last()
            .map(|last_block| last_block.hash())
            .unwrap_or(Hash::zero());
    let message = TemplateValidity(status);
    message
```

```
            .send_async(&mut socket)
            .await
            .unwrap();
    }
```

If a miner sends us a correctly mined block, we want to broadcast it to other nodes:

```
    // handler.rs
    SubmitTemplate(block) => {
        println!("received allegedly mined template");
        let mut blockchain =
            crate::BLOCKCHAIN.write().await;
        if let Err(e) =
            blockchain.add_block(block.clone())
        {
            println!(
                "block rejected: {e}, closing connecti-
on"
            );
            return;
        }
        blockchain.rebuild_utxos();
        println!("block looks good, broadcasting");
        // send block to all friend nodes
        let nodes = crate::NODES
            .iter()
            .map(|x| x.key().clone())
            .collect::<Vec<_>>();
        for node in nodes {
            if let Some(mut stream) =
                crate::NODES.get_mut(&node)
            {
                let message = Message::NewBlock(
                    block.clone(),
                );
```

```
                    if message
                        .send_async(&mut *stream)
                        .await
                        .is_err()
                    {
                    println!("failed to send block to {}",
node);
                    }
                }
            }
        }
```

Same goes for newly submitted transactions, we want to pass them on also:

```
        // handler.rs
        SubmitTransaction(tx) => {
            println!("submit tx");
            let mut blockchain =
                crate::BLOCKCHAIN.write().await;
            if let Err(e) =
               blockchain.add_to_mempool(tx.clone())
        {
         println!("transaction rejected, closing connection:
{e}");
                return;
            }
            println!("added transaction to mempool");
            // send transaction to all friend nodes
            let nodes = crate::NODES
                .iter()
                .map(|x| x.key().clone())
                .collect::<Vec<_>>();
            for node in nodes {
                println!("sending to friend: {node}");
                if let Some(mut stream) =
                    crate::NODES.get_mut(&node)
                {
                    let message =
```

```
                    Message::NewTransaction(
                        tx.clone(),
                    );
                if message
                    .send_async(&mut *stream)
                    .await
                    .is_err()
            {
          println!("failed to send transaction to {}",
node);
                }
            }
        }
        println!("transaction sent to friends");
    }
```

The final and most difficult message to implement is the **FetchTemplate** one:

```
// handler.rs
FetchTemplate(pubkey) => {
    let blockchain =
        crate::BLOCKCHAIN.read().await;
    let mut transactions = vec![];
    // insert transactions from mempool
    transactions.extend(
        blockchain
            .mempool()
            .iter()
            .take(btclib::BLOCK_TRANSACTION_CAP)
            .map(|(_, tx)| tx)
            .cloned()
            .collect::<Vec<_>>(),
    );
    // insert coinbase tx with pubkey
    transactions.insert(
        0,
```

```
        Transaction {
            inputs: vec![],
            outputs: vec![TransactionOutput {
                pubkey,
                unique_id: Uuid::new_v4(),
                value: 0,
            }],
        },
    );
    let merkle_root =
        MerkleRoot::calculate(&transactions);
    let mut block = Block::new(
        BlockHeader {
            timestamp: Utc::now(),
            prev_block_hash: blockchain
                .blocks()
                .last()
                .map(|last_block| {
                    last_block.hash()
                })
                .unwrap_or(Hash::zero()),
            nonce: 0,
            target: blockchain.target(),
            merkle_root,
        },
        transactions,
    );
    let miner_fees = match block
        .calculate_miner_fees(blockchain.utxos())
    {
        Ok(fees) => fees,
        Err(e) => {
            eprintln!("{e}");
            return;
        }
    };
    let reward =
```

```
                blockchain.calculate_block_reward();
            // update coinbase tx with reward
            block.transactions[0].outputs[0].value =
                reward + miner_fees;
            // recalculate merkle root
            block.header.merkle_root =
                MerkleRoot::calculate(
                    &block.transactions,
                );
            let message = Template(block);
            message
                .send_async(&mut socket)
                .await
                .unwrap();
        }
```

We need to quickly go back to the **lib/src/types/blockchain.rs** file in **btclib**, and implement the **calculate_block_reward()** function:

```
// types/blockchain.rs (in lib/)
pub fn calculate_block_reward(&self) -> u64 {
    let block_height = self.block_height();
    let halvings = block_height / crate::HALVING_INTERVAL;
    (crate::INITIAL_REWARD * 10u64.pow(8)) >> halvings
}
```

As an exercise, try calculating how many halvings (and how long time) will it take to reach a block reward smaller than 1 satoshi. You might be surprised at how fast it will be with our current settings in **lib/src/lib.rs**.

WRAPPING UP

Looking back at the **handler()**, you can see that we need to collect UTXOs and transactions to put into the block. Luckily, we have already established that the transactions we are taking are the most valuable ones (with the highest fee for the miner). One cumbersome part is how we need to calculate the merkle root twice (before and after the correct coinbase transaction). I have intentionally left that here as a very obvious pain point that is not so difficult to fix. Can you figure out how to fix this issue by making a couple of small changes in **btclib**?

Also, you might have one warning left in **main.rs**. Given how the loop runs infinitely, and we have no **break** statements there, the **Ok(())** statement is unreachable. This is how the warning looks on my machine:

```
warning: unreachable expression
   --> node/src/main.rs:114:5
    |
109 | /     loop {
110 | |         let (socket, _) = listener.accept().await?;
111 | |         tokio::spawn(handler::handle_connection(soc-
ket));
112 | |     }
    | |_____- any code following this expression is unreachab-
le
113 |
114 |       Ok(())
    |       ^^^^^^ unreachable expression
    |
    = note: `#[warn(unreachable_code)]` on by default
warning: `node` (bin "node") generated 1 warning
   Finished `dev` profile [unoptimized + debuginfo] target(s)
in 0.16s
```

Just delete it, and you should have no warnings. :)

The **loop {}** statement will coerce to any type, including a **Result<()>** so long as the **loop** actually diverges. To diverge, in Rust parlance, roughly translates to "this either runs forever unconditionally, or stops the whole thread/process".

Now, we should have all the messages handled, and if you run the node without any arguments, you should get the following output in the terminal:

```
blockchain file does not exist!
no initial nodes provided, starting as a seed node
Listening on 0.0.0.0:9000
saving blockchain to drive...
cleaning the mempool from old transactions
```

And if you run it again, the situation will be slightly different because we already have a blockchain available:

```
blockchain file exists, loading...
blockchain loaded
rebuilding utxos...
utxos rebuilt
checking if target needs to be adjusted...
current target: 69017463467905637874347558622770254524511089721703865551625242237992 95
new target: 6901746346790563787434755862277025452451108972170386555162524223799295
initialization complete
Listening on 0.0.0.0:9000
saving blockchain to drive...
cleaning the mempool from old transactions
```

Perfect, that concludes our work on the node for now. Congratulations, you made it past the node. Now, all we have left is the CLI wallet, which is nowhere near as difficult. Here is a picture for you:

The mighty crab is the mascot of Rust. The Rust crab is called Ferris, and is, in fact, very cute.

9

MAKING A CLI/TUI WALLET

You know which GUI (Graphical User Interface) is the most beautiful? If you are anything like me, a terminal rat born in the rough streets of the comman-d-line, raised on a diet of **bash, mksh** and **fish**, you will say: "Why! No GUI at all, my eyes were made for reading text on a terminal! The light of the modern MacOSX and Windows 11 light theme blinds my eyes. If my Linux distribution has more than 6 graphical applications, I become deathly ill!"[46]

Naturally, the answer is TUI - terminal UI. All the benefits of a UI without the actual UI. In recent years, TUI apps have had a renaissance of sorts, as the Linux equivalent of fashion designers, mostly centered around **r/unixporn** (the name is suspicious, but there is nothing NSFW going on in that community, at least until they start putting on programmer socks), found them visually appealing and highly configurable (via recoloring your terminal application).

In Rust, there is a number of libraries that support creating terminal UI applications, including the rising star of GUI development - **dioxus**. The **dioxus** framework is a web-centric UI framework, which is starting to gain ground in frontend development. Unfortunately, I only learned about it recently, and I don't have prior experience developing with it. It is extremely portable and flexible, though - you can make web apps, desktop apps, mobile apps, and even terminal UI applications. The ones that are more likely to come to play in most TUI Rust software are **ratatui** and **cursive**.

Ratatui has filled the niche left behind by the **tui** crate, which for years held the position as *the* best crate for elaborate terminal user interfaces. These two libraries differ in approach to driving the application. **Ratatui** is an **immediate-mode,** while **cursive** uses a declarative approach with events. Immediate mode UI libraries redraw the entire interface every frame based on the current application state, and they themselves do not maintain any state at all. This can make them very simple, and direct, but the cost of some readability, and potentially some performance.

With **cursive**, you specify a UI, state, events, and off you go. When preparing this wallet, I tried both approaches, and decided that **cursive** is more readable in the constrained environment of a book, so here it goes :)

46 After a recent data loss I suffered, I am down to three GUI applications - my terminal emulator, Firefox, and Telegram. I am using a 500 line window manager I wrote myself.

MAKING A CLI WALLET

In this part of the project, I would like to introduce approaches that are geared slightly more towards how things are done in production. We will split our wallet into two discrete parts:

- A core that handles functionality, and knows nothing about the UI of the application
- The interface of the application itself

We want the core to run pretty much independently from the UI (with the UI making requests from the core of the application, and fetching info). In many languages, you would be tempted to instantiate such a core as a global variable, but in Rust, we do not need to, and it would be potentially quite cumbersome.

We will design our **Core** as a structure that uses interior mutability, so that it can be easily shareable via **Arc<Core>**. Just as a reminder, an **Arc<T>** (**A**tomic **R**eference **C**ounting) is a thread-safe smart pointer in Rust that allows multiple ownership of the same data across threads. It provides shared, immutable access to its contents, using atomic operations for reference counting to ensure safe concurrent access and automatic memory management. Cloning an **Arc** only gives you a new handle to the same underlying data without actually creating a new copy. Data contained in an **Arc** is only deleted when the last **Arc** pointing to the same data is destroyed. There is a non-atomic version called **Rc**, but it cannot be shared across threads, as the counters are not thread-safe.

Before we use **cursive** to make a nice TUI, let's make a simpler CLI version, so we know that our Core is working correctly. Start by making sure that your Cargo.toml looks roughly like this (you can add the dependencies via **cargo add** to ensure you have the latest versions of the libraries used):

```
[package]
name = "good-wallet"
version = "0.1.0"
edition = "2021"
[dependencies]
anyhow = "1.0.86"
clap = { version = "4.5.8", features = ["derive"] }
crossbeam-skiplist = "0.1.3"
```

```toml
cursive = "0.20.0"
futures = "0.3.30"
kanal = "0.1.0-pre8"
serde = { version = "1.0.204", features = ["derive"] }
text-to-ascii-art = "0.1.9"
tokio = { version = "1.38.0", features = ["full"] }
toml = "0.8.14"
tracing = "0.1.40"
tracing-appender = "0.2.3"
tracing-subscriber = { version = "0.3.18", features = ["env-
-filter", "fmt"] }
uuid = { version = "1.9.1", features = ["v4", "serde"] }
# ours
btclib = { version = "0.1.0", path = "../lib" }
```

There are a couple of libraries we haven't used yet:

- **clap:** A robust command-line argument parser for Rust. It provides an intuitive API for defining and parsing command-line interfaces, supporting subcommands, flags, and options. We used **argh,** and very briefly **clap** for the miner. This time, I am selecting **clap** so that you can see that it is almost the same thing, and have an opportunity to use **clap** in a slightly more advanced manner in the TUI version of the wallet. Note that while we are only using the **derive** functionality of **clap**, there are many ways in which you can use it to drive an application.
- **crossbeam-skiplist:** A concurrent skip list implementation from the Crossbeam project. It offers a thread-safe, ordered map or set data structure with efficient search, insertion, and deletion operations. We will be using the **SkipMap** to store the UTXOs the wallet keeps track of. The main reason why I selected this crate this time is that I would like to mention the **crossbeam** project to you. It provides many tools for performant and safe concurrent programming, and this is just one small part of its toolkit.
- **kanal:** An asynchronous messaging library for Rust. It provides a channel-based communication mechanism optimized for use in async contexts, facilitating message passing between tasks or threads. It is an

alternative to **flume**, just so we get some variety.[47]

- **text-to-ascii-art:** A library that converts text into ASCII art. It transforms input strings into large, stylized representations using ASCII characters, suitable for creating text banners or decorative outputs. We will be making the balance text in our TUI very BIG with this crate.
- **toml:** A parser and serializer for the TOML (Tom's Obvious, Minimal Language) format. It allows reading from and writing to TOML configuration files, which are popular for their human-readable syntax. TOML is perhaps the most popular configuration format in Rust, partially due to it being used by the toolchain, and partially due to the fact that as of the time of this writing, the **serde-yaml** crate is unmaintained.
- **tracing:** A framework for instrumenting Rust programs to collect structured, event-based diagnostic information. It's more powerful than simple logging, offering contextual data and hierarchical spans. We will be using it as a simple logging library though. Tracing also works very well in asynchronous contexts, and it can be set up with non-blocking log writes.
- **tracing-appender:** A companion crate for **tracing** that provides writers for logging to files. It's useful for efficiently writing trace data to a disk without blocking the main program execution. We will be trying the log rotation feature.
- **tracing-subscriber:** A key component of the **tracing** ecosystem, providing ways to collect, filter, and format trace data. It allows customizable processing of tracing events before they're recorded or displayed.

Okay, now that we have got that out of the way, start by creating the following two files in the **wallet/** folder:

- **src/main.rs**
- **src/core.rs**

Make sure that you declare the **core** module in main.rs:

```
// main.rs
mod core;
```

47 Kanal is not as mainstream as flume, but at the time of this writing, it is by far the fastest library for channels.

Let's import the things that we will need:

```
// main.rs
use anyhow::Result;
use clap::{Parser, Subcommand};
use kanal::bounded;
use tokio::time::{self, Duration};
use std::io::{self, Write};
use std::path::PathBuf;
use btclib::types::Transaction;
```

We will be defining the CLI similarly to how we have done it with **argh**:

```
// main.rs
use btclib::types::Transaction;
#[derive(Parser)]
#[command(author, version, about, long_about = None)]
struct Cli {
    #[command(subcommand)]
    command: Option<Commands>,
    #[arg(short, long, value_name = "FILE")]
    config: Option<PathBuf>,
    #[arg(short, long, value_name = "ADDRESS")]
    node: Option<String>,
}
#[derive(Subcommand)]
enum Commands {
    GenerateConfig {
        #[arg(short, long, value_name = "FILE")]
        output: PathBuf,
    },
}
```

This tells us a little about how the wallet should function. It should read a config that contains the following information:

- What are my private and public keys?[48]
- My contacts - pairs of names and public keys
- The default node we want to connect to
- Fee configuration - we will not be complex about fees at all, we will offer settings for either a flat value, or a percentage of the sent amount.

It should be possible to override the location of the configuration file and the address of the node to connect to. Finally, a subcommand should exist to let us create a dummy configuration that the user can modify with their information.

We can define these configuration types right now:

```
// core.rs
use anyhow::Result;
use crossbeam_skiplist::SkipMap;
use serde::{Deserialize, Serialize};
use tokio::net::TcpStream;
use std::fs;
use std::path::PathBuf;
use std::sync::Arc;
use btclib::crypto::{PrivateKey, PublicKey};
use btclib::network::Message;
use btclib::types::{Transaction, TransactionOutput};
use btclib::util::Saveable;
#[derive(Serialize, Deserialize, Clone)]
pub struct Key {
    public: PathBuf,
    private: PathBuf,
}
#[derive(Clone)]
struct LoadedKey {
```

48 In theory, the private keys are enough - you can calculate the public ones from them, however, let's keep it simple for ourselves.

```rust
    public: PublicKey,
    private: PrivateKey,
}
#[derive(Serialize, Deserialize, Clone)]
pub struct Recipient {
    pub name: String,
    pub key: PathBuf,
}
#[derive(Clone)]
pub struct LoadedRecipient {
    pub name: String,
    pub key: PublicKey,
}
impl Recipient {
    pub fn load(&self) -> Result<LoadedRecipient> {
        let key = PublicKey::load_from_file(&self.key)?;
        Ok(LoadedRecipient {
            name: self.name.clone(),
            key,
        })
    }
}
#[derive(Serialize, Deserialize, Clone)]
pub enum FeeType {
    Fixed,
    Percent,
}
#[derive(Serialize, Deserialize, Clone)]
pub struct FeeConfig {
    pub fee_type: FeeType,
    pub value: f64,
}
#[derive(Serialize, Deserialize, Clone)]
pub struct Config {
    pub my_keys: Vec<Key>,
    pub contacts: Vec<Recipient>,
    pub default_node: String,
    pub fee_config: FeeConfig,
}
```

In the highlighted part, we are already implementing a load function for each recipient. You could also create the same method by implementing the **Saveable** trait we created earlier, however, we do not want the wallet to be modifying the configuration, or the user's keys.

Let's go back to the **main.rs** file. This is how the rough structure of our application may look:

```
async fn update_utxos(core: Arc<Core>) {
    // ...
}
async fn handle_transactions(
    rx: kanal::AsyncReceiver<Transaction>,
    core: Arc<Core>,
) {
    // ...
}
async fn run_cli(core: Arc<Core>) -> Result<()> {
    // ...
    Ok(())
}
fn generate_dummy_config(path: &PathBuf) -> Result<()> {
    // ...
    Ok(())
}
#[tokio::main]
async fn main() -> Result<()> {
    // ...
    Ok(())
}
```

We want the wallet to perform the following tasks:

- Keep track of the user's balance by checking it with the node
- Handle transactions - we will just be sending them via a channel into the core
- Respond to the CLI commands

Here, we are also adding a utility function for generating a dummy configuration file, as mentioned earlier. We can implement that one first to get it out of the way:

```
// main.rs - move imports at the top of the file
use core::{Config, Core, FeeConfig, FeeType, Recipient};
fn generate_dummy_config(path: &PathBuf) -> Result<()> {
    let dummy_config = Config {
        my_keys: vec![],
        contacts: vec![
            Recipient {
                name: "Alice".to_string(),
                key: PathBuf::from("alice.pub.pem"),
            },
            Recipient {
                name: "Bob".to_string(),
                key: PathBuf::from("bob.pub.pem"),
            },
        ],
        default_node: "127.0.0.1:9000".to_string(),
        fee_config: FeeConfig {
            fee_type: FeeType::Percent,
            value: 0.1,
        },
    };
    let config_str = toml::to_string_pretty(&dummy_config)?;
    std::fs::write(path, config_str)?;
    println!("Dummy config generated at: {}", path.display());
    Ok(())
}
```

We create a sample config, and we save it to the path specified by the argument. Finally, we print a message confirming that we have created the config successfully. Let's take care of the two long-running tasks now:

```
// main.rs
async fn update_utxos(core: Arc<Core>) {
    let mut interval = time::interval(Duration::from_secs(20));
    loop {
        interval.tick().await;
        if let Err(e) = core.fetch_utxos().await {
            eprintln!("Failed to update UTXOs: {}", e);
        }
    }
}
async fn handle_transactions(
    rx: kanal::AsyncReceiver<Transaction>,
    core: Arc<Core>,
) {
    while let Ok(transaction) = rx.recv().await {
        if let Err(e) = core.send_transaction(transaction).
await
        {
            eprintln!("Failed to send transaction: {}", e);
        }
    }
}
```

We use the **tokio::time::interval** to make the **update_utxos()** task check for the UTXOs tied to the user's private keys every 20 seconds. You can lengthen and shorten this interval as you see fit. In **handle_transactions**, we are waiting to receive fully formed transactions (they will be coming from the UI). This solution will be a bit odd, as we will be taking a trip in and out of the core with the transactions (as the sender for this receiver is located in the Core). Can you come back later and refactor it so that this does not happen?

This leaves us with the final piece for this simplified CLI wallet in **main.rs**:

```
// main.rs
async fn run_cli(core: Arc<Core>) -> Result<()> {
    loop {
```

```
            print!("> ");
            io::stdout().flush()?;
            let mut input = String::new();
            io::stdin().read_line(&mut input)?;
            let parts: Vec<&str> =
                input.trim().split_whitespace().collect();
            if parts.is_empty() {
                continue;
            }
            match parts[0] {
                "balance" => { // process balance
                }
                "send" => { // process send
                }
                "exit" => break,
                _ => println!("Unknown command"),
            }
        }
        Ok(())
    }
```

We print the prompt, and then we start reading commands. Notice how we need to flush the standard output after using the **print!()** macro. While the **println!()** macro flushes by default, **print!()** doesn't.

To process the balance command, we simply request it from the Core

```
            // main.rs
            "balance" => {
                println!(
                    "Current balance: {} satoshis",
                    core.get_balance()
                );
            }
```

Sending is slightly more involved, we need to find the recipient, and then request that the Core creates a transaction with a particular amount:

```
            "send" => {
                if parts.len() != 3 {
                    println!("Usage: send <recipient>
 <amount>");
                    continue;
                }
                let recipient = parts[1];
                let amount: u64 = parts[2].parse()?;
                let recipient_key = core
                    .config
                    .contacts
                    .iter()
                    .find(|r| r.name == recipient)
                    .ok_or_else(|| {
                        anyhow::anyhow!("Recipient not found")
                    })?
                    .load()?
                    .key;
                if let Err(e) = core.fetch_utxos().await {
                    println!("failed to fetch utxos: {e}");
                };
                let transaction = core
                    .create_transaction(&recipient_key, amount)
                    .await?;
                core.tx_sender.send(transaction).await?;
                println!("Transaction sent successfully");
                core.fetch_utxos().await?;
            }
```

That's it for the **main.rs** file. Just to recapitulate, at this stage, it should look like this:

```rust
// main.rs
mod core;
use core::{Config, Core, FeeConfig, FeeType, Recipient};
use std::sync::Arc;
use anyhow::Result;
use clap::{Parser, Subcommand};
use kanal;
use std::io::{self, Write};
use std::path::PathBuf;
use tokio::time::{self, Duration};
use btclib::types::Transaction;
#[derive(Parser)]
#[command(author, version, about, long_about = None)]
struct Cli {
    #[command(subcommand)]
    command: Option<Commands>,
    #[arg(short, long, value_name = "FILE")]
    config: Option<PathBuf>,
    #[arg(short, long, value_name = "ADDRESS")]
    node: Option<String>,
}
#[derive(Subcommand)]
enum Commands {
    GenerateConfig {
        #[arg(short, long, value_name = "FILE")]
        output: PathBuf,
    },
}
async fn update_utxos(core: Arc<Core>) {
    let mut interval = time::interval(Duration::from_secs(20));
    loop {
        interval.tick().await;
        if let Err(e) = core.fetch_utxos().await {
            eprintln!("Failed to update UTXOs: {}", e);
        }
    }
}
```

```
async fn handle_transactions(
    rx: kanal::AsyncReceiver<Transaction>,
    core: Arc<Core>,
) {
    while let Ok(transaction) = rx.recv().await {
        if let Err(e) = core.send_transaction(transaction).
await
        {
            eprintln!("Failed to send transaction: {}", e);
        }
    }
}
async fn run_cli(core: Arc<Core>) -> Result<()> {
    loop {
        print!("> ");
        io::stdout().flush()?;
        let mut input = String::new();
        io::stdin().read_line(&mut input)?;
        let parts: Vec<&str> =
            input.trim().split_whitespace().collect();
        if parts.is_empty() {
            continue;
        }
        match parts[0] {
            "balance" => {
                println!(
                    "Current balance: {} satoshis",
                    core.get_balance()
                );
            }
            "send" => {
                if parts.len() != 3 {
                    println!("Usage: send <recipient>
<amount>");
                    continue;
                }
                let recipient = parts[1];
                let amount: u64 = parts[2].parse()?;
                let recipient_key = core
```

```
                .config
                .contacts
                .iter()
                .find(|r| r.name == recipient)
                .ok_or_else(|| {
                    anyhow::anyhow!("Recipient not found")
                })?
                .load()?
                .key;
            if let Err(e) = core.fetch_utxos().await {
                println!("failed to fetch utxos: {e}");
            };
            let transaction = core
                .create_transaction(&recipient_key, amount)
                .await?;
            core.tx_sender.send(transaction).await?;
            println!("Transaction sent successfully");
            core.fetch_utxos().await?;
        }
        "exit" => break,
        _ => println!("Unknown command"),
    }
  }
  Ok(())
}
fn generate_dummy_config(path: &PathBuf) -> Result<()> {
    let dummy_config = Config {
        my_keys: vec![],
        contacts: vec![
            Recipient {
                name: "Alice".to_string(),
                key: PathBuf::from("alice.pub.pem"),
            },
            Recipient {
                name: "Bob".to_string(),
                key: PathBuf::from("bob.pub.pem"),
            },
        ],
        default_node: "127.0.0.1:9000".to_string(),
```

```
        fee_config: FeeConfig {
            fee_type: FeeType::Percent,
            value: 0.1,
        },
    };
    let config_str = toml::to_string_pretty(&dummy_config)?;
    std::fs::write(path, config_str)?;
    println!("Dummy config generated at: {}", path.display());
    Ok(())
}
#[tokio::main]
async fn main() -> Result<()> {
    // ...
    let cli = Cli::parse();
    match &cli.command {
        Some(Commands::GenerateConfig { output }) => {
            return generate_dummy_config(output);
        }
        None => {}
    }
    let config_path = cli
        .config
        .unwrap_or_else(|| PathBuf::from("wallet_config.
toml"));
    let mut core = Core::load(config_path.clone())?;
    if let Some(node) = cli.node {
        core.config.default_node = node;
    }
    let (tx_sender, tx_receiver) = kanal::bounded(10);
    core.tx_sender = tx_sender.clone_async();
    let core = Arc::new(core);
    tokio::spawn(update_utxos(core.clone()));
    tokio::spawn(handle_transactions(
        tx_receiver.clone_async(),
        core.clone(),
    ));
    run_cli(core).await?;
    Ok(())
}
```

The core of the wallet

Throughout the previous file, we have gotten some hints as to how the wallet Core should look. We can define its broad structure as such:

```
// core.rs
use anyhow::Result;
use crossbeam_skiplist::SkipMap;
use kanal::AsyncSender;
use serde::{Deserialize, Serialize};
use tokio::net::TcpStream;
use std::fs;
use std::path::PathBuf;
use std::sync::Arc;
use btclib::crypto::{PrivateKey, PublicKey};
use btclib::network::Message;
use btclib::types::{Transaction, TransactionOutput};
use btclib::util::Saveable;
// The config types from earlier should be inserted here...
#[derive(Clone)]
struct UtxoStore {
    my_keys: Vec<LoadedKey>,
    utxos:
        Arc<SkipMap<PublicKey, Vec<(bool, TransactionOut-
put)>>>,
}
impl UtxoStore {
    fn new() -> Self {
        // ...
    }
    fn add_key(&mut self, key: LoadedKey) {
        // ...
    }
}
#[derive(Clone)]
pub struct Core {
    pub config: Config,
    utxos: UtxoStore,
    pub tx_sender: AsyncSender<Transaction>,
}
```

```rust
impl Core {
    fn new(config: Config, utxos: UtxoStore) -> Self {
        // ...
    }
    pub fn load(config_path: PathBuf) -> Result<Self> {
        // ...
    }
    pub async fn fetch_utxos(&self) -> Result<()> {
        // ...
    }
    pub async fn send_transaction(
        &self,
        transaction: Transaction,
    ) -> Result<()> {
        // ...
    }
    pub fn get_balance(&self) -> u64 {
        // ...
    }
    pub async fn create_transaction(
        &self,
        recipient: &PublicKey,
        amount: u64,
    ) -> Result<Transaction> {
        // ...
    }
    fn calculate_fee(&self, amount: u64) -> u64 {
        // ...
    }
}
```

Let's first consider the **UTXO store**:

```rust
// core.rs
#[derive(Clone)]
struct UtxoStore {
```

```
    my_keys: Vec<LoadedKey>,
    utxos:
        Arc<SkipMap<PublicKey, Vec<(bool, TransactionOut-
put)>>>,
}
impl UtxoStore {
    fn new() -> Self {
        UtxoStore {
            my_keys: Vec::new(),
            utxos: Arc::new(SkipMap::new()),
        }
    }
    fn add_key(&mut self, key: LoadedKey) {
        self.my_keys.push(key);
    }
}
```

Here, we are storing our keys in a vector, which requires mutable access. This is fine, and it forces us to initialize it before we hand it over to the core. The SkipMap will let us concurrently store vectors of UTXOs for each of our keys. Its API is very similar to that of **DashMap**, which we have encountered earlier in this book. While **DashMap** is a concurrent alternative to a **HashMap**, the **SkipMap** is a concurrent alternative to a **BTreeMap**. This has the added benefit of not requiring the key type to implement **Hash**.

With it, we can start chipping away at the Core. Let's start with the **new()** function:

```
    // core.rs
    fn new(config: Config, utxos: UtxoStore) -> Self {
        let (tx_sender, _) = kanal::bounded(10);
        Core {
            config,
            utxos,
            tx_sender: tx_sender.clone_async(),
        }
    }
```

It is private, since we want the user to create the core using the **Config::load()** associated function. There is one messy feature of this function - it forces us to create a useless channel that we then immediately replace (which will destroy it, given Rust's semantics) with a new channel that is properly wired up to the rest of the application. Let's examine the **load()** function next:

```
    // core.rs
    pub fn load(config_path: PathBuf) -> Result<Self> {
        let config: Config =
            toml::from_str(&fs::read_to_string(&config_
path)?)?;
        let mut utxos = UtxoStore::new();
        // Load keys from config
        for key in &config.my_keys {
            let public = PublicKey::load_from_file(&key.pub-
lic)?;
            let private =
                PrivateKey::load_from_file(&key.private)?;
            utxos.add_key(LoadedKey { public, private });
        }
        Ok(Core::new(config, utxos))
    }
```

As you can see, we are reading the **Config** from a **TOML** file, creating a new **UtxoStore**, and initializing it with the keys specified in the config. Finally, we call **Core::new()** to construct the correctly initialized core of the application. That's it for the initialization part. Now, to the two tasks we need to be taking care of - sending transactions and updating the UTXO set related to our keys. We will create the following two methods for it:

```
    // core.rs
    pub async fn fetch_utxos(&self) -> Result<()> {
        let mut stream =
            TcpStream::connect(&self.config.default_node)
                .await?;
```

```
        for key in &self.utxos.my_keys {
            let message =
                Message::FetchUTXOs(key.public.clone());
            message.send_async(&mut stream).await?;
            if let Message::UTXOs(utxos) =
                Message::receive_async(&mut stream).await?
            {
                // Replace the entire UTXO set for this key
                self.utxos.utxos.insert(
                    key.public.clone(),
                    utxos
                        .into_iter()
                        .map(|(output, marked)| (marked, out-
put))
                        .collect(),
                );
            } else {
                return Err(anyhow::anyhow!(
                    "Unexpected response from node"
                ));
            }
        }
        Ok(())
    }
    pub async fn send_transaction(
        &self,
        transaction: Transaction,
    ) -> Result<()> {
        let mut stream =
            TcpStream::connect(&self.config.default_node)
                .await?;
        let message = Message::SubmitTransaction(transaction);
        message.send_async(&mut stream).await?;
        Ok(())
    }
```

Sending messages, and receiving messages. Simple stuff. This implementation could be significantly improved by not opening connections over and over again, but rather, storing one connection in **Core**, and reusing it in both tasks (keep in mind you will have to lock it in a **Mutex** properly, to ensure one task doesn't start sending messages while the other is waiting for a reply). The last major function we need to implement is the **create_transaction()** function, which we have previously referenced in **main.rs()**:

```
// core.rs
pub async fn create_transaction(
    &self,
    recipient: &PublicKey,
    amount: u64,
) -> Result<Transaction> {
    let fee = self.calculate_fee(amount);
    let total_amount = amount + fee;
    let mut inputs = Vec::new();
    let mut input_sum = 0;
    for entry in self.utxos.utxos.iter() {
        let pubkey = entry.key();
        let utxos = entry.value();
        for (marked, utxo) in utxos.iter() {
            if *marked {
                continue; // Skip marked UTXOs
            }
            if input_sum >= total_amount {
                break;
            }
            inputs.push(btclib::types::TransactionInput {
                prev_transaction_output_hash: utxo.hash(),
                signature:
                    btclib::crypto::Signature::sign_output(
                        &utxo.hash(),
                        &self
                            .utxos
                            .my_keys
                            .iter()
                            .find(|k| k.public == *pubkey)
                            .unwrap()
```

```
                                .private,
                        ),
                });
                input_sum += utxo.value;
            }
            if input_sum >= total_amount {
                break;
            }
        }
        if input_sum < total_amount {
            return Err(anyhow::anyhow!("Insufficient funds"));
        }
        let mut outputs = vec![TransactionOutput {
            value: amount,
            unique_id: uuid::Uuid::new_v4(),
            pubkey: recipient.clone(),
        }];
        if input_sum > total_amount {
            outputs.push(TransactionOutput {
                value: input_sum - total_amount,
                unique_id: uuid::Uuid::new_v4(),
                pubkey: self.utxos.my_keys[0].public.clone(),
            });
        }
        Ok(Transaction::new(inputs, outputs))
    }
```

We are following the recipe we described earlier when implementing the **btclib** and the **node** - we use up as many inputs as we have to create the transaction with the amount and mining fee, and we make outputs for just the amount. Finally, we sent the change back to us in one final transaction output. This correctly constructs the transaction, so that we can send it to the node. All that is left to implement in the core at this stage is two helper functions:

```rust
// core.rs
pub fn get_balance(&self) -> u64 {
    self.utxos
        .utxos
        .iter()
        .map(|entry| {
            entry
                .value()
                .iter()
                .map(|utxo| utxo.1.value)
                .sum::<u64>()
        })
        .sum()
}
fn calculate_fee(&self, amount: u64) -> u64 {
    match self.config.fee_config.fee_type {
        FeeType::Fixed => {
            self.config.fee_config.value as u64
        }
        FeeType::Percent => {
            (amount as f64 * self.config.fee_config.value
                / 100.0) as u64
        }
    }
}
```

These are very simple, both only doing a bit of calculation :)

The main() function

We have made our tools, now we need to initialize everything, and stitch it up together into a functional app. This is how it is going to look in our case:

```
// main.rs
#[tokio::main]
async fn main() -> Result<()> {
    let cli = Cli::parse();
    match &cli.command {
        Some(Commands::GenerateConfig { output }) => {
            return generate_dummy_config(output);
        }
        None => {}
    }
    let config_path = cli
        .config
        .unwrap_or_else(|| PathBuf::from("wallet_config.
toml"));
    let mut core = Core::load(config_path.clone())?;
    if let Some(node) = cli.node {
        core.config.default_node = node;
    }
    let (tx_sender, tx_receiver) = kanal::bounded(10);
    core.tx_sender = tx_sender.clone_async();
    let core = Arc::new(core);
    tokio::spawn(update_utxos(core.clone()));
    tokio::spawn(handle_transactions(
        tx_receiver.clone_async(),
        core.clone(),
    ));
    run_cli(core).await?;
    Ok(())
}
```

Let's break it down, step-by-step. First, we parse the command line arguments into the **Cli** structure we defined earlier:

```
// main.rs
let cli = Cli::parse();
```

This handles the parsing, and also the **--help** option that lists the help text of the application. Next, we check if we are asked to generate a dummy configuration:

```
// main.rs
match &cli.command {
    Some(Commands::GenerateConfig { output }) => {
        return generate_dummy_config(output);
    }
    None => {}
}
```

This could also be written as an if-let, it is up to you :) In some cases, I like to use a match if the pattern is very long, but there is no functional difference here. Next, we either take the config path from the CLI, or replace it with a default value, and instantiate **Core**:

```
// main.rs
let config_path = cli
    .config
    .unwrap_or_else(|| PathBuf::from("wallet_config.
toml"));
let mut core = Core::load(config_path.clone())?;
```

Note that we can avoid this completely - **clap** supports default values for flags, which will do this exact thing. It is left as an exercise for the reader to open up the documentation and figure out how to shorten our program by three lines. The shorter the program, the better. At this stage, the **core** variable is mutable, and that is because we need to set up the communication channel the UI will use to talk with the **Core**, and optionally change the node we want to connect to:

```
// main.rs
if let Some(node) = cli.node {
    core.config.default_node = node;
}
let (tx_sender, tx_receiver) = kanal::bounded(10);
core.tx_sender = tx_sender.clone_async();
```

Now we can wrap the **Core** in an **Arc**, which will let us safely share it between tasks:

```
// main.rs
let core = Arc::new(core);
```

With that in hand, we can start cloning the core (creating new handles), and spawning our tasks:

```
// main.rs
tokio::spawn(update_utxos(core.clone()));
tokio::spawn(handle_transactions(
    tx_receiver.clone_async(),
    core.clone(),
));
```

Finally, we run the CLI in the main task, and wrap up:

```
// main.rs
run_cli(core).await?;
Ok(())
```

At this stage, the project should be able to compile, and run. If you generate a key with **key_gen**, start a node, and start mining with that key, and open a wallet with the same key, you can view the amount of bitcoins you have increasing. If you make another set of keys, and configure a **contact** properly, then you should be also able to send bitcoins to the recipient. Keep in mind that this is bitcoin-like, and if there are no miners currently mining, no transactions can be processed.

TUI WALLET VERSION

Alright, let's make the TUI version now. If you are tracking the project in Git or another version control system (which is a very good idea), then consider committing this version of the wallet to your repository. You can make both the CLI and the TUI interfaces available as an extra exercise.

Logging and the util module

Since the TUI version cannot log messages into the standard output, we will be using **tracing** to report what's going on in the application outside of the UI. Insert the following line into every file:

```
use tracing::*;
```

This will make the tracing macros available for use:

```
error!("For critical issues that need immediate attention");
warn!("For potential problems or unusual situations that
aren't immediately threatening");
info!("For general operational messages about the app's state
and major operations");
debug!("For detailed information useful during development and
troubleshooting");
trace!("For very fine-grained information, even more detailed
than debug");
```

We will be using them at various places to make it clearer what is going on. Note that this is not enough to make the application print anything anywhere - we will need to set up a subscriber for that. We can take care of it right away.

Create a new **util.rs** module, and add the following import statements:

```
// util.rs
use anyhow::Result;
use std::panic;
use std::path::PathBuf;
use tracing::*;
use tracing_appender::rolling::{RollingFileAppender, Rotati-
on};
use tracing_subscriber::{fmt, prelude::*, EnvFilter};
use crate::core::{Config, Core, FeeConfig, FeeType, Recipi-
ent};
```

Next, we will create two functions - one to set up tracing itself, and another to set up a panic hook that will make tracing log panics that occur in our application:

```
// util.rs
/// Initialize tracing to save logs into the logs/ folder
pub fn setup_tracing() -> Result<()> {
    let file_appender = RollingFileAppender::new(
        Rotation::DAILY,
        "logs",
        "wallet.log",
    );
    tracing_subscriber::registry()
        .with(fmt::layer().with_writer(file_appender))
        .with(
            EnvFilter::from_default_env()
                .add_directive(tracing::Level::TRACE.into()),
        )
        .init();
```

```
    Ok(())
}
/// Make sure tracing is able to log panics occurring in the
wallet
pub fn setup_panic_hook() {
    panic::set_hook(Box::new(|panic_info| {
        let backtrace =
            std::backtrace::Backtrace::force_capture();
        error!("Application panicked!");
        error!("Panic info: {:?}", panic_info);
        error!("Backtrace: {:?}", backtrace);
    }));
}
```

Setting up a panic hook is a fairly common practice in much bigger applications, as you can use it to save crash information to the disk, or even send it over a network as a crash reporting mechanism.

While we are at it, let's also move the **generate_dummy_config()** function here:

```
// util.rs
/// Generate a dummy config
pub fn generate_dummy_config(path: &PathBuf) -> Result<()> {
    let dummy_config = Config {
        my_keys: vec![],
        contacts: vec![
            Recipient {
                name: "Alice".to_string(),
                key: PathBuf::from("alice.pub.pem"),
            },
            Recipient {
                name: "Bob".to_string(),
                key: PathBuf::from("bob.pub.pem"),
            },
        ],
        default_node: "127.0.0.1:9000".to_string(),
```

```
        fee_config: FeeConfig {
            fee_type: FeeType::Percent,
            value: 0.1,
        },
    };
    let config_str = toml::to_string_pretty(&dummy_config)?;
    std::fs::write(path, config_str)?;
    info!("Dummy config generated at: {}", path.display());
    Ok(())
}
```

Note that if you did not make it public before, you will have to now. Finally, let's also add two functions that will be useful in the future:

```
// util.rs
/// Convert satoshis to a BTC string
pub fn sats_to_btc(sats: u64) -> String {
    let btc = sats as f64 / 100_000_000.0;
    format!("{} BTC", btc)
}
// util.rs
/// Make it big lmao
pub fn big_mode_btc(core: &Core) -> String {
    text_to_ascii_art::convert(sats_to_btc(core.get_balance()))
        .unwrap()
}
```

I have left the **sats_to_btc()** function public, but in my implementation, it is only used inside **big_mode_btc()**. Therefore, its entire existence is at your discretion. It may come in handy later, or it might not.

The **text_to_ascii_art** crate will print our text in a manner similar to how the **figlet** UNIX tool works - essentially a big font made from block characters.

You can play around with the formatting in **sats_to_btc()** or **big_mode_btc()** to make it look like you want it to look.

Finally, don't forget to declare the module in **main.rs**:

```
mod util;
```

Core updates

Let's start by making a couple of changes to the **core**. Unfortunately, we will have to grapple with the fact that by default, **cursive** is not **async**. We can manage with the following two measures taken - using the synchronous **Sender** with an asynchronous **AsyncReceiver,** and using **tokio's task::spawn_blocking(),** which lets Tokio manage a non-async task from an asynchronous context. The latter will, however, be a problem for the **main.rs** file.

So, let's replace the **AsyncSender:**

```
// core.rs
use kanal::Sender;
```

We will also replace it in **Core** struct, and while we are at it, we will also start having a single shared stream:

```
// core.rs
pub struct Core {
    pub config: Config,
    utxos: UtxoStore,
    pub tx_sender: Sender<Transaction>,
    pub stream: Mutex<TcpStream>,
}
```

Making this change will immediately force us to modify all methods related to the **tx_sender** and the **stream.** For the **stream**:

```
// core.rs
use tokio::net::TcpStream;
use tokio::sync::Mutex;
/// Create a new Core instance.
fn new(
    config: Config,
    utxos: UtxoStore,
    stream: TcpStream,
) -> Self {
    let (tx_sender, _) = kanal::bounded(10);
    Core {
        config,
        utxos,
        tx_sender,
        stream: Mutex::new(stream),
    }
}
/// Load the Core from a configuration file.
pub async fn load(config_path: PathBuf) -> Result<Self> {
    info!("Loading core from config: {:?}", config_path);
    let config: Config =
        toml::from_str(&fs::read_to_string(&config_
path)?)?;
    let mut utxos = UtxoStore::new();
    let stream =
        TcpStream::connect(&config.default_node).await?;
    // Load keys from config
    for key in &config.my_keys {
        debug!("Loading key pair: {:?}", key.public);
        let public = PublicKey::load_from_file(&key.public)?;
        let private =
            PrivateKey::load_from_file(&key.private)?;
        utxos.add_key(LoadedKey { public, private });
    }
    Ok(Core::new(config, utxos, stream))
}
```

I have also taken the liberty of starting to add documentation comments to the items in the module. Apart from the initialization functions, we also need to update the methods that perform the tasks:

```
/// Fetch UTXOs from the node for all loaded keys.
pub async fn fetch_utxos(&self) -> Result<()> {
    debug!(
        "Fetching UTXOs from node: {}",
        self.config.default_node
    );
    for key in &self.utxos.my_keys {
        let message =
            Message::FetchUTXOs(key.public.clone());
        message
            .send_async(&mut *self.stream.lock().await)
            .await?;
        if let Message::UTXOs(utxos) =
            Message::receive_async(
                &mut *self.stream.lock().await,
            )
            .await?
        {
            debug!(
                "Received {} UTXOs for key: {:?}",
                utxos.len(),
                key.public
            );
            // Replace the entire UTXO set for this key
            self.utxos.utxos.insert(
                key.public.clone(),
                utxos
                    .into_iter()
                    .map(|(output, marked)| (marked, output))
                    .collect(),
            );
        } else {
            error!("Unexpected response from node");
            return Err(anyhow::anyhow!(
                "Unexpected response from node"
```

```
                ));
            }
        }
        info!("UTXOs fetched successfully");
        Ok(())
    }
    /// Send a transaction to the node.
    pub async fn send_transaction(
        &self,
        transaction: Transaction,
    ) -> Result<()> {
        debug!(
            "Sending transaction to node: {}",
            self.config.default_node
        );
        let message = Message::SubmitTransaction(transaction);
        message
            .send_async(&mut *self.stream.lock().await)
            .await?;
        info!("Transaction sent successfully");
        Ok(())
    }
```

Finally, we will also need to be able to send a transaction asynchronously:

```
    /// Prepare and send a transaction asynchronously.
    pub fn send_transaction_async(
        &self,
        recipient: &str,
        amount: u64,
    ) -> Result<()> {
        info!(
            "Preparing to send {} satoshis to {}",
            amount, recipient
        );
        let recipient_key = self
```

```
            .config
            .contacts
            .iter()
            .find(|r| r.name == recipient)
            .ok_or_else(|| {
                anyhow::anyhow!("Recipient not found")
            })?
            .load()?
            .key;
        let transaction =
            self.create_transaction(&recipient_key, amount)?;
        debug!("Sending transaction asynchronously");
        self.tx_sender.send(transaction)?;
        Ok(())
    }
```

Although this name may be a bit of a misnomer. We are not actually sending a transaction via Rust's async here, but rather, we are sending it into the asynchronous part of the application. If you can think of a better way to name this method, go for it :) Now, these changes may be a bit harder to keep track of, so here is the entire file at this stage. I have added a couple more log messages and documentation comments, which you may elect to include in your implementation as well.

```
// core.rs
use anyhow::Result;
use crossbeam_skiplist::SkipMap;
use kanal::Sender;
use serde::{Deserialize, Serialize};
use tokio::net::TcpStream;
use tokio::sync::Mutex;
use tracing::{debug, error, info};
use std::fs;
use std::path::PathBuf;
use std::sync::Arc;
use btclib::crypto::{PrivateKey, PublicKey};
use btclib::network::Message;
```

```rust
use btclib::types::{Transaction, TransactionOutput};
use btclib::util::Saveable;
/// Represent a key pair with paths to public and private
keys.
#[derive(Serialize, Deserialize, Clone)]
pub struct Key {
    pub public: PathBuf,
    pub private: PathBuf,
}
/// Represent a loaded key pair with actual public and private
keys.
#[derive(Clone)]
struct LoadedKey {
    public: PublicKey,
    private: PrivateKey,
}
/// Represent a recipient with a name and a path to their pu-
blic key.
#[derive(Serialize, Deserialize, Clone)]
pub struct Recipient {
    pub name: String,
    pub key: PathBuf,
}
/// Represent a loaded recipient with their actual public key.
#[derive(Clone)]
pub struct LoadedRecipient {
    pub key: PublicKey,
}
impl Recipient {
    /// Load the recipient's public key from file.
    pub fn load(&self) -> Result<LoadedRecipient> {
        debug!("Loading recipient key from: {:?}", self.key);
        let key = PublicKey::load_from_file(&self.key)?;
        Ok(LoadedRecipient { key })
    }
}
/// Define the type of fee calculation.
#[derive(Serialize, Deserialize, Clone)]
pub enum FeeType {
```

```
    Fixed,
    Percent,
}
/// Configure the fee calculation.
#[derive(Serialize, Deserialize, Clone)]
pub struct FeeConfig {
    pub fee_type: FeeType,
    pub value: f64,
}
/// Store the configuration for the Core.
#[derive(Serialize, Deserialize, Clone)]
pub struct Config {
    pub my_keys: Vec<Key>,
    pub contacts: Vec<Recipient>,
    pub default_node: String,
    pub fee_config: FeeConfig,
}
/// Store and manage Unspent Transaction Outputs (UTXOs).
#[derive(Clone)]
struct UtxoStore {
    my_keys: Vec<LoadedKey>,
    utxos:
        Arc<SkipMap<PublicKey, Vec<(bool, TransactionOut-
put)>>>,
}
impl UtxoStore {
    /// Create a new UtxoStore.
    fn new() -> Self {
        UtxoStore {
            my_keys: Vec::new(),
            utxos: Arc::new(SkipMap::new()),
        }
    }
    /// Add a new key to the UtxoStore.
    fn add_key(&mut self, key: LoadedKey) {
        debug!("Adding key to UtxoStore: {:?}", key.public);
        self.my_keys.push(key);
    }
```

```
}
/// Represent the core functionality of the wallet.
pub struct Core {
    pub config: Config,
    utxos: UtxoStore,
    pub tx_sender: Sender<Transaction>,
    pub stream: Mutex<TcpStream>,
}
impl Core {
    /// Create a new Core instance.
    fn new(
        config: Config,
        utxos: UtxoStore,
        stream: TcpStream,
    ) -> Self {
        let (tx_sender, _) = kanal::bounded(10);
        Core {
            config,
            utxos,
            tx_sender,
            stream: Mutex::new(stream),
        }
    }
    /// Load the Core from a configuration file.
    pub async fn load(config_path: PathBuf) -> Result<Self> {
        info!("Loading core from config: {:?}", config_path);
        let config: Config =
            toml::from_str(&fs::read_to_string(&config_
path)?)?;
        let mut utxos = UtxoStore::new();
        let stream =
            TcpStream::connect(&config.default_node).await?;
        // Load keys from config
        for key in &config.my_keys {
            debug!("Loading key pair: {:?}", key.public);
            let public = PublicKey::load_from_file(&key.pub-
lic)?;
            let private =
                PrivateKey::load_from_file(&key.private)?;
```

```
            utxos.add_key(LoadedKey { public, private });
        }
        Ok(Core::new(config, utxos, stream))
    }
    /// Fetch UTXOs from the node for all loaded keys.
    pub async fn fetch_utxos(&self) -> Result<()> {
        debug!(
            "Fetching UTXOs from node: {}",
            self.config.default_node
        );
        for key in &self.utxos.my_keys {
            let message =
                Message::FetchUTXOs(key.public.clone());
            message
                .send_async(&mut *self.stream.lock().await)
                .await?;
            if let Message::UTXOs(utxos) =
                Message::receive_async(
                    &mut *self.stream.lock().await,
                )
                .await?
            {
                debug!(
                    "Received {} UTXOs for key: {:?}",
                    utxos.len(),
                    key.public
                );
                // Replace the entire UTXO set for this key
                self.utxos.utxos.insert(
                    key.public.clone(),
                    utxos
                        .into_iter()
                        .map(|(output, marked)| (marked, out-
put))
                        .collect(),
                );
            } else {
                error!("Unexpected response from node");
                return Err(anyhow::anyhow!(
```

```
                "Unexpected response from node"
            ));
        }
    }
    info!("UTXOs fetched successfully");
    Ok(())
}
/// Send a transaction to the node.
pub async fn send_transaction(
    &self,
    transaction: Transaction,
) -> Result<()> {
    debug!(
        "Sending transaction to node: {}",
        self.config.default_node
    );
    let message = Message::SubmitTransaction(transaction);
    message
        .send_async(&mut *self.stream.lock().await)
        .await?;
    info!("Transaction sent successfully");
    Ok(())
}
/// Prepare and send a transaction asynchronously.
pub fn send_transaction_async(
    &self,
    recipient: &str,
    amount: u64,
) -> Result<()> {
    info!(
        "Preparing to send {} satoshis to {}",
        amount, recipient
    );
    let recipient_key = self
        .config
        .contacts
        .iter()
        .find(|r| r.name == recipient)
        .ok_or_else(|| {
```

```
            anyhow::anyhow!("Recipient not found")
        })?
        .load()?
        .key;
    let transaction =
        self.create_transaction(&recipient_key, amount)?;
    debug!("Sending transaction asynchronously");
    self.tx_sender.send(transaction)?;
    Ok(())
}
/// Get the current balance of all UTXOs.
pub fn get_balance(&self) -> u64 {
    let balance = self
        .utxos
        .utxos
        .iter()
        .map(|entry| {
            entry
                .value()
                .iter()
                .map(|utxo| utxo.1.value)
                .sum::<u64>()
        })
        .sum();
    debug!("Current balance: {} satoshis", balance);
    balance
}
/// Create a new transaction.
pub fn create_transaction(
    &self,
    recipient: &PublicKey,
    amount: u64,
) -> Result<Transaction> {
    debug!(
        "Creating transaction for {} satoshis to {:?}",
        amount, recipient
    );
    let fee = self.calculate_fee(amount);
    let total_amount = amount + fee;
```

```
        let mut inputs = Vec::new();
        let mut input_sum = 0;
        for entry in self.utxos.utxos.iter() {
            let pubkey = entry.key();
            let utxos = entry.value();
            for (marked, utxo) in utxos.iter() {
                if *marked {
                    continue;
                } // Skip marked UTXOs
                if input_sum >= total_amount {
                    break;
                }
                inputs.push(btclib::types::TransactionInput {
                    prev_transaction_output_hash: utxo.hash(),
                    signature:
                        btclib::crypto::Signature::sign_output(
                            &utxo.hash(),
                            &self
                                .utxos
                                .my_keys
                                .iter()
                                .find(|k| k.public == *pubkey)
                                .unwrap()
                                .private,
                        ),
                });
                input_sum += utxo.value;
            }
            if input_sum >= total_amount {
                break;
            }
        }
        if input_sum < total_amount {
            error!("Insufficient funds: have {} satoshis, need
{} satoshis", input_sum, total_amount);
            return Err(anyhow::anyhow!("Insufficient funds"));
        }
        let mut outputs = vec![TransactionOutput {
            value: amount,
```

```
            unique_id: uuid::Uuid::new_v4(),
            pubkey: recipient.clone(),
        }];
        if input_sum > total_amount {
            outputs.push(TransactionOutput {
                value: input_sum - total_amount,
                unique_id: uuid::Uuid::new_v4(),
                pubkey: self.utxos.my_keys[0].public.clone(),
            });
        }
        info!("Transaction created successfully");
        Ok(Transaction::new(inputs, outputs))
    }
    /// Calculate the fee for a transaction.
    fn calculate_fee(&self, amount: u64) -> u64 {
        let fee = match self.config.fee_config.fee_type {
            FeeType::Fixed => {
                self.config.fee_config.value as u64
            }
            FeeType::Percent => {
                (amount as f64 * self.config.fee_config.value
                    / 100.0) as u64
            }
        };
        debug!("Calculated fee: {} satoshis", fee);
        fee
    }
}
```

I have highlighted one small final change - making the **Key** fields public, we are going to need that in a different part of the program.

Setting up tasks

We have the core extracted, we have a utils module, let's also evict and expand the long-running tasks. We are going to have four tasks to maintain:

- The one for updating UTXOs
- Handling transactions
- The **spawn_blocking** task running the **UI**
- And a final task that will update the balance display in the **UI** dynamically

Let's move all the imports we need:

```
// tasks.rs
use cursive::views::TextContent;
use tokio::task::JoinHandle;
use tokio::time::{self, Duration};
use tracing::*;
use std::sync::Arc;
use btclib::types::Transaction;
use crate::core::Core;
use crate::ui::run_ui;
use crate::util::big_mode_btc;
```

As you can see, we are hallucinating a **ui::run_ui** function in the style of Chat-GPT 3.5. We will implement it later, of course. First, let's define the task for updating utxos. This one is very simple, we will take what we had previously in the **CLI** version of the wallet, and wrap it in a **tokio::spawn()**:

```
// tasks.rs
pub async fn update_utxos(core: Arc<Core>) -> JoinHandle<()> {
   tokio::spawn(async move {
       let mut interval =
           time::interval(Duration::from_secs(20));
       loop {
           interval.tick().await;
           if let Err(e) = core.fetch_utxos().await {
               error!("Failed to update UTXOs: {}", e);
           }
       }
   })
}
```

We can do the same thing with **handle_transactions()**:

```
// tasks.rs
pub async fn handle_transactions(
    rx: kanal::AsyncReceiver<Transaction>,
    core: Arc<Core>,
) -> JoinHandle<()> {
    tokio::spawn(async move {
        while let Ok(transaction) = rx.recv().await {
            if let Err(e) =
                core.send_transaction(transaction).await
            {
                error!("Failed to send transaction: {}", e);
            }
        }
    })
}
```

Notice that on the highlighted line, we are using the **async** function **send_transaction()**. We can do that here, and you can rely on this task also if you reintroduce the **CLI** interface from the first version of the wallet. We can tackle the final two tasks at the same time:

```
// tasks.rs
pub async fn ui_task(
    core: Arc<Core>,
    balance_content: TextContent,
) -> JoinHandle<()> {
    tokio::task::spawn_blocking(move || {
        info!("Running UI");
        if let Err(e) = run_ui(core, balance_content) {
            eprintln!("UI ended with error: {e}");
        };
    })
}
pub async fn update_balance(
```

```
    core: Arc<Core>,
    balance_content: TextContent,
) -> JoinHandle<()> {
    tokio::spawn(async move {
        loop {
            tokio::time::sleep(Duration::from_millis(500)).
await;
            info!("updating balance string");
            balance_content.set_content(big_mode_btc(&core));
        }
    })
}
```

The **balance_content** is of type **TextContent**. This type is very similar to **Arc**, but is a specialized string-like type for the **cursive** library. It lets us update text displayed in the UI from a completely different part of the application, which in our case is the **update_balance** task. At this point, this is what the file should look like:

```
// tasks.rs
use cursive::views::TextContent;
use tokio::task::JoinHandle;
use tokio::time::{self, Duration};
use tracing::*;
use std::sync::Arc;
use btclib::types::Transaction;
use crate::core::Core;
use crate::ui::run_ui;
use crate::util::big_mode_btc;
pub async fn update_utxos(core: Arc<Core>) -> JoinHandle<()> {
    tokio::spawn(async move {
        let mut interval =
            time::interval(Duration::from_secs(20));
        loop {
            interval.tick().await;
            if let Err(e) = core.fetch_utxos().await {
```

```
                error!("Failed to update UTXOs: {}", e);
            }
        }
    })
}
pub async fn handle_transactions(
    rx: kanal::AsyncReceiver<Transaction>,
    core: Arc<Core>,
) -> JoinHandle<()> {
    tokio::spawn(async move {
        while let Ok(transaction) = rx.recv().await {
            if let Err(e) =
                core.send_transaction(transaction).await
            {
                error!("Failed to send transaction: {}", e);
            }
        }
    })
}
pub async fn ui_task(
    core: Arc<Core>,
    balance_content: TextContent,
) -> JoinHandle<()> {
    tokio::task::spawn_blocking(move || {
        info!("Running UI");
        if let Err(e) = run_ui(core, balance_content) {
            eprintln!("UI ended with error: {e}");
        };
    })
}
pub async fn update_balance(
    core: Arc<Core>,
    balance_content: TextContent,
) -> JoinHandle<()> {
    tokio::spawn(async move {
        loop {
            tokio::time::sleep(Duration::from_millis(500)).
await;
            info!("updating balance string");
```

```
            balance_content.set_content(big_mode_btc(&core));
        }
    })
}
```

Remember, that just like with the previous modules, you have to declare **mod tasks** in the **main.rs** file of the wallet. With that out of the way, we need to tackle the UI now.

Cursive user interface

Since we have already added **cursive** to the dependencies, we can just go ahead and create the **ui** module with the following imports:

```
// ui.rs
use crate::core::Core;
use anyhow::Result;
use cursive::event::{Event, Key};
use cursive::traits::*;
use cursive::views::{
    Button, Dialog, EditView, LinearLayout, Panel, ResizedView,
    TextContent, TextView,
};
use cursive::Cursive;
use std::sync::{Arc, Mutex};
use tracing::*;
```

This is how I imagined the UI when conceiving the wallet:

- We have two buttons, one to create a transaction and the other to exit the wallet
    - In the dialog window for creating a transaction, I can choose whether I will be specifying the amount in sats, or in BTC. I will

        enter the name of the recipient into an input field.
    - This means that I should also have a button that lets me switch between the two different units.

- The main screen of the wallet displays my balance in big text in BTC (in today's wallets for real BTC, it is almost more practical to display your balance in sats, rather than a tiny fraction of a BTC, but hey, we can all dream of having a full coin).

- Below the main screen, there are two views:
    - Left view lists the paths to my keys.
    - Right view lists contacts added to the wallet.

First, let's tackle the units by making an **enum** that tracks the setting, and a function that lets me convert between different units:

```
// ui.rs
#[derive(Clone, Copy)]
enum Unit {
    Btc,
    Sats,
}
/// Convert an amount between BTC and Satoshi units.
fn convert_amount(amount: f64, from: Unit, to: Unit) -> f64 {
    match (from, to) {
        (Unit::Btc, Unit::Sats) => amount * 100_000_000.0,
        (Unit::Sats, Unit::Btc) => amount / 100_000_000.0,
        _ => amount,
    }
}
```

Note that because we go through floats, we are losing some precision. If you want to, you can refactor this function to use our old friend **bigdecimal** we previously utilized in the target calculations in **btclib**.

Now, let's create stubs for the functions that we are going to use to compose our cursive view:

```rust
// ui.rs
/// Initialize and run the user interface.
pub fn run_ui(
    core: Arc<Core>,
    balance_content: TextContent,
) -> Result<()> {
    // ...
}
/// Set up the Cursive interface with all necessary components
and callbacks.
fn setup_siv(
    siv: &mut Cursive,
    core: Arc<Core>,
    balance_content: TextContent,
) {
    // ...
}
/// Set up the menu bar with "Send" and "Quit" options.
fn setup_menubar(siv: &mut Cursive, core: Arc<Core>) {
    // ...
}
/// Set up the main layout of the application.
fn setup_layout(
    siv: &mut Cursive,
    core: Arc<Core>,
    balance_content: TextContent,
) {
    // ...
}
/// Create the information layout containing keys and con-
tacts.
fn create_info_layout(core: &Arc<Core>) -> LinearLayout {
    // ...
}
/// Display the send transaction dialog.
fn show_send_transaction(s: &mut Cursive, core: Arc<Core>) {
    // ...
```

```
}
/// Create the layout for the transaction dialog.
fn create_transaction_layout(
    unit: Arc<Mutex<Unit>>,
) -> LinearLayout {
    // ...
}
/// Create the layout for selecting the transaction unit (BTC
or Sats).
fn create_unit_layout(unit: Arc<Mutex<Unit>>) -> LinearLayout
{
    // ...
}
/// Switch the transaction unit between BTC and Sats.
fn switch_unit(s: &mut Cursive, unit: Arc<Mutex<Unit>>) {
    // ...
}
/// Process the send transaction request.
fn send_transaction(
    s: &mut Cursive,
    core: Arc<Core>,
    unit: Unit,
) {
    // ...
}
/// Display a success dialog after a successful transaction.
fn show_success_dialog(s: &mut Cursive) {
    // ...
}
/// Display an error dialog when a transaction fails.
fn show_error_dialog(
    s: &mut Cursive,
    error: impl std::fmt::Display,
) {
    // ...
}
```

You can see that the instance of **Cursive** is traditionally bound to the **siv** variable. We have made a function for every part of the UI, and finally, we made a function **run_ui()** that kickstarts the user interface. We can take care of it first:

```
// ui.rs
/// Initialize and run the user interface.
pub fn run_ui(
    core: Arc<Core>,
    balance_content: TextContent,
) -> Result<()> {
    info!("Initializing UI");
    let mut siv = cursive::default();
    setup_siv(&mut siv, core.clone(), balance_content);
    info!("Starting UI event loop");
    siv.run();
    info!("UI event loop ended");
    Ok(())
}
```

On the first two highlighted lines, we are instantiating a default configuration of Cursive, and handing it off to the **setup_siv()** function that will compose the UI. The last highlighted line starts the event loop. This is the major difference between **cursive** and **ratatui/tui**. In the latter, it is your responsibility to build an event loop for yourself, if that's something you want to do.

Since we have already mentioned it, we can take a look at the **setup_siv()** function next:

```
// ui.rs
/// Set up the Cursive interface with all necessary components
and callbacks.
fn setup_siv(
    siv: &mut Cursive,
    core: Arc<Core>,
    balance_content: TextContent,
) {
```

```
    siv.set_autorefresh(true);
    siv.set_window_title("BTC wallet".to_string());
    siv.add_global_callback('q', |s| {
        info!("Quit command received");
        s.quit()
    });
    setup_menubar(siv, core.clone());
    setup_layout(siv, core, balance_content);
    siv.add_global_callback(Event::Key(Key::Esc), |siv| {
        siv.select_menubar()
    });
    siv.select_menubar();
}
```

I want the application to be as responsive as possible, so I enabled autorefresh which sets the FPS to 30. If the terminal supports it, we are setting the name to **BTC wallet**:

```
    // ui.rs
    siv.set_window_title("BTC wallet".to_string());
```

Just to make quitting easier, we can also bind a global callback to the Q key that will kill the application:

```
    // ui.rs
    siv.add_global_callback('q', |s| {
        info!("Quit command received");
        s.quit()
    });
```

We then hand off the **Cursive** instance to the **setup_menubar()** and **setup_layout()** functions respectively:

```
// ui.rs
setup_menubar(siv, core.clone());
setup_layout(siv, core, balance_content);
```

Finally, we add an Escape key callback that will select the menu bar, and finalize the setup function by selecting it. We can tackle the **menu bar** layout now, as it is very simple:

```
// ui.rs
/// Set up the menu bar with "Send" and "Quit" options.
fn setup_menubar(siv: &mut Cursive, core: Arc<Core>) {
    siv.menubar()
        .add_leaf("Send", move |s| {
            show_send_transaction(s, core.clone())
        })
        .add_leaf("Quit", |s| s.quit());
    siv.set_autohide_menu(false);
}
```

If you are older than me, you may be familiar with DOS programs that had tree menus spanning from a top menu bar. These were later reincarnated into the standard Windows menus to the note of **File..., Edit..., View..., Tools..., Help** that have become a staple in many user-facing applications written over the last two decades or so. Cursive lets us make the same types of menus, but in this case, we are only inserting two buttons, rather than creating any submenu. This is why we are using the **.add_leaf()** method on the **MenuBar** rather than adding a subtree, which has a method of a similar name.

The **Send** button will display the dialogue for creating and sending a transaction, whereas the **Quit** button will just terminate the **Cursive** event loop, which we can wire up to lead to the termination of the whole program later on in the **main()** function.

We also disable the **auto hide** feature of the menu, so that the user always knows it is available. Let's take a look at the **show_send_transaction()** function now:

```
// ui.rs
/// Display the send transaction dialog.
fn show_send_transaction(s: &mut Cursive, core: Arc<Core>) {
    info!("Showing send transaction dialog");
    let unit = Arc::new(Mutex::new(Unit::Btc));
    s.add_layer(
        Dialog::around(create_transaction_layout(unit.clone()))
            .title("Send Transaction")
            .button("Send", move |siv| {
                send_transaction(
                    siv,
                    core.clone(),
                    *unit.lock().unwrap(),
                )
            })
            .button("Cancel", |siv| {
                debug!("Transaction cancelled");
                siv.pop_layer();
            }),
    );
}
```

This one is a bit more involved. In **Cursive**, different views can be reused, and one view can wrap over another. That's what we are doing on the highlighted line. Dialog can have buttons on the bottom, and I believe that it looks better than if we were to place those buttons inside the dialog. However, you can experiment with either option. **Cursive** works on the basis of layers, so if we want to render one window over another, such as a dialog, we add a layer. If we want to quickly destroy it, we just pop the layer - the model resembles a stack data structure. Notice how we are using an **Arc<Mutex<Unit>>** to safely share the unit settings between the UI and the transaction sender.

Let's take a look at the transaction sender, which pulls the information from the UI, converts the units, and uses the **Core::send_transaction_async()** method to submit a transaction to the core:

```
// ui.rs
/// Process the send transaction request.
fn send_transaction(
    s: &mut Cursive,
    core: Arc<Core>,
    unit: Unit,
) {
    debug!("Send button pressed");
    let recipient = s
        .call_on_name("recipient", |view: &mut EditView| {
            view.get_content()
        })
        .unwrap();
    let amount: f64 = s
        .call_on_name("amount", |view: &mut EditView| {
            view.get_content()
        })
        .unwrap()
        .parse()
        .unwrap_or(0.0);
    let amount_sats =
        convert_amount(amount, unit, Unit::Sats) as u64;
    info!(
        "Attempting to send transaction to {} for {} satoshis",
        recipient, amount_sats
    );
    match core
        .send_transaction_async(recipient.as_str(), amount_
sats)
    {
        Ok(_) => show_success_dialog(s),
        Err(e) => show_error_dialog(s, e),
    }
}
```

Notice the highlighted lines. **Cursive** lets you name particular views, and then pull information out of them elsewhere by using the **call_on_name()** function that lets you mutably access the view in question. If we are successful in pulling out the information, we send the transaction, and react to the result:

```
// ui.rs
match core
    .send_transaction_async(recipient.as_str(), amount_
sats)
{
    Ok(_) => show_success_dialog(s),
    Err(e) => show_error_dialog(s, e),
}
```

This is how the two dialogues are constructed:

```
// ui.rs
/// Display a success dialog after a successful transaction.
fn show_success_dialog(s: &mut Cursive) {
    info!("Transaction sent successfully");
    s.add_layer(
        Dialog::text("Transaction sent successfully")
            .title("Success")
            .button("OK", |s| {
                debug!("Closing success dialog");
                s.pop_layer();
                s.pop_layer();
            }),
    );
}
/// Display an error dialog when a transaction fails.
fn show_error_dialog(
    s: &mut Cursive,
    error: impl std::fmt::Display,
) {
    error!("Failed to send transaction: {}", error);
    s.add_layer(
```

```
        Dialog::text(format!(
            "Failed to send transaction: {}",
            error
        ))
        .title("Error")
        .button("OK", |s| {
            debug!("Closing error dialog");
            s.pop_layer();
        }),
    );
}
```

This concludes this path in the tree, let's return to **show_send_transaction()**, and see how we can implement **create_transaction_layout()**. It will essentially be the two input fields, and a unit switcher:

```
// ui.rs
/// Create the layout for the transaction dialog.
fn create_transaction_layout(
    unit: Arc<Mutex<Unit>>,
) -> LinearLayout {
    LinearLayout::vertical()
        .child(TextView::new("Recipient:"))
        .child(EditView::new().with_name("recipient"))
        .child(TextView::new("Amount:"))
        .child(EditView::new().with_name("amount"))
        .child(create_unit_layout(unit))
}
```

As you can see, we are naming the two **EditViews** so that we can refer to them from the **send_transaction()** function we implemented earlier. The missing piece here is the unit layout, where we want to do show the name of the unit, and add a button that switches between one unit and another:

```rust
// ui.rs
/// Create the layout for selecting the transaction unit (BTC
or Sats).
fn create_unit_layout(unit: Arc<Mutex<Unit>>) -> LinearLayout
{
    LinearLayout::horizontal()
        .child(TextView::new("Unit: "))
        .child(
            TextView::new_with_content(TextContent::new("BTC"))
                .with_name("unit_display"),
        )
        .child(Button::new("Switch", move |s| {
            switch_unit(s, unit.clone())
        }))
}
/// Switch the transaction unit between BTC and Sats.
fn switch_unit(s: &mut Cursive, unit: Arc<Mutex<Unit>>) {
    let mut unit = unit.lock().unwrap();
    *unit = match *unit {
        Unit::Btc => Unit::Sats,
        Unit::Sats => Unit::Btc,
    };
    s.call_on_name("unit_display", |view: &mut TextView| {
        view.set_content(match *unit {
            Unit::Btc => "BTC",
            Unit::Sats => "Sats",
        });
    });
}
```

Now we have to go all the way back, almost to the very beginning and implement **setup_layout()**:

```rust
// ui.rs
/// Set up the main layout of the application.
fn setup_layout(
```

```
    siv: &mut Cursive,
    core: Arc<Core>,
    balance_content: TextContent,
) {
    let instruction =
        TextView::new("Press Escape to select the top menu");
    let balance_panel =
        Panel::new(TextView::new_with_content(balance_content))
            .title("Balance");
    let info_layout = create_info_layout(&core);
    let layout = LinearLayout::vertical()
        .child(instruction)
        .child(balance_panel)
        .child(info_layout);
    siv.add_layer(layout);
}
```

We start off by making a **TextView** that lets the user know that we can use **Escape** to select the top menu bar, then we show the balance, and then the other info. Finally, we combine these into a vertical layout. The info layout is very simple, but a little long, since we need to pull information out of the core:

```
// ui.rs
/// Create the information layout containing keys and con-
tacts.
fn create_info_layout(core: &Arc<Core>) -> LinearLayout {
    let mut info_layout = LinearLayout::horizontal();
    let keys_content = core
        .config
        .my_keys
        .iter()
        .map(|key| format!("{}", key.private.display()))
        .collect::<Vec<String>>()
        .join("\n");
    info_layout.add_child(ResizedView::with_full_width(
        Panel::new(TextView::new(keys_content))
            .title("Your keys"),
```

```
    ));
    let contacts_content = core
        .config
        .contacts
        .iter()
        .map(|contact| contact.name.clone())
        .collect::<Vec<String>>()
        .join("\n");
    info_layout.add_child(ResizedView::with_full_width(
        Panel::new(TextView::new(contacts_content))
            .title("Contacts"),
    ));
    info_layout
}
```

To ensure that the two boxes are not tiny, we are using **ResizedView**. This will motivate the **Panel**-wrapped **TextViews** to take up as much space as they can, which will make them split the available space between the two of them. Note that **ResizedView** is very configurable. We are composing these two into a horizontal layout so that we have one big balance panel and two smaller panels under it, side to side. That's it for the UI.

At this stage, it should look like this:

```
// ui.rs
use crate::core::Core;
use anyhow::Result;
use cursive::event::{Event, Key};
use cursive::traits::*;
use cursive::views::{
    Button, Dialog, EditView, LinearLayout, Panel, ResizedView,
    TextContent, TextView,
};
use cursive::Cursive;
use std::sync::{Arc, Mutex};
```

```rust
use tracing::*;
#[derive(Clone, Copy)]
enum Unit {
    Btc,
    Sats,
}
/// Convert an amount between BTC and Satoshi units.
fn convert_amount(amount: f64, from: Unit, to: Unit) -> f64 {
    match (from, to) {
        (Unit::Btc, Unit::Sats) => amount * 100_000_000.0,
        (Unit::Sats, Unit::Btc) => amount / 100_000_000.0,
        _ => amount,
    }
}
/// Initialize and run the user interface.
pub fn run_ui(
    core: Arc<Core>,
    balance_content: TextContent,
) -> Result<()> {
    info!("Initializing UI");
    let mut siv = cursive::default();
    setup_siv(&mut siv, core.clone(), balance_content);
    info!("Starting UI event loop");
    siv.run();
    info!("UI event loop ended");
    Ok(())
}
/// Set up the Cursive interface with all necessary components
and callbacks.
fn setup_siv(
    siv: &mut Cursive,
    core: Arc<Core>,
    balance_content: TextContent,
) {
    siv.set_autorefresh(true);
    siv.set_fps(30);
    siv.set_window_title("BTC wallet".to_string());
```

```rust
    siv.add_global_callback('q', |s| {
        info!("Quit command received");
        s.quit()
    });
    setup_menubar(siv, core.clone());
    setup_layout(siv, core, balance_content);
    siv.add_global_callback(Event::Key(Key::Esc), |siv| {
        siv.select_menubar()
    });
    siv.select_menubar();
}
/// Set up the menu bar with "Send" and "Quit" options.
fn setup_menubar(siv: &mut Cursive, core: Arc<Core>) {
    siv.menubar()
        .add_leaf("Send", move |s| {
            show_send_transaction(s, core.clone())
        })
        .add_leaf("Quit", |s| s.quit());
    siv.set_autohide_menu(false);
}
/// Set up the main layout of the application.
fn setup_layout(
    siv: &mut Cursive,
    core: Arc<Core>,
    balance_content: TextContent,
) {
    let instruction =
        TextView::new("Press Escape to select the top menu");
    let balance_panel =
        Panel::new(TextView::new_with_content(balance_content))
            .title("Balance");
    let info_layout = create_info_layout(&core);
    let layout = LinearLayout::vertical()
        .child(instruction)
        .child(balance_panel)
        .child(info_layout);
```

```
    siv.add_layer(layout);
}
/// Create the information layout containing keys and con-
tacts.
fn create_info_layout(core: &Arc<Core>) -> LinearLayout {
    let mut info_layout = LinearLayout::horizontal();
    let keys_content = core
        .config
        .my_keys
        .iter()
        .map(|key| format!("{}", key.private.display()))
        .collect::<Vec<String>>()
        .join("\n");
    info_layout.add_child(ResizedView::with_full_width(
        Panel::new(TextView::new(keys_content))
            .title("Your keys"),
    ));
    let contacts_content = core
        .config
        .contacts
        .iter()
        .map(|contact| contact.name.clone())
        .collect::<Vec<String>>()
        .join("\n");
    info_layout.add_child(ResizedView::with_full_width(
        Panel::new(TextView::new(contacts_content))
            .title("Contacts"),
    ));
    info_layout
}
/// Display the send transaction dialog.
fn show_send_transaction(s: &mut Cursive, core: Arc<Core>) {
    info!("Showing send transaction dialog");
    let unit = Arc::new(Mutex::new(Unit::Btc));
    s.add_layer(
        Dialog::around(create_transaction_layout(unit.clone()))
            .title("Send Transaction")
```

```
            .button("Send", move |s| {
                send_transaction(
                    s,
                    core.clone(),
                    *unit.lock().unwrap(),
                )
            })
            .button("Cancel", |s| {
                debug!("Transaction cancelled");
                s.pop_layer();
            }),
    );
}
/// Create the layout for the transaction dialog.
fn create_transaction_layout(
    unit: Arc<Mutex<Unit>>,
) -> LinearLayout {
    LinearLayout::vertical()
        .child(TextView::new("Recipient:"))
        .child(EditView::new().with_name("recipient"))
        .child(TextView::new("Amount:"))
        .child(EditView::new().with_name("amount"))
        .child(create_unit_layout(unit))
}
/// Create the layout for selecting the transaction unit (BTC
or Sats).
fn create_unit_layout(unit: Arc<Mutex<Unit>>) -> LinearLayout
{
    LinearLayout::horizontal()
        .child(TextView::new("Unit: "))
        .child(
            TextView::new_with_content(TextContent::new("BTC"))
                .with_name("unit_display"),
        )
        .child(Button::new("Switch", move |s| {
            switch_unit(s, unit.clone())
        }))
}
/// Switch the transaction unit between BTC and Sats.
```

```
fn switch_unit(s: &mut Cursive, unit: Arc<Mutex<Unit>>) {
    let mut unit = unit.lock().unwrap();
    *unit = match *unit {
        Unit::Btc => Unit::Sats,
        Unit::Sats => Unit::Btc,
    };
    s.call_on_name("unit_display", |view: &mut TextView| {
        view.set_content(match *unit {
            Unit::Btc => "BTC",
            Unit::Sats => "Sats",
        });
    });
}
/// Process the send transaction request.
fn send_transaction(
    s: &mut Cursive,
    core: Arc<Core>,
    unit: Unit,
) {
    debug!("Send button pressed");
    let recipient = s
        .call_on_name("recipient", |view: &mut EditView| {
            view.get_content()
        })
        .unwrap();
    let amount: f64 = s
        .call_on_name("amount", |view: &mut EditView| {
            view.get_content()
        })
        .unwrap()
        .parse()
        .unwrap_or(0.0);
    let amount_sats =
        convert_amount(amount, unit, Unit::Sats) as u64;
    info!(
        "Attempting to send transaction to {} for {} satoshis",
        recipient, amount_sats
    );
```

```
    match core
        .send_transaction_async(recipient.as_str(), amount_
sats)
    {
        Ok(_) => show_success_dialog(s),
        Err(e) => show_error_dialog(s, e),
    }
}
/// Display a success dialog after a successful transaction.
fn show_success_dialog(s: &mut Cursive) {
    info!("Transaction sent successfully");
    s.add_layer(
        Dialog::text("Transaction sent successfully")
            .title("Success")
            .button("OK", |s| {
                debug!("Closing success dialog");
                s.pop_layer();
                s.pop_layer();
            }),
    );
}
/// Display an error dialog when a transaction fails.
fn show_error_dialog(
    s: &mut Cursive,
    error: impl std::fmt::Display,
) {
    error!("Failed to send transaction: {}", error);
    s.add_layer(
        Dialog::text(format!(
            "Failed to send transaction: {}",
            error
        ))
        .title("Error")
        .button("OK", |s| {
            debug!("Closing error dialog");
            s.pop_layer();
        }),
    );
}
```

Remember to have the UI modular declared in your **main.rs** file, if you haven't done so already. Now that we have the Core, the UI, and the tasks completed, all that is left is updating the main file to start the new UI and the other tasks.

The main file

First, let's make sure we are importing all the new stuff from the modules we created in the last couple sections:

```
// main.rs
use anyhow::Result;
use clap::{Parser, Subcommand};
use cursive::views::TextContent;
use tracing::{debug, info};
use std::path::PathBuf;
use std::sync::Arc;
mod core;
mod tasks;
mod ui;
mod util;
use core::Core;
use tasks::{
    handle_transactions, ui_task, update_balance, update_utxos,
};
use util::{
    big_mode_btc, generate_dummy_config, setup_panic_hook,
    setup_tracing,
};
```

The CLI configuration stays almost the same as it was before. However, this time, we can be smarter about it, and use the **Clap** frame work's functionality to provide default values where applicable:

```
#[derive(Parser)]
#[command(author, version, about, long_about = None)]
struct Cli {
    #[command(subcommand)]
    command: Option<Commands>,
    #[arg(short, long, value_name = "FILE", default_value_os_t
= PathBuf::from("wallet_config.toml"))]
    config: PathBuf,
    #[arg(short, long, value_name = "ADDRESS")]
    node: Option<String>,
}
#[derive(Subcommand)]
enum Commands {
    GenerateConfig {
        #[arg(short, long, value_name = "FILE", default_value_
os_t = PathBuf::from("wallet_config.toml"))]
        output: PathBuf,
    },
}
```

And all that is left now is the main function. First, let's take a look at it as a whole:

```
#[tokio::main]
async fn main() -> Result<()> {
    setup_tracing()?;
    setup_panic_hook();
    info!("Starting wallet application");
    let cli = Cli::parse();
    match &cli.command {
        Some(Commands::GenerateConfig { output }) => {
            debug!("Generating dummy config at: {:?}", output);
            return generate_dummy_config(output);
        }
        None => (),
    }
```

```
    info!("Loading config from: {:?}", cli.config);
    let mut core = Core::load(cli.config.clone()).await?;
    if let Some(node) = cli.node {
        info!("Overriding default node with: {}", node);
        core.config.default_node = node;
    }
    let (tx_sender, tx_receiver) = kanal::bounded(10);
    core.tx_sender = tx_sender;
    let core = Arc::new(core);
    info!("Starting background tasks");
    let balance_content = TextContent::new(big_mode_btc(&co-
re));
    tokio::select! {
        _ = ui_task(core.clone(), balance_content.clone()).
await => (),
        _ = update_utxos(core.clone()).await => (),
        _ = handle_transactions(tx_receiver.clone_async(),
core.clone()).await  => (),
        _ = update_balance(core.clone(), balance_content).await
=> (),
    }
    info!("Application shutting down");
    Ok(())
}
```

There we go. First, we start by setting up our logging tools - the tracing subscriber (a subscriber is what collects the logging events from across the app and saves them somewhere, in simple terms), and the panic hook, which responds to and extracts information from panics happening across the application, so that we can log them as well:

```
    setup_tracing()?;
    setup_panic_hook();
```

Then we parse and process the command line arguments:

```
info!("Starting wallet application");
let cli = Cli::parse();
match &cli.command {
    Some(Commands::GenerateConfig { output }) => {
        debug!("Generating dummy config at: {:?}", output);
        return generate_dummy_config(output);
    }
    None => (),
}
```

We load the core with the config, and complete its setup:

```
info!("Loading config from: {:?}", cli.config);
let mut core = Core::load(cli.config.clone()).await?;
if let Some(node) = cli.node {
    info!("Overriding default node with: {}", node);
    core.config.default_node = node;
}
let (tx_sender, tx_receiver) = kanal::bounded(10);
core.tx_sender = tx_sender;
```

From this point onwards, we no longer need **Core** to be mutable, so we wrap it in an **Arc**, so that we can clone it into every task:

```
let core = Arc::new(core);
```

Then, we can finally instantiate all tasks and run the application:

```
    info!("Starting background tasks");
    let balance_content = TextContent::new(big_mode_btc(&co-
re));
    tokio::select! {
        _ = ui_task(core.clone(), balance_content.clone()).
await => (),
        _ = update_utxos(core.clone()).await => (),
        _ = handle_transactions(tx_receiver.clone_async(),
core.clone()).await  => (),
        _ = update_balance(core.clone(), balance_content).await
=> (),
    }
    info!("Application shutting down");
    Ok(())
```

We create the **balance_content**, and we put all our tasks into a **select!**. A **select!** will poll all futures until one of them completes. If a future is completed, all the other ones will be dropped. The way we are using the **select!** is to ensure that when one task exits (due to an error or due to natural causes such as quitting the UI), all of them do. This pattern is very common in Tokio programs.

You should now be able to compile the wallet without error, and if you configure it to connect to a running node and have a miner running with one of the private keys you have added to the config, you should see your BTC balance slowly increase.

That's it. We have successfully created a pretty nice BTC wallet. However, there is a lot of space for improvement in terms of functionality and ergonomics.

This is the last part of the project, and we are now successfully at its end. Therefore, here is a picture of an echidna[49]

49 Knuckles is my favorite, although I am quite partial to Shadow The Hedgehog as well. Introducing guns and edgy humor into a children's game was the best idea SEGA ever had!

10

CONCLUSION AND NEXT STEPS

Well, we have finished the project, what now?

EVALUATING OUR PROJECT

It is clear that while we have laid down a basic framework to get our hands dirty with building a bitcoin-like system in Rust, there is a lot we have kept simple on purpose. This was all about making things clear and easy to grasp, rather than packing it with complex features or optimizing for speed.

In our journey, we‘ve prioritized learning and understanding over perfecting every line of code. That said, our code could definitely be slicker and more efficient. Right now, it‘s more of a solid starting point than a finished product. We have got a lot of room to beef up our code, especially when it comes to Rust specifics.

Looking ahead, there are heaps of ways to kick things up a notch. We could dive deeper into Rust‘s powerful features - for example, advanced memory management (you can write the node such that it does not need any global variables) or concurrency models (as we mentioned earlier, the miner could be multi-threaded, and you could make a better mine function that lets you split the **nonce** space) - to really tailor our system for better performance and security. Rust is always evolving, and so can our project. By leveraging more of Rust‘s capabilities, we can make our simulated bitcoin network faster, safer, and more robust.

And it‘s not just about beefing up what we have. We could expand on the basics, like enhancing network functionalities or introducing more refined validation processes. All these improvements are not just upgrades - they are new opportunities to learn and experiment.

To sum it up, we have made a solid start, but there is a whole lot more we can do. This project is a great launchpad for anyone curious about bitcoin or Rust, and there‘s plenty of space to tweak, tinker, and expand. You can make many improvements, but first and foremost, have fun doing them.

RECOMMENDED READING FROM BRAIINS

This is not the first book released under the Braiins umbrella. We have been active in creating and publishing books for several years at this point, and if you are interested, you can check out other books from **Braiins Publishing**. Our books mostly focus on bitcoin, and the Austrian school of economics and mining. Both the technical and economic aspects of bitcoin are covered. To date, we have published the following books:

- Bitcoin Mining Handbook
- Bitcoin Mining Economics
- Bitcoin: Separation of Money and State

The latest offering of Braiins books can be found at the following website: https://braiins.com/books

We have also published the **mining handbook** in Spanish, and we have published other books in Czech. If you are curious about the Czech language books, you can visit **Bitperia**:
https://www.bitperia.cz/

Bitperia is also an excellent Czech-language source for everything bitcoin. Stay tuned for more releases from Braiins Publishing!

OTHER RESOURCES FOR RUST AND BTC

This book may be over now, but your journey is not.[50] There is more to learn about Rust, and more to learn about bitcoin. In our bitcoin implementation, we have made a number of simplifications, small changes and less-than-ideal solutions to the issues of implementing a blockchain. It is up to you, if you want to take this project anywhere further. After all, it is a toy project, and toys are meant to be played with, and often are facsimiles of concepts and objects from the real world. There is no financial profit to be made from our toy blockchain, but you can make it your own. You know the codebase well, and you can certainly think of places where you could make improvements or implement new features.

If you now look at the real, big, monumental project that is the main bitcoin

50 I'm still thinking about Rome.

implementation, you already have some idea of how it works internally, and how the different components talk to one another. Of course, there are things we have not covered in this book, and that can be interesting for you to learn about from a technical perspective. For example, mining pools. It may be kind of ironic to consider that a bitcoin-implementing book from Braiins, **the operators of the first bitcoin mining pool**, does not mention pools at all. But that would have only added complexity with little benefit for the purposes of teaching Rust and the major, overarching technical aspects of bitcoin.

That can be one thing you can try to implement. Read up on how the concept of pools work, implement a pool that talks to your toy blockchain, and edit your toy miner program so that it talks to your pool instead of to the node directly. Then there are always things like nicer logging, smarter storage solutions, and so on. Before I leave you to your own devices, let me recommend you a couple of resources about Rust, and bitcoin, so that you can further your own education in these two subjects.

Rust

For a more in-depth look at Rust, and if you have more time on your hands, you can follow up by checking out the official **The Rust Programming Language** book[51], otherwise known in the community as **TRPL**. It covers Rust from top to bottom, and is a very hefty read of about 500 pages in its paper version.

Again, a more practical counterpart could be **Rust By Example**, which contains many runnable code excerpts that show you how to solve the most common problems in Rust.

It might also be a good idea at this stage to flip through **Rust Design Patterns** if you want to get familiar with ways we solve certain categories of problems in Rust.

An interesting take on learning Rust in a very practical way is the **Learning Rust with Entirely Too Many Linked Lists** book. Lists are a great tool for demonstrating key Rust concepts, and *Too Many Linked Lists* leans heavily into it.

51 Freely available at https://doc.rust-lang.org/book/, or bundled locally with your toolchain - do rustup doc --book.

Advanced resources

Rust has a complex underbelly of interesting concepts and under-the-hood oddities that are documented in the ***Nomicon***, a book of Rust dark arts. It is not necessary to know most of these things for day-to-day usage of Rust, but it can help you make pragmatic decisions in a couple of situations, especially regarding performance and interactions with C/C++ code. It is an indispensable resource for writing unsafe Rust correctly.

If you are willing to invest in a paper book, a great advanced Rust resource is the **Rust for Rustaceans book by Jon Gjengset**. He also creates a great YouTube series called **Crust of Rust**, where he goes into the nitty gritty implementation details of parts of the standard library and considerations that must be taken into account when implementing them. The videos are a similar level of resources as the Nomicon - not necessary for most work, but a nice-to-have.

Finally, it is time to go domain-specific:

- For macros, see **The Little Book of Rust Macros**
- Embedded development is best described in the **Rust Embedded Book**
- For performance, see **The Rust Performance Book**
- and there are many others, which are usually not that difficult to find...

Bitcoin

For those who wish to delve deeply into the technical aspects of bitcoin, beginning with *Mastering Bitcoin* by Andreas M. Antonopoulos is highly recommended. Often referred to as the definitive guide, it explores Bitcoin's technical foundation extensively, covering everything from blockchain basics to sophisticated details of its protocol.

For a more hands-on approach, *Programming Bitcoin* by Jimmy Song provides practical code examples that teach the bitcoin software from the ground up. This book is perfect for developers looking to build their understanding through programming exercises that tackle real-world scenarios.

If you're interested in the patterns and principles underlying bitcoin, *Bitcoin and Cryptocurrency Technologies* by Arvind Narayanan et al. offers a comprehensive look at the design and technology of bitcoin and other cryptocurrencies. This academic approach helps clarify not only how but why bitcoin functions as it does.

An intriguing resource for those who want to engage with bitcoin through a blend of theory and practical challenges is *Grokking Bitcoin* by Kalle Rosenbaum. This book breaks down complex concepts into understandable parts using clear visuals and explanations, focusing heavily on the mechanics of bitcoin transactions.

Advanced Resources

Bitcoin's more intricate workings are laid out in The Book of Satoshi by Phil Champagne, which compiles the writings of Satoshi Nakamoto. While not a technical guide per se, it provides essential context and foundational philosophies directly from bitcoin's creator, alongside technical commentary.

For developers looking to delve into advanced bitcoin programming and integration, *Advanced Bitcoin Scripting* by Glenn Willen is invaluable. It covers sophisticated aspects of bitcoin's scripting language, enabling the creation of more complex smart contracts and innovations on the bitcoin blockchain.

Specialized Topics

- For those interested in security aspects, *Bitcoin Security Fundamentals* is crucial.
- In terms of economic implications and digital currency policy, *The Economics of Bitcoin* offers a detailed analysis.
- For mining-specific insights, *Bitcoin Mining and Blockchain Dynamics* provides a technical exploration of the mining process and its impact on blockchain stability.

Final words and opinions of Lukáš Hozda, Gentleman (not written by Laurence Stern)

Ending books is difficult because there is always more to say. For a book like this one, this is especially the case, as there is always more to learn, more to discover and the space of possible improvements and changes one can make to a project is infinite. I hope you liked the journey presented in this book. I tried to keep it largely organic, similar to how one would develop a project in real life. An iterative process, where you account for some things ahead, but others pop up as you go, and sometimes you need to go back and change what you previously had, or extend older pieces of the programs or libraries with new functionality.

Anyways, that's it. Before you go, enjoy this drawing of a honey badger.[52] I hear it is an important animal in bitcoin. Like a Rust-powered honey badger, bitcoin doesn't care and keeps on running. :) You can also reach out to me (or Braiins) on our social media pages. I would love to hear how you liked my book, so that I can flex in front of everyone.

52 Listen, some time ago, I splurged my hard-earned Braiins money on a drawing tablet, and by god, I am gonna use it.

Made in United States
North Haven, CT
04 November 2026

21760289R00241